A Yorkshire Lass
at the Court of
THATCHER

For my husband Brian
and sons Jonathan and Nicholas
without whose help and support
I would never have reached Westminster
and this book would not have been written!

A Yorkshire Lass
at the Court of
THATCHER

*An autobiographical review of the
Thatcher and Major years
by a political rebel*

'My View'

ELIZABETH J. PEACOCK

PEN & SWORD
POLITICS

First published in Great Britain in 2013 by
PEN & SWORD POLITICS
an imprint of
Pen and Sword Books Ltd
47 Church Street
Barnsley
South Yorkshire S70 2AS

ISBN 978 1 78303 292 1

Printed and bound in England by
CPI Group (UK) Ltd, Croydon, CR0 4YY

Typeset in Sabon by CHIC GRAPHICS

Pen & Sword Books Ltd incorporates the imprints of
Pen & Sword Books Ltd incorporates the imprints of Pen & Sword
Archaeology, Atlas, Aviation, Battleground, Discovery, Family History,
History, Maritime, Military, Naval, Politics, Railways, Select, Social History,
Transport, True Crime, and Claymore Press, Frontline Books, Leo Cooper,
Praetorian Press, Remember When, Seaforth Publishing and Wharncliffe.

For a complete list of Pen and Sword titles please contact
Pen and Sword Books Limited
47 Church Street, Barnsley, South Yorkshire, S70 2AS, England
E-mail: enquiries@pen-and-sword.co.uk
Website: www.pen-and-sword.co.uk

Contents

The Major Years

Life After Westminster

Acknowledgements

The author wishes to record her thanks to those who helped or played a part in the activities referred to in this book. As so many people have been involved I am inevitably going to omit someone so I apologize in advance.

I must start by thanking the book-writing team, which includes my husband Brian who did most of the drafting with the help of my huge archive.

I am, of course, indebted to the Rt Hon. Cheryl Gillan MP, a dear friend, for agreeing to write the Foreword.

I particularly thank the late Doug Brewer, OBE, my constituency president and chief canvasser. Never did an individual work harder and longer for the Conservative cause.

Members of the Batley & Spen Conservative Association Executive Committee.

Thanks are also due to the 'office team', the late Lorna Humphreys who ran my London office and then Martin Casey who took over after Lorna's untimely death.

The late Mary Bentley, Kath Wrightson and Margaret Bates who all worked incredibly hard in the constituency.

Thanks must also go to the members of the Patrons Club.

Members of the Batley & Spen Business Association and all those who joined our canvassing teams at each election.

I hope all those who appear in this story are reasonably happy with the way they are depicted!

Foreword

We are a rare breed, us Conservative women. So rare that, even now, Elizabeth Peacock is a trail-blazer; an inspiration to younger women like me, who may otherwise have been put off politics altogether. So, I am honoured to have been asked to write this foreword to a long-overdue book.

Elizabeth's story is of a life built upon strong Conservative principles, a struggle in the face of adversity and an inherent belief that government should, in her words, 'be available to help those in need'.

Having been proud to call her a friend for over twenty years, her endearing quality is that she is dogged and determined. Accused in 1987 of being 'a bloody nuisance', she had the stomach for a fight, as demonstrated continuously throughout her fourteen-year parliamentary career. An essential quality if one is to be heard and respected in the bear pit that is the Commons.

She clearly got her fortitude from her upbringing. Her father was disabled as a result of a motorbike accident and had a small business, which failed. She was the second of four daughters and spent time in council-provided accommodation. However, this was no impediment to her progress and her determination to this day. Elizabeth exemplifies the strong work ethic her early years so clearly gave her.

By the time Elizabeth was elected to Westminster, she was already well known in her native Yorkshire. After initially volunteering to support the now Sir Nicholas Winterton, in his by-election she became a North Yorkshire county councillor, vehemently opposing colleagues when they sought to scrap the historic York grammar schools, a decision which to this day she believes played a part in seeing her rejected from the Conservatives' parliamentary candidates list.

Undeterred, she declined help from Conservative Central Office and was duly elected as MP for Batley and Spen.

It is easy to forget now, but she served in uncertain times. While she was elected on the crest of the Thatcher wave in 1983, she witnessed the Falklands War and the miners' strikes first-hand. Like all good parliamentarians, however, Elizabeth's chief concern was with her constituents.

Foreword

MPs of Elizabeth Peacock's calibre are rare. She has a unique sense of humour and a great sense of duty. When the modern emphasis is on the sound-bite and the individual, who largely enters believing that he or she is destined for imminent ministerial office, Elizabeth's intake never entered politics seeking a ministerial career.

I have always found colleagues surprising when away from the hustle and bustle of Westminster. I have been fortunate to have had numerous overseas travel companions and my time spent buying pearls under Elizabeth's tutelage in Hong Kong remains one of my fondest memories. It was subsequent to this trip that I discovered her talent for making exquisite jewellery.

In such a male-dominated environment, it is seldom mentioned how difficult this career can be for women. All too often a choice needs to be made between work and family; Elizabeth did both. She remains a shining example for women of all political persuasions of what can be accomplished.

The Rt Hon. Cheryl Gillan MP

Introduction

Over the years since I left Westminster several people have said: 'Elizabeth, you appeared to have an exciting and interesting time at Westminster; you should write it down for us all to enjoy.' I have even had several offers to do the writing.

More recently the question has changed in emphasis:

> As one of only twenty-three women in your early years you should use your experience to give us your opinions of the Thatcher and Major government years. You were never fully in government but you had one of the best seats available from which to comment.

Some time ago I did decide that I would put something on record, if only for the Peacock archives, but would only do so if my husband Brian would get involved with the project. This was important as he was also in a unique position in these years as husband of one of the twenty-three women elected to Westminster in 1983. As a businessman he did not get involved in the political scene during weekdays but then spent many of his Friday nights driving me to supper club events around Yorkshire. During weekends he went to the constituency and to some national events and was my election campaign strategy advisor. He clearly had a close view of my years at Westminster and he eventually, despite the Denis Thatcher comparison comments, agreed to help but it had to be my book. The question was who would be interested in the nuisance I became at Westminster because of my independent views and who would be interested in my measure of the Thatcher and Major years? To answer these questions we decided that we must track my political activities, with some comments on the characters at Westminster ('Characters in the Commons'), placing this all within national government endeavours.

Placing this in context, it is now thirty years since this era began and fifteen years since it ended. Since then we have moved on through New Labour, the regime of Tony Blair and Gordon Brown and back to the new Conservatism of Cameron. Furthermore, most people have today forgotten the dark days of the 'winter of discontent' during the dying weeks of the Wilson and Callaghan government in 1979 which preceded Margaret Thatcher.

We need to evaluate the importance of the Thatcher and Major years. What did this period do for Britain? From this we can assess where Margaret Thatcher and John Major stand in the league table of successful prime ministers.

It could be argued that now is an appropriate time to review their performance and policies some fifteen years after the end point of the era. This gives us the opportunity to stand back and measure the consequences and results of their policies and decisions but is not too long to test memories.

It is true to say that both Margaret Thatcher and John Major are positioned controversially within political history depending upon your own political viewpoint.

Most of us would say that Margaret Thatcher put the 'Great' back into Great Britain, that she really was the 'Iron Lady' and 'not for turning'. On the other hand there are those who cannot bear to use her name and to this day blame her and her policies for everything that went wrong. They brand her as a heartless woman; something that I know is patently not true.

Equally John Major gained the reputation of a 'grey man'; a title he did not deserve and something which time has shown he never warranted.

My story is not, of course, limited to the two main players but includes the teams of people who helped or in some cases hindered progress. Their influence is considerable and has to be measured in terms of their success as team players or good 'spoilers' when in opposition.

I comment on the characters involved in the political scene, having convinced myself that I held a fairly unique position at Westminster during most of these years. Admittedly I was never a major player but I was always in a position to view the events of the day with a woman's open mind. In 1983 women at Westminster were rare, so I was privileged. When I was elected I was only the 115th woman to be elected since Nancy Astor in 1919. Additionally I was elected for a Yorkshire constituency which made me different, as did my un-Tory background. This gave and still gives me the drive to challenge conformity and to speak my mind.

When elected as a county councillor in North Yorkshire and again as Member of Parliament for Batley and Spen I always said that I represented all my constituents and would do my utmost for them, regardless of how they had voted. As my political career existed with a 'knife-edge' majority I was well appraised of the 'other side' of the argument on issues of the day. As a consequence I often took a contrary position to my party, voting with the opposition. This in some eyes branded me as an unreliable nuisance and a rebel. I have always considered myself an independent-minded Yorkshire woman with a commonsense approach to politics; in other words a 'commonsense Conservative'. As we will discover, this approach has led me into difficulties and still does today. How did this brand of commonsense Conservatism arise? Where did it come from?

As we will see later I come from a poor background which would not normally embrace Tory politics. However, my family was very supportive wishing that I, with my sisters, should achieve something in life. I have always been somewhat restless with a degree of ambition which has driven me along. After an education limited by the family financial position, I got involved in running businesses and in public and political life.

People often ask, with your background why did you fight under a Conservative flag?

There never really seemed to be an alternative; I was always in favour of free enterprise and opportunity for all together with a tough line on crime. This was a mix the Labour Party could not offer, nor could the halfway house, the Liberals.

However, with my background I understood that there is an under-privileged community that needs and deserves help if it is prepared to help itself. This gave me a compassionate approach to Conservative politics. The next question was how I could balance these conflicting forces, hardline with compassionate Conservative politics. The answer is easy: come from Yorkshire!

Look at every issue in the round and apply a commonsense formula. This formula got me to Westminster and kept me there for fourteen happy years but it has led me into difficulties on the way and branded me a rebel. The media have often said: 'Elizabeth, we do not understand your politics. On some issues you are hardline right-wing and on others you are liberal left-wing. Please explain.' The answer is that under a Conservative banner I apply a down-to-earth independent mind to issues and look for the commonsense solution. People seem to like it. One other early guideline was that I must enjoy political life while campaigning, both at Westminster and in the constituency. We must have fun as well as work hard.

I was certainly not going to be overcome by the system. If I did not enjoy it I would give up.

Commonsense Conservatism
I arrived at this brand of political philosophy by elimination.

I considered the Labour offer but knew from my early experience that the party had little time for people with my background who they assumed were already Labour supporters. They could never have matched my get-up-and-go spirit or tolerated my independent approach; it would not have worked. So I had to look again! The Liberals of my youth were a halfway house led by an interesting man, Jo Grimond. However, they seemed to be a one-man band with nowhere to go!

Conservatism was the answer. I was attracted by the balanced Harold Macmillan approach, apparently influenced by his experience gained in the Great War. This followed the Disraeli 'One Nation thinking' perpetuated by the Primrose League and seemingly influencing the Edward Heath style. The trouble with Heath governments was a lack of dynamism as they flip-flopped about, apparently lacking direction. The Thatcher approach brought the dynamism with an iron determination which could in some circumstances be too positive. The answer was to take the best of these strands of Conservatism and apply a measure of common sense.

Coming from Yorkshire I had an open mind on most issues. I was determined that I would follow an independent line, if I needed to. My test for commonsense Conservatism was always: 'What would be best for Yorkshire? What would the majority of sensible Yorkshire folk want me to do on this issue or problem? Could I provide a commonsense position?' If these thoughts were positive, that was my line and still is!

I did realize that becoming a Member of Parliament, albeit from a background like mine, opens doors and creates new horizons. An informed backbencher is offered the opportunity from time to time to meet world leaders in many spheres of activity. It somewhat amazed me that a lass from Yorkshire could get into conversation with the President of the United States, which I did with Ronald Reagan and George Bush Senior. I did also meet Bill Clinton but much to my regret could just say 'Hello'!

At the risk of being accused of name-dropping, I had the opportunity to meet many world leaders including Nelson Mandela, Chief Buthelezi, Benazir Bhutto (who I greatly admired), President Gorbachev, and Shimon Peres from Israel. On the world scene the highlight for a Catholic girl was the opportunity to make a presentation to Pope John Paul II in a private audience; what a charming man.

A final observation as we launch the project is the informality of Westminster and government within the working structure. Outside the Chamber first names are in use with the exception of the prime minister. Chancellor of the Exchequer Nigel Lawson was 'Nigel'.

The honour bestowed on an MP is much greater than their electors realize!

Chapter 1

My Early Years and My Drive to Westminster

As already stated, I never intended that I should write an autobiography as many of my former colleagues have already written theirs and there is not much room left on the shelves. However, as one of only twenty-three women in the House in 1983 and having been re-elected in 1987 and 1992 I had a unique view of the Thatcher and Major years with an equally unique northern perspective. I now attempt to give the reader some idea of my background and its influence on my political views. I describe my early years and my drive to get into the House and importantly why I would want to do so. Equally it might help the reader understand why I sometimes found it necessary to rebel against my own government and so became branded as a rebel.

I was one of four daughters in what would now be called a very poor family. My father was severely disabled as the result of a motorbike accident as a young man. This restricted the sort of work he could do but he was determined that he should work. However, during my younger years he was often unemployed so I know all about families where there is not much money, particularly in the days when there were no benefits and certainly no housing support. The rent still had to be paid!

For many years my father traded as a cobbler but had great difficulty in making a living as people did not like paying for shoe repairs. He was born in Skipton, Yorkshire where I grew up, and there he remained. My mother moved to Skipton from the Durham area at the age of 18 to be a nurse, met my father and stayed. My father would traditionally have seen his family going to work in one of the local mills as many of my contemporaries did. My mother was determined that we would not and struggled throughout her life to ensure we had a good start. She was a devout Catholic and resolved that we should be educated at the local

1

convent school to give her daughters a solid basic education from which we all ultimately benefited. Fortunately all four of us passed our 11-plus examination. We lived initially in a small back-to-back house in Victoria Street in the town, moving at some point to a council house of somewhat inferior design on Sharphaw Avenue. I suppose my childhood could be described as hard-up but it was a loving, close family that took an active part in church and town events.

Interestingly in my case I do not recall that we ever discussed politics or took much interest in the electoral process. The local councillors didn't canvass for votes; they just expected to get a Labour vote. I suspect my father voted Labour but he would never say so. Clearly my mother did not support Labour but again would never disclose who she did support. At an early age I realized that local government had problems and that the local council did not look after its property or its tenants and I know that influenced my thoughts.

Born in 1937, I received a good basic education at St Stephen's School and then at St Monica's Convent and did well in the important subjects. As I reached school leaving age my father was again unemployed and as I had two younger sisters someone needed to go to work and earn some money to help support the family. It had to be me but my mother looked to the future and insisted that I take a shorthand and typing course to equip me with skills. With the course completed, I worked in an office at the local hospital and one of the textile mills. This experience helped me in later years.

So I left school with no formal qualifications but a determination to gain experience and make my own mark in life. However, I was never happy with office work. My real interests lay in hair, beauty and fashion and somewhat by chance a good friend offered me the opportunity to train as a hairstylist. This I grabbed, even though the initial pay was lower than I was earning at the time. Following a rapid training period in Yorkshire, Manchester and London I was given the challenge of starting up and managing a new hair and fashion business in Keighley. This quickly grew into a reasonable-sized high street business which promoted charity fashion shows. The latter gave me my first experience of public speaking to a sizeable audience that proved invaluable in later years.

During this period I met my husband-to-be Brian but it took some years to get him to the altar as he was more interested in business, skiing and playing with his sports and racing cars! My ring spent as much of its time on a chain round my neck as it did on my finger. We did eventually marry and we have been good friends for these past fifty years!

The Gates family, 1944. Dorothy and John Gates with Josephine, Margaret and Elizabeth.

Elizabeth Gates, 1945.

Elizabeth Gates, 1962.

Modelling clothes for a charity fashion show, 1960.

Attending a dinner in Skipton in a dress designed and made by the wearer.

Brian Peacock and Elizabeth Gates in 1956 at Leeds University Ball.

Brian had studied bacteriology and biochemistry at Leeds University and joined the family dairy business, West Marton Dairies, with operations in West Yorkshire, Lancashire and Westmorland. This concern became part of the Associated Dairies and Farm Stores Group created by like-minded Yorkshire dairy and farming businesses that became the launch pad for the now famous Asda supermarkets.

Shortly after we married, Brian decided he wanted to strike out on his own by buying a share in an international food consultancy business in Sherborne, Dorset. This proved unsatisfactory so we moved to Cheshire to allow him to take up a management role with the CWS (Co-operative Wholesale Society) in Manchester. These moves brought us into contact with new people and widened our thinking.

When our children were born I gave up work as I believed, and still do, that looking after a family properly as they grow up is a full-time job. My husband Brian agreed but did not think women in this position should sit around drinking coffee. He encouraged me to get involved with the community as an outlet for my restless spirit. I was appointed a school governor in Macclesfield in the early '70s and became very interested in education; something that has lasted to this day. During this period the Labour government and Shirley Williams were bringing in comprehensive schools which I could not see working in the longer term. This together with my business background convinced me that the only cause I could support was the Conservative Party, which surprised me.

By chance at the same time someone asked me to run people to the polling stations at a by-election in Macclesfield, that of Nicholas Winterton. I did so and became a member of the local branch and rather quickly a member of the Macclesfield Constituency Executive.

Equally by good luck I had an opportunity to experience the world of international aid and politics. Building on my interest in business, I had been for several years a member of the UK Business and Professional Women's Organization. During my presidential year of the Macclesfield club, in 1975, I was awarded the Business and Professional Women's International Travel Award which allowed me to attend the WHO/FAO conference in Rome. The conference was concentrating on feeding the world with a demand for international aid to vulnerable areas to bolster agriculture and improve food transportation. This I found fascinating and challenging. On my return I was faced with a year of speaking engagements all around the UK, with a demand for magazine contributions. From this pressure I gained the experience of describing the work of WHO/FAO to

My wedding to Brian Peacock, February 1963.

a diverse range of audiences and answering the inevitable questions. This was obviously good training for a political career which I began to think would be interesting but beyond my horizon.

Also during my Business and Professional Women's presidential year I was nominated and appointed as a magistrate for the Macclesfield Bench, the youngest in the country at the time. I found the work to be a very significant challenge, particularly when I was required to sit in the Knutsford Crown Court with a judge. Inevitably, as a young magistrate with a young family I was recruited to the juvenile bench which brought me into contact with the working of the 1969 Children and Young Persons Act. I was soon outraged by its implications and took the view that Westminster must be full of a bunch of idiots, putting this sort of Act together. They obviously had no idea how things worked at the sharp end. In typical style I soon made my thoughts known on the issue. Even then I was becoming outspoken as I felt no one at Westminster was listening to the common sense of people on the ground. I pestered Nicholas Winterton, who was by then our Member of Parliament, on the issue; so much so that he got fed up with me and said: 'Just get involved yourself and get things changed.' Exactly the catalyst I needed to head me towards a political career!

I instantly realized that having limited senior school education I was at a disadvantage but I was determined to pick up the challenge under a Conservative banner. To expand my experience and develop my political knowledge which was at the time limited I decided to train as a Conservative agent learning to run a constituency, hopefully serving a Conservative Member of Parliament and getting involved in running elections.

Luckily my husband recognized this change of direction and the determination expressed to get involved in politics, not only at the local level but hopefully nationally. He did voice the opinion that I must walk before I could run by first serving at local council level.

Setting off along this new career path was an interesting experience. Thankfully I soon learnt the ropes and was given the task of helping to

The author as President of Macclesfield Business and Professional Women receiving guest speaker Nicholas Winterton MP, 1973.

run the 1979 by-election in Knutsford where the well-known MP John Davies had died and was replaced by Jock Bruce-Gardyne. This followed helping with campaigns in Stockport and Moss Side in Manchester; all very educational!

By the summer of 1979 I was a fully-fledged Conservative agent who really wanted to have a go myself. However, I was election agent for Peter Rost MP who was defending his South Derbyshire Erewash seat. Thankfully we had a good campaign and we got him elected to join the new Margaret Thatcher team at Westminster. Throughout the campaign I realized I would love to have a go myself but in truth 1979 would have been too early for me to stand for Westminster. I was not ready, I needed local council experience and our sons were still too young. I had constantly said that bringing up my family was my most important job and realized that politics must follow in later years. However, my involvement as a juvenile bench magistrate, my frustration with the Children and Young Persons Act, the challenge from Nicholas Winterton and my experience as an election agent got me more and more into the political scene. Consequently in 1978 I was asked to stand for a Cheshire county council seat in a winnable area and said 'yes' as a first stepping-stone.

Then things suddenly changed: just as I was making progress with my political ambitions my husband was offered a new job in Yorkshire that he really wanted to accept. He was offered a position at director level with Northern Dairies/Dale Farm within the Northern Foods Group working with colleagues he had known in earlier years in the Yorkshire dairy scene. He was to be based at Holme-on-Spalding-Moor near York.

It was great moving back to 'God's own county' and a new house but I had to resign all my Cheshire commitments and concentrate on settling two boys into a new school in York. After some discussion we chose Nunthorpe Grammar School because of its approach and its headmaster G.I. Cushing and we found a well-situated house in Old Earswick. Being bright boys who were fully involved in sport, our sons were quickly drawn into the academic work and playing in the cricket and rugby teams and they did not miss their Macclesfield school, the King's School.

In the early months I felt lost but recognized that I had to start again and was determined to do just that. I decided that I would get a job to get me into local community affairs and hopefully into the Yorkshire political scene. As luck would have it I was offered the position of assistant director of the York Council for Voluntary Service with the specific remit to manage a series of charitable trusts that had the objective of helping the people of York. This got me into the local community scene and gave me knowledge of Yorkshire political issues.

Having transferred my political allegiance to the Thirsk and Malton constituency I was offered the chance to stand for North Yorkshire County Council. Thank goodness I was back where I had got to in Cheshire. I now had the challenge of taking the rural ward Flaxton No 3 and getting myself onto North Yorkshire County Council. Flaxton No 3 was held by the Conservatives but had been neglected for some time. The Liberals were set to take the seat. However, we were determined as a family that we would tackle the task and set about leafleting the whole area for the first time in many years. We had few Conservative helpers with the exception of my now long-term friend Carol Raylor who usefully knew the area well. We had a good campaign, even though Brian complained about the sheepdogs that vigorously greeted him on the farms, only to be bitten by a Yorkshire terrier! I was elected to the county council much to the surprise of the Liberals, albeit with a small majority. I joined at a time when there was an interesting mix of characters on all sides of the party divide with the 'old school' of Conservatives in command. The characters included a good sprinkling of ex-military men who I am sure did not approve of women councillors and particularly women who took an independent line but they were wonderful 'old boys'. Among their ranks was Colonel van Straubenzee who regularly turned up at County Hall perfectly dressed but with his regimental tie holding his trousers up!

The county council soon became an eye-opener. The Conservative group was in control but that did not, in some areas, mean we were following what I considered to be true Conservative principles.

It was a time of great educational change nationally and in Yorkshire with a Conservative council scrapping perfectly excellent York grammar schools in favour of a sixth-form college. I took instant exception to this crazy plan and campaigned vigorously against the idea; so much so that I led a delegation to Westminster for a meeting with Secretary of State for Education Keith Joseph and his Minister of State Rhodes Boyson to protest against these plans.

When the issue came to council, I had to vote against. Rebellion number one against my own party when I had just got my foot on the first level of a political career! Little did I know that it would happen again!

I still believe the Conservatives in North Yorkshire were wrong to change their educational policies as they had excellent grammar schools in York and elsewhere. I am sure that time has proved me right because grammar schools in Skipton and Ripon were not touched and still remain strong today.

At about that time I applied to have my name added to the list of suitable candidates to fight a parliamentary seat for the party. After a selection process I was unceremoniously rejected for several reasons. I was told very positively that I was not of a true Conservative background, I had no higher education and limited political experience. Also I had not always supported party policy as I had recently opposed the education plans for North Yorkshire. With these points taken together I was deemed unsuitable as a candidate, and an unreliable member of the party. Of course I was disappointed but I was determined to overcome this rejection which to this day has never been removed from my record. I decided there and then so be it: if the party takes policy routes which are not in the best interest of the people I represent, then I will vote against that policy regardless of the consequences. I never went into politics to gain preference and position; I just went into politics to get things done, hopefully to the benefit of everyone within my constituency regardless of their vote. This rejection, however, spurred me on. I talked to my friends who were on the candidates list and asked them to let me have details of northern parliamentary constituencies who were planning to select a candidate for the likely 1983 general election, so that I could apply direct to the constituencies.

The timing was right. Our sons were heading through their education with Jonathan, the eldest, going to Oxford to study law. Nicholas was planning to follow in two years' time with law in mind but with rugby to the forefront as he had played for Yorkshire Schoolboys.

I soon discovered that it was not easy for a woman to be selected to fight a parliamentary seat. I always got the questions: 'What about your husband and family? Should you really be at home looking after them?'

I have often said it is easier for a woman to get elected than selected in the first place. I had to overcome this prejudice to get selected. I really wanted a Yorkshire seat but I needed experience of the selection process, so off I went for interviews in Grimsby to fight Austin Mitchell, to Blackburn to fight Jack Straw and to Doncaster North. I usually got onto the short list but thankfully as it turned out was not successful; the men always won!

Suddenly along came the new seat of Batley and Spen which looked like a good challenge, albeit a likely Labour win but one very difficult to judge. Yes, I was selected after a good fight with local candidates and the announcement made in local papers before it was discovered that I was not on the party approved list. After a few days' discussion the party accepted the selection on the basis that 'she will not win so there's no problem'.

I was selected on 29 March 1983 and therefore had just six weeks before the general election to prove them wrong. I did know this part of Yorkshire fairly well but did not know many of the electors. However, Brian had business connections in the area and so we knew some of the 'movers and shakers'.

The constituency was new, being a mix of Brighouse and Spenborough and Batley and Morley. It had no money or agent but it did have a constituency secretary, Mary Bentley, who had fought and won in several general elections. So with my 19-year-old son we fought my first general election from the boot of my car and from Mary's kitchen table in Scholes – it was a great experience.

Throughout the campaign I had the support of a number of dedicated Conservatives who encouraged me, and while many have now passed on, the remainder are firm friends. This team was led by my president the late Doug Brewer, a local solicitor, who had been fighting elections for years and who subsequently supported me when I got into political scrapes at Westminster. I was always in Doug's debt for his support. My other great helper at the time was Eric Marshall who had interesting and wide-ranging friendships in the Asian community in Batley. Eric proved to be an invaluable contact, particularly with the Asian businessmen.

My View

Yes, we did win and I rode to Westminster on the tails of Margaret Thatcher's coat. My early life was over and my political life had commenced: I had made it to Westminster from Yorkshire as one of the few women in the House with a very un-Conservative background. Maybe I was lucky but sometimes you have to make your own luck. Suddenly I was now the Member of Parliament for Batley and Spen; only the 115th woman elected to Parliament since Nancy Astor in 1919 and the first Conservative MP for Batley since the 1930s when a National Liberal was elected.

Chapter 2

Prelude to the Thatcher Years
(1975–79)

Preparing the pitch

To understand the Thatcher era it is important to understand the political scene that brought her to power in 1979. The 1970s were a period of almost constant political upheaval nationally and an equally important period of political awakening for me.

Nationally Edward Heath had got himself into a tangle with the trade unions and staged a battle with the miners without the necessary long-term planning. For me, I moved politically from a keen local activist in Cheshire to a trainee, then qualified Conservative agent which gave me full exposure to the current political scene that I hoped might some day take me to Westminster. I somehow had never been switched on by Edward Heath and his Conservative brand of politics and policies. His government did not seem to have a goal or objective; he was an enigma and his politics were the same. I quite understood why the country decided that they wanted a change in 1974 and put Harold Wilson into Downing Street. However, Ted did have political talent and ability. You cannot become Tory leader or prime minister without.

I had personal experience of Edward's enigmatic style in the 1980s when I eventually arrived at Westminster. As will be explained, I shared an office with Angela Rumbold for four years and in the next office on one side we had ex-paratrooper Jim Spicer, the MP for Dorset, who was in our office on a regular basis trying to get us to use the House of Commons gym. On the other side we had Ted Heath and I don't remember entering his office or him ours in all those years. We always knew when he was in because his bodyguards sat on a chaise longue in the corridor outside reading newspapers and looking for someone to engage in conversation. The surprise was that suddenly I received an invitation for me and my husband to go to a drinks party at Ted's then London home. Being rather curious as to the objective, I accepted and we went. On arrival we discovered that those present were Ted's friends and supporters. He remembered that we had not been before when we asked about his many photographs around the house. He then took us on a complete tour of the place, looking at his collection of watercolours and sailing photographs while discussing the political scene. I never did understand why he invited us as by then I had begun to express my independent views and he was seeking allies for a comeback. He was clearly disappointed as I never had a real conversation with him again, just a passing of the time of day when we met. An unusual man who was rejected by the country, then the party. His style opened the door for change, firstly to Wilson and then to Thatcher.

From the day that Margaret Thatcher defeated Ted Heath in 1975 for the leadership of the Conservative Party she was preparing herself for eventual government. This was at the time a tall order as Ted had got himself and the party into a tangle with the electorate. He had gone to the country to fight an election, providing a challenge to voters to decide 'who runs the country'. They decided very positively that he should not as his brand of Conservatism was 'wishy-washy' and so he paid the price.

Margaret had, as a first task, to give credibility to the idea of a woman leading the party and to restore the confidence of the Conservative Party. This was all rather difficult with a former prime minister in your ranks who was sulking and plotting with his equally defeated colleagues. She accepted this challenge and took the attack to the Labour Party led initially by Harold Wilson and latterly by Jim Callaghan. Labour managed to shoot themselves in the foot with the help of the unions getting Britain into a terrible financial state. Britain really did become the 'sick man of Europe'. As a consequence Labour only managed to cling to power with the help of a pact with the Liberals: the Lib-Lab pact.

So during these years (1975–79), circumstances could have forced an election at any time that could have taken Margaret to Downing Street. Using her typical positive approach she prepared herself for power with a small dedicated team. The question remains even today as to whether the Conservative Party totally endorsed her early efforts. Some members of the party looked for a Heath comeback as they were doubtful about a woman as leader and I believe many were not in favour of her positive Conservatism. In these four years Margaret Thatcher was taking positive and fundamental steps planning to change Britain for the better, while I was still dreaming of a campaign to get me to Westminster.

Historically it has been recognized that those prime ministers who have subsequently been considered to be a success have taken their most bold and positive steps in the early days of their reign. Margaret had planned these bold steps because she knew an election could come at short notice.

For example, there is evidence to show that Balfour in the early 1930s took positive action as soon as he entered Downing Street. There is equally clear evidence from the very successful 1945 Labour government that Clement Attlee grabbed the reins at once and drove his team forward. He transformed Britain in five years from its 1930s attitude into a modern society, using his big majority to great effect. This he did in the most difficult post-war circumstances of continued austerity and rationing. On the other hand at a much later date Tony Blair, with a similar-sized majority and great initial plans for change, failed to achieve an equivalent momentum!

Not so Margaret Thatcher; she knew what she wanted to do from the word go after the 1979 election. She had planned in advance and her determination pushed through those plans, regardless of the difficult circumstances and roadblocks laid by some of her Conservative colleagues. She was determined to attack the issues that had branded Britain the 'sick man of Europe' based on the ills of the economy and outrageous trade union behaviour. These were difficult matters to take on, leading inevitably to unpopularity, even before she was in power. She eventually took a two-pronged approach that proved a success: she sorted the economy and changed the trade unions but she certainly had difficulties along the way. A normal person may have wilted under the pressure of planning for office but Margaret Thatcher did not; she was built of sterner stuff. Love her or hate her, she certainly was different.

By early 1974 the Heath government had provided a lot of difficulties for the Conservatives including strikes and three-day working weeks, so in February a general election was called. The result was that the Conservative government had a majority of seventeen which should have been manageable but the country was not happy with the situation as it appeared unstable. When the police were unable to control striking miners at Sketchley gas-works, Ted Heath decided to go to the country and fight under the banner 'Who runs the country', seeking confirmation to continue. The electors decided otherwise and Heath was defeated, handing over to Harold Wilson.

Things did not get better as Harold Wilson could not repeat the successes of his first administration and always appeared to be on the back foot. The trade unions dominated his government, even with negotiation based on beer and sandwiches in Downing Street. Wilson could not get the unions to take a sensible approach to industry. When 'Sunny Jim' Callaghan took over in 1976 he did not make progress either. In essence the Labour Party and the Wilson–Callaghan government had lost control of Britain to the unions. By 1976 the government was crumbling and the Labour majority was dwindling as deaths of Labour members resulted in their seats going to Tories or Liberals. By 1978 Callaghan was in real trouble so he did a deal with David Steel and the Liberals to form a Lib-Lab pact. This pact extended the life of the Labour government through the winter into 1979. This period became known as the 'winter of discontent' due to the great number of strikes around the country resulting in household rubbish not being collected and the dead not being buried.

The Lib-Lab axis was clearly unstable but the pact was held in place until spring 1979 by a handful of votes including some from minority parties. In late spring 1979 my predecessor in Batley, the well-liked and sensible Labour MP Dr Alfred Broughton, could not go through the lobby to vote due to ill health and the government fell. Sadly Dr Broughton died shortly afterwards. The whips had an important part to play in holding the government in power for so long. The well-respected Labour whip Walter Harrison MP for Wakefield and the Conservative whip and future Speaker Bernard Weatherill played a dramatic part in the eventual downfall of the government (see 'Speakers').

I always understood in a close-run political situation as in 1974 why the country chose Harold Wilson: he was a down-to-earth and charming Yorkshire man. Obviously I was not in the House when he was prime minister but I met him several times in the 1980s when we attended Scout tea parties organized by the Speaker, when Harold would bring out a photograph of his favourite Huddersfield Town football team. He was a crafty politician in his day but maybe not strong enough to handle the unions, this weakness being compounded when Jim Callaghan took the reins. This was somewhat surprising as they had some strong players on their team, especially those from Yorkshire including Denis Healey and Merlyn Rees (Home Office).

Later on in my career I discovered that these two senior Labour politicians could also tolerate a lowly Tory backbencher. Denis Healey, my future fellow Yorkshire MP, was in the Chancellor of the Exchequer seat with plenty of problems throughout the Wilson/Callaghan period. He got plenty of stick from the media which he weathered with true Yorkshire grit. In 1993 when Denis won the Yorkshire Man of the Year Award and I won the Yorkshire Woman of the Year Award we got into hot water with the TV producers for being too jovial and fooling about on the programme. He had the audience in stitches with me as the fall guy!

As is obvious, I was not in the House during this historic period and some would say that I am not really qualified to pass an opinion on the events. However, I have often spoken to my colleagues who were there and to media who reported on the events. This has given me enough knowledge to share my view.

My View

I will make no further comment on the Lib-Lab pact, other than to say its performance helped Mrs Thatcher into Downing Street.

With the passage of thirty years it has become somewhat difficult to remember the chaos of the 1975–79 years with the trade unions attempting to run the country by sidelining the government. Anarchy reigned; trade union leaders grabbed power with the support of militant members and the help of parts of the media. The economy was out of control and the country was heading for disaster. It was obvious that things had to change. The alternative was Mrs Thatcher and the Conservatives. Not too surprisingly, on election day this resulted in a 44-seat Conservative majority and Margaret Thatcher became the first woman prime minister of Great Britain.

As the party had elected her as leader in 1975 her determination and self-confidence were soon recognized, as was her intense political stance. Those who worked with her in the early days noted her pleasing personal style. As a potential prime minister she had a great ability to put the finger on populist issues. There has always been discussion as to whether she used her femininity to get her own way. The gender issue as first woman party leader and eventual prime minister will never be answered.

Probably the issue that initially highlighted her approach to governing was her economics which had always been different from earlier Tory leaders. It was positively laissez-faire liberalism.

Her greatest problem was the views and reactions of her Cabinet colleagues who had voted almost to a man for Ted Heath in the leadership battle and were not always as supportive as I might have expected.

Whatever might be said or written about Margaret Thatcher and her legacy to the nation, no one can truthfully deny that during her premiership she was formidable, courageous and played a significant role in reversing Britain's prestige and position in the world as we will discuss later.

I am convinced that really successful prime ministers set the agenda before they get to Downing Street and that when they do arrive, they hit the ground running. Margaret did just that! She had to work hard to move the party along from the low-key Conservatism of Ted Heath to her style of positive Conservatism. By 1979 she was making some progress but she still had too many 'wets' (as she labelled them) within her team; a problem she would have for several more years. However, she had their measure (just) and her determination won out.

The Thatcher Years

* * *

Chapter 3

Early Attack
(1979-83)

The Thatcher revolution

As I have outlined, I was deeply involved in the political scene in these years attempting to follow my plan to get to Westminster. I knew I could not achieve my goal in 1979; my children were too young and I needed a stronger political background. This I was gaining as part of the team fighting by-elections in Knutsford, Moss Side (Manchester) and elsewhere. In 1979 I was the election agent for Peter Rost, Member of Parliament for Erewash in South Derbyshire, so played a minor part in the Conservative success.

The 1979 election was fought around the previous government's record under the strain of Irish terrorism. This was due to the recent assassination of Shadow Secretary of State for Northern Ireland Airey Neave by a car bomb on the ramp of the House of Commons car park. This caused the stepping-up of security for ministers and MPs. Inevitably Labour then had to fight on the government's record which was not good following the 'winter of discontent'. They tried hard to avoid left-wing issues of abolition of the House of Lords and nuclear weapons. This put Jim Callaghan on the defensive from the beginning and he was never able to put a dent in the Conservative lead in the polls.

In the early days of Mrs Thatcher's leadership various commentators had referred to her as rather inexperienced. This had changed by the end of the campaign, the same commentators now noting her uncompromising headmistress style.

When Margaret Thatcher won the 1979 general election with a workable 44-seat majority it was a defining point in British politics and history. Not only did it bring the first woman into the role of prime minister, it brought someone with determination for change and someone with a clear understanding of what the nation needed. Clearly I was not at Westminster but I took a daily interest in the political scene as I was equally determined that I should somehow get to Westminster at the next election. As a consequence my views of these years are those of a committed bystander. The 'Thatcher revolution' had begun.

Taking a view of this period in 2012 emphasizes the changes that have been achieved in the intervening years and the difficulties faced by Mrs Thatcher as she took office. As I have outlined earlier, the steps Margaret took in this period laid down the success of her period in Downing Street when she put the 'Great' back into Great Britain. She set the scene for her government at the Conservative conference in October 1980 with the memorable statement: 'You turn if you want to; the lady's not for turning.' This statement was designed to confront the Liberal 'wet' Heathite wing of the party, who advocated a U-turn regarding her liberalization of the economy.

As we come to analyze the events and challenges of this period we can see three major issues to be addressed. At this point in time some thirty years later it is difficult to recognize the mess the country was in after the 'winter of discontent' and the shambles the outgoing Labour government and its Lib-Lab pact had left behind. The pact had held the Labour government in place for an additional two years but had been powerless to act against the trade unions.

The first challenge to the incoming government was to tackle the economic ills, re-structure British industry and reform the activities of the trade unions, taking them out of the political arena. Inflation was out of control at 10 per cent and rising, with sky-high oil prices and government costs rising by the day.

The second challenge was Britain's relationship with Europe. We had been taken into the European Union against the better judgement of many people on terms which did not seem favourable to Britain. This turned into an ongoing battleground throughout the Thatcher years.

The third and really defining challenge for Margaret Thatcher was not even on the horizon when she took office, namely the Falklands problem and subsequent conflict. Her stance in dealing with this later issue together with the resolution of the war pushed her right up into the elite of British prime ministers where she remains today despite her subsequent later problems.

As we all expected, Mrs Thatcher hit the ground running as soon as she knew she had won the election with a workable majority. She had, with the typical approach of a determined woman, planned ahead and decided her early plan of campaign.

Within hours of the result she had a Cabinet in place. Whether it really was the Cabinet she would have chosen with a totally free hand, we will never know. It had some stunning players: Geoffrey Howe as Chancellor, Willie Whitelaw at the Home Office, Peter Carrington as Foreign Secretary and the guru of the philosophy Keith Joseph at Industry. However, this was probably not strength in depth as some of the other players were in post to balance the Heathite factors within the Conservative Party which was a coalition within. As Margaret would later say, they were 'wets' and not 'one of us'. They were not true Thatcherites, not providing the sort of action she required. This structure held back her early years and had to be corrected in a later re-shuffle.

Economic ills: the need for re-structure of British industry and trade unions

Britain and the whole economy were in serious trouble in 1979. Inflation was out of control and industry was faced with wage demands and related strikes, these being driven by a union movement which was under militant control. Additionally, public spending had been allowed to grow and had become unsustainable.

But where to start? Margaret Thatcher had a plan but she really needed new thinking in government and within the Conservative ranks and it was not initially available.

Tax rates were too high; the top rate of 83 per cent and standard rate of 33 per cent had to be reduced, together with the removal of dividend and exchange controls. The outgoing Labour government had tried using price controls to stem inflation but they had not worked and had to be abolished.

To balance the budget public spending had to be reduced across most areas with the exception of the NHS, defence, and law and order. This led to early opposition to Mrs Thatcher's plans from sectors of the Conservative Party who could not understand the concept of cutting budgets in this manner, and those people concerned within her Cabinet being branded 'wets' as described above. Such a banner was pinned on those who did not follow the great lady's thinking or who got in her way, as did Norman St John-Stevas, a real character.

Despite her endeavours, by the spring of 1980 the economic situation had worsened and positive steps were needed. Social security costs were too high due to the level of unemployment, sickness, injury, maternity and invalidity payments and had to be reviewed. Action was required to counter the widely-held view: 'Why work? Benefit payments are better than a wage.' In truth this was an area that Margaret Thatcher never solved and a problem that remains today thirty years on.

What she did recognize, however, was the fact that since 1945 Britain had retained a culture of government interference in industry from the totally nationalized industries to economic controls on private business, something that successive Conservative governments had failed to address in the intervening years. The Thatcher philosophy of the 'free market' without government involvement and interference was outside the scope of much contemporary thinking. This is something we do not understand today. The concept put Mrs Thatcher on a collision course with many of her government team, making it difficult to get things done to her satisfaction.

Additionally it was soon realized that wage demands, lack of price competitiveness in the markets and associated strikes were not the only problem. Low industrial productivity, the lowest in Europe, was the underlying issue and had to be corrected by placing some control over trade union activities. Margaret realized that government control of industry was the wrong way to go to provide a solution to these problems.

I always realized that the crucial step was the introduction of legislation to deal with trade union power, where militants had gained key positions throughout the union movement. This new legislation was designed to control secondary picketing, ban closed shops and introduce better rules on ballots. The TUC and some unions recognized the implications of these controls and were prepared to listen to government but there was little willingness to co-operate and progress was difficult. The unions would not face the economic facts, preferring the monopoly or a government-protected route for British industry.

Even within government there was a difficulty as Jim Prior, the minister responsible, did not see eye-to-eye with Margaret Thatcher on the policy to follow but she got her way in the end. This basic concept of bringing union activity under control transformed British industry and was a positive example of the role played by Margaret Thatcher in shaping modern Britain by her resolve.

To get what was needed the government had to fight through the Commons, the Lords and in the courts. They had to withstand argument and strikes across the industrial landscape. One example was British Steel, which to remain competitive could not afford the union demand for increased wages. This led to a strike, as did disputes between newspaper proprietors and the National Union of Journalists. Margaret summed the whole problem up in her speech to Conservative trade unionists in November 1979:

> British Steel would like to import coking coal to make its steel more competitive. But the miners NUM opposes this saying 'buy our coking coal' even if it is more expensive. If British Steel agree they must, in turn, say to the car manufacturers 'buy our steel' even if it is more expensive, but then British Leyland and other car manufacturers have to ask the consumer 'please buy our cars' even if they are more expensive. But we are all consumers and as consumers we need a choice and we want to buy the best value for money. If foreign cars or washing machines are cheaper or better than the British goods, the consumer wants the choice. The trouble is trade unionists as producers want a protected market for their products, but the same trade unionists, as consumers, want an open market. They cannot both win but they can both lose. (Margaret Thatcher, *The Downing Street Years*)

For some years the British Steel Corporation had accumulated serious losses. If the government was serious about turning it around, there would have to be plant closures, a wage freeze and a re-organization of working practices that inevitably would lead to a strike. The unacceptable alternative was to allow the losses to continue. The government decided on positive action and the strike was called and eventually resolved with the management gaining better control. The situation at British Leyland was somewhat similar, with very poor financial results leading to the prospect of liquidation. The solution demanded plant closures and huge job losses, all in the face of trade union obstruction on every issue. Politically the company had to be supported by a re-structure plan that, against the better judgement of government members, required an injection of £900 million of taxpayers' funds.

The coal industry had played a major part in the downfall of Ted Heath and his government in 1974 and looked as though it would cause serious problems for the Thatcher government in 1981 with Arthur Scargill heading the miners' union (NUM).

Since 1974 the industry had developed several profitable new pits but because of difficulties with the unions on closures most of the old unprofitable pits had remained open causing overall losses for the National Coal Board. This had to be corrected so the NCB resolved to close fifty of these pits and conflict seemed inevitable. Somewhat mysteriously, a joint government, NUM and NCB meeting agreed to the closure of twenty-three pits, so with other concessions on redundancy and finance a coal strike was averted by negotiation.

Throughout the whole of the period of union unrest I know the government was making progress with the 1980 Employment Act that would ban secondary picketing, change the rules on closed shops and make the unions responsible for unlawful actions of their members.

By the autumn of 1980 these challenges had taken their toll on the popularity of Margaret Thatcher and her government. The government was struggling; unemployment was now 2 million and rising. The recession was deepening with oil prices doubling and world inflation rising. However, Mrs Thatcher was convinced that she was following the right strategy to achieve a fundamental change in Britain. The problem was that people did not understand where she was going. To emphasize this she had to explain, which she did. She nailed her flag to the mast at the Conservative conference with that now-famous statement: 'You turn if you want to; the lady's not for turning.'

With her resolve confirmed and better understood, the policy continued placing importance on restraining public expenditure, trade union reform and developing a sound monetary policy. On public expenditure the 'wets' decision was one of 'borrow and spend', providing support for industry and creating employment with an associated increase in taxes to provide the funds, labelled the 'wet approach'. The alternative Thatcher approach was to keep taxes low to encourage industry and employment and let the market decide. She eventually won the argument but with plenty of drama along the way.

A world recession created real problems for public expenditure and monetary policy development. Geoffrey Howe played a significant part working with Margaret Thatcher to address the issues, though the two of them were to have their differences in later years. The steps they took did not correct the financial position which continued to deteriorate during 1981 and created a huge private and public debate on monetary policy between Geoffrey Howe and Mrs Thatcher and her advisor Alan Walters.

Throughout the first two years of her government Margaret Thatcher had suffered leaks and dissent from within her government due to dislike of her new brand of Conservatism. By January 1981 she had decided there had to be change so she removed several people from the government including Norman St John-Stevas, Francis Pym and Angus Maude (he resigned), bringing in the talented Leon Brittan, Norman Tebbit and Kenneth Baker who were in line with her thinking. However, dissenters remained who could not handle this 'free market' Conservatism. Maybe she should have had a wider reshuffle.

To add to her problems urban riots in 1981 placed even greater pressure on Mrs Thatcher and her team. In April riots broke out in Brixton, shops were looted and cars destroyed with up to 150 police officers injured and over 200 people arrested. The cause was related to growing unemployment. In July riots broke out in Southend, Toxteth in Liverpool and Moss Side, Manchester with fighting and hostility towards the police. The Labour Party blamed Conservative economic policy, while others cited police brutality. Despite a thorough investigation by Lord Scarman, the causes remain obscure but they put pressure on the government.

As a consequence of this pressure, dissent within the Cabinet continued to the prime minister's annoyance. The dissenters believed it was unacceptable for unemployment to be heading towards 3 million and that the government should spend to stimulate the economy. The prime minister did not agree, stating that a smaller part of the nation's income should go to the government, thus freeing funds for the private sector to create jobs. The Cabinet was split on the issue with the 'wets' increasing their arguments and leaving the prime minister vulnerable to overthrow. However, with the aid of Willie Whitelaw, Keith Joseph and Geoffrey Howe the Thatcherite policy won the day. To consolidate her position a further change in the Cabinet team was inevitable and this occurred in September 1981 with Ian Gilmour, Christopher Soames and Mark Carlisle leaving the government, Jim Prior moving to the post of Northern Ireland Secretary and Cecil Parkinson replacing Peter Thorneycroft as party chairman. I believe these moves fundamentally changed the philosophy of government and Margaret Thatcher had a team made up of those considered 'one of us'.

Throughout 1978 to 1981 I was busy working with the party, firstly in Macclesfield and the local association in a voluntary capacity and later as a trainee party agent. In this later role I was in the thick of the political scene. My first job as a trainee was to work with the Stockport Association preparing for what looked like an immediate election in the autumn of

1978 when the Lib-Lab pact seemed shaky. I got the job of preparing the election literature working with the candidate Dr David Skidmore, a dynamic and competent surgeon at the local hospital. The election did not happen but the experience of starting a campaign from scratch was great. Dr Skidmore never did get to Westminster but he would have added interest to the House. In later years he did make the news as he was near the Grand Hotel in Brighton when the IRA bomb exploded and he courageously went into the bombed building with the firemen to give skilled medical assistance to the victims; a very brave man!

I worked on two by-elections of differing style and demand which looking back were valuable for my own political career. Moss Side, Manchester was a Labour stronghold but we had a lively local candidate who was determined to make a mark. We did not win but I learnt how to handle a campaign in a difficult constituency.

Knutsford (1979) was a great contest; a Tory stronghold that had become vacant due to the death of the sitting member John Davies who was a government minister. Despite a potentially good Conservative majority we had a strong campaign with a confident but somewhat different candidate Jock Bruce-Gardyne. We won quite easily but I have since been convinced that you have to campaign with maximum effort to win any by-election.

By the time the 1979 general election came along I had learnt how to read the political scene and could run an election campaign myself which I did for Peter Rost MP in Erewash, Derbyshire. This gave me the confidence to run my own campaign in Batley and Spen later.

I found the economic actions taken to be impressive but with serious side-effects. Before the 1979 election the Conservatives had pledged to cut public spending and borrowing, reduce inflation and taxation to encourage enterprise and provide a climate for growth. Public expenditure was curbed but with the proportion of gross domestic product (GDP) above the level agreed with the IMF by the Wilson/Callaghan government. The public sector borrowing requirement fell from 5.7 per cent of GDP to 2.75 per cent by 1983. This in turn had an influence on inflation; the Retail Price Index at 21.9 per cent in 1980 falling to 4 per cent by 1983. All this had a serious effect on unemployment which rose to 2 million in 1980 and to 3 million in 1982 (the highest since 1933). Minimum lending rate was replaced by a more flexible system to manage interest rates.

I was pleased to see that the privatization of state assets became the norm because almost any business runs better as a private company. To my delight, state-owned trading companies such as British Aerospace, Britoil, the National Freight Corporation, Cable and Wireless, and Amersham International among others were privatized with other sales scheduled for future years.

The Thatcher initiative to allow council-house tenants to buy their council houses was progressed with vigour. Many tenants were given the right to buy their homes; a great inspired policy.

Labour Party split

After two years in office it looked as though Mrs Thatcher was to be a one-term prime minister. Then quite suddenly the scene changed: the Labour Party split, which made more Labour seats winnable so I was happy.

The behaviour of the Labour Party in this to some extent came to the rescue of the Thatcher project as the Labour split failed to react to the change in Conservatism. The 1979 Labour Party conference approved new rules for re-selection of Labour MPs and gave the unions and constituency members a share in electing the party leader. This created a divergent split in the party, with Tony Benn and the Left gaining confirmation of these rule changes and the freedom to lobby for unilateral disarmament and withdrawal from the Common Market. This caused the party Right led by Roy Jenkins, David Owen, Shirley Williams and William Rogers to form the Social Democratic Party which quickly formed an alliance with the Liberals and at the same time split the opposition. This gave me hope but I was unlikely to find a safe Tory seat to fight; however, a Labour-held seat with an SDP split would be promising.

The international scene

During these early Thatcher years I thought that Margaret Thatcher and her government looked to be more successful on the international scene in the 1979–83 period than they were on the domestic front. The overriding theme was to match the military and political challenges of communism within the Soviet countries who were pressing on with the development of nuclear weapons. This provided an ongoing need to measure the military balance between the NATO Alliance and the Warsaw Pact forces.

Early in her premiership Mrs Thatcher became the first foreign leader to visit Ronald Reagan in Washington after his election in November 1979. These two hit it off at once and cemented a real understanding between the USA and Great Britain that was firmer than anything before or since. The threat of nuclear development in the Soviet bloc led by President Brezhnev was recorded, thus causing Britain to head towards the purchase of the Trident nuclear deterrent system, an issue that caused me plenty of problems during the 1979 and 1983 elections.

This close relationship also had the benefit of allowing joint consideration of economic challenges, especially the policy aimed at reducing budgetary deficits. In my opinion these Thatcher/Reagan discussions laid the foundation for better economic conditions from 1983 onwards. Margaret Thatcher gave the impression of being a driven person who, in the presence of a relaxed personality like Ronald Reagan, contributed at the highest level. Having also met Ronald Reagan at a later date I can clearly understand how these two people could develop a positive and helpful understanding.

Margaret had the good sense to use this advantage when building relationships with the Soviet bloc. Russia was at this time involved in a failing campaign in Afghanistan that produced the stimulant for the development of Muslim radicalism and subsequent terrorism that has caused ongoing problems. In truth Margaret Thatcher made a great success of these worldwide negotiations and relationship-building but they were lost on the British public because of the problems being experienced on the home front.

A major factor in Mrs Thatcher's early years was, of course, the Falklands conflict but as the outcome was very important to the Thatcher project I have decided that we should give it separate consideration (see Chapter Four).

The European scene

Relations with our European colleagues were constantly strained during the early 1980s with the main players qualifying for a good 'handbagging' as they conspired against Britain and Mrs Thatcher. Maybe it was because of her forthright personality or maybe it was because she was a woman leading in a man's world. It is true that she openly considered the European Union to be interventionist, protectionist and ultimately federalist; all parameters at odds with the Thatcher philosophy and she said so! This was an approach that was bound to create opposition and confrontation, especially when it was clear that the EU was controlled by a French/ German axis.

It was clearly evident that Margaret had some difficulties working with Giscard d'Estaing and Helmut Schmidt who referred to her as 'the Iron

Lady'. It was no secret that she could not get along with Giscard. Despite these difficulties Margaret Thatcher insisted that her government should take an active part in European affairs and that Britain's European credentials should be improved.

The big battleground was the EU budget and its implications for Britain. Mrs Thatcher considered that the British contribution was too high and as insufficient benefit was coming to Britain it should therefore be reduced. Too much support was being given to agriculture with insufficient emphasis on structural and investment programmes. The EU Commission acknowledged that it was possible to achieve a balanced portfolio. This allowed Mrs Thatcher to insist that a reduction in Britain's net contribution should last as long as the problem existed and is still in place in 2012! The inequality still applies so the reduced contribution remains relevant, albeit the components of the discussion may have changed.

The hard Thatcher line was exposed to widespread EU opposition in Dublin and Luxembourg but eventually Peter Carrington and Ian Gilmour, under Thatcher guidance, finalized a deal in May 1984 at Foreign Secretary level which benefits Britain to this day.

My View

The early years of the Thatcher reign (1979–81) were turbulent with Margaret wanting to move dynamically forward with her revolutionary politics. She was, however, constrained by her more liberal Cabinet which she was forced to reshuffle twice to get a Cabinet more in her mould. She was beset by economic problems that were intensified by the actions of the trade unions which were out of control. Positive steps were taken to correct these items by new legislation.

The Cabinet reshuffle of September 1981 and the advent of the Falklands War proved crucial to the continuation of the Thatcher project. Indeed, an election or an event of political significance in the autumn of 1981 could have seen Margaret Thatcher ousted as she did not have a cohesive team at the time. Fortunately the Cabinet re-structure brought together a team that could work in harmony using the Thatcher philosophy of prudence and hardline policies. In retrospect, perhaps the reshuffle should have come earlier but it is difficult to judge the circumstances at this point in time. Just maybe Mrs Thatcher was too nice and therefore failed to change the team earlier; a concept that many people would find difficult to accept!

She and the government in this two-year period were just not popular; unemployment was too high and people were not happy. An election at that point would have seen Mrs Thatcher disappear. An election did not happen and as we shall see, the Falklands War changed the scene completely.

However, I have often wondered whether the problems with her Shadow Cabinet pre-1979 and her Cabinet in her early years could be put down wholly to a difference in political outlook or whether like many men they were unhappy working for and being dominated by a dynamic woman. It is not unknown for some men to say: 'I will not work for a woman boss.' In this case did the 'wets' join the team but were not good team players?

Chapter 4

The Falklands War

A defining moment

Until I began to analyze the first Thatcher government (1979–83) I had not realized the nature and importance of the Falklands War and how it was handled by Mrs Thatcher. In retrospect I now appreciate this had an effect on my eventual political career. The first two Thatcher years had been difficult and put in question a future Conservative government. The Falklands saved the situation and changed the scene. For that reason alone I now look at the war in some depth.

As I have already commented and history has recorded, the Thatcher government was in a fairly serious position at the end of 1981 with many domestic problems and a big fight in Europe. History also shows that the handling of the Falklands War in early 1982 when Argentina invaded the Falkland Islands completely transformed the Thatcher project. The positive approach and determined leadership of Margaret Thatcher elevated her into the position of a world-class stateswoman with a distinctive place in British and world history. It also lifted the prospects of the Conservative Party from a potentially difficult position in the public esteem to an election-winning organization. However, the whole incident got off to a difficult start that even today takes some explaining and leaves questions in the mind. It is true to say that during this period I, like many others, followed the daily events. It was much later in my time at Westminster that I worked on the detail as the issue would reappear from time to time in debate.

History records that the British first arrived in the Falkland Islands (Argentine – Las Malvinas) in 1690 and populated the islands in 1833. Being off-shore from Argentina the islands have been subject to a sovereignty claim by the Argentines for much of the time, despite fierce opposition from the British settlers. Over the years there have been discussions on how to resolve the dispute including a meeting as late as February 1982 on a so-called 'lease-back' deal.

In the early 1980s Argentina suffered political instability which placed General Leopoldo Galtieri in the presidency with the personal objective of adding Las Malvinas to Argentina. Suddenly, and to the surprise of the Thatcher government, the Argentines invaded and claimed the Falkland Islands on 2 April 1982.

The first official reaction to a possible invasion was when Defence Secretary John Nott recorded on 31 March that there had been Argentine press speculation of an invasion and that the Argentine fleet was at sea.

Obviously detailed planning for the invasion must have been made by the Argentines. There was speculation in their press and the subsequent resignation of senior British figures there suggests that some knowledge was available and not adequately acted upon. What has never been explained is the role of the Foreign Office and the diplomatic service who failed to report the threat.

What we do know is that when John Nott first raised the matter with Margaret Thatcher on the evening of 31 March 1982 in her office in the House of Commons she made instant and positive decisions which were to confirm her premiership.

Sir Henry Leach Chief of Naval Staff had been asked to join the meeting and during the discussion offered to pull together a task force of naval vessels carrying troops and aircraft, capable of retaking the Falkland Islands should they be invaded. Margaret made the decision to proceed there and then and he left the meeting to begin organizing such a task force; issue management Thatcher-style!

Mrs Thatcher also decided she would speak to her friend President Reagan and ask him to put pressure on Galtieri not to invade. This, of course, was to no avail and the Falkland Islands were invaded. As I was later to realize, an incident of this gravity automatically leads to a debate in the House of Commons which necessitates bringing members back from all parts of the world. The idea of a task force gained support on the assumption that there would be no fighting. John Nott ran into real trouble in the House for having pushed for defence cuts and Peter Carrington and his Foreign Office team had similar problems for not knowing about the Argentine invasion plan. This led to the subsequent resignations of Peter Carrington, Humphrey Atkins and Richard Luce, whereas John Nott remained in post to handle the task force issue.

Having held detailed discussions with Falkland Islands Governor Rex Hunt, Mrs Thatcher decided that the government had to be put on a war footing and followed the advice of Harold Macmillan, her predecessor as prime minister, by forming a War Cabinet without Treasury involvement arguing cost constraint. This was to the great annoyance of Chancellor Geoffrey (now Lord) Howe but turned out to be a good decision as the War Cabinet could concentrate on winning. Equally decisively Margaret picked a competent operational team: Sir John Fieldhouse with overall command of the task force, Rear Admiral Sandy Woodward as commander of the surface ships with Major General Jeremy Moore and his deputy Brigadier Julian Thompson directing land forces; a winning team as they worked well together. This demonstrated a positive example of Thatcher leadership with clear objectives and the necessary planning to achieve success, something I witnessed at first hand in later years. Consequently the task force was dispatched to the South Atlantic with a speed and efficiency which surprised the world.

From the beginning the British government made it clear that the issue was not just a dispute between Britain and Argentina but was a matter of principle on the use of force to seize disputed territory. I have never really understood the American attitude to the dispute; it never seemed to have logic despite our close relationship. On this occasion they just sat on the fence as they did not want to let their British friends down nor did they want to depose Galtieri. The British government position was that the Falkland islanders themselves should decide whether they wanted to be linked to Britain or Argentina; in other words, it was a matter for self-determination.

By 12 April the task force was arriving at Ascension Island, halfway to the Falklands, which began to put real pressure on Argentina. The American negotiation was still not making progress in Iraq and Afghanistan.

By 16 April the two aircraft carriers HMS *Hermes* and HMS *Invincible* had reached Ascension Island and rules of engagement were being put in place for the final leg from Ascension to the Falklands. At this point Galtieri indicated, via President Reagan, that he did not want conflict but did not offer to withdraw from the Falklands; a response which added to British and Thatcher determination.

On 23 April Margaret Thatcher and Britain gave a warning to Argentina that any approach by their warships or aircraft which could amount to a threat to British forces would be considered hostile and would receive a response. The new Foreign Secretary Francis Pym was working with the Americans to find a compromise solution that would prevent war. Some members of government considered that this proposal had some attraction, so it had to be considered by the War Cabinet. How realistic this was I have never been able to establish.

However, Margaret Thatcher, supported by Willie Whitelaw, did not approve of a compromise plan and it was rejected. Mrs Thatcher makes it very clear in her memoirs that had the Pym compromise plan been agreed she would have resigned as prime minister and the Thatcher dream would have ended.

By 26 April an exclusion zone with a radius of 200 nautical miles was announced based on Port Stanley, with a positive plan to recapture the Falkland Islands despite the presence of the Argentine aircraft carrier ARA *25 de Mayo* and its Exocet missiles. Proof of the intent to recapture the Falklands was given by bombing Argentine positions around the islands including Port Stanley.

Our submarine HMS *Conqueror* was ordered to follow the Argentine cruiser the *General Belgrano* and its escort ships which were engaged in a movement likely to endanger the task force. Despite some naval opposition, something had to be done. Mrs Thatcher agreed that the rules of engagement could be changed and the *Belgrano* was attacked and sunk with the loss of many lives. This caused a political storm in Britain and elsewhere but was a crucial act in winning the war. The sinking of the *Belgrano* was taken up by Labour MP Tam Dalyell as a major issue that he continued to raise for years during his time in the House. His argument seemed to be that we attacked the *Belgrano* after it had turned away from the task force and that Margaret Thatcher was to blame for the ensuing loss of life. The Exocet attack the next day on our destroyer HMS *Sheffield* in retaliation and its subsequent loss with many lives was a significant setback for Britain which I believe confirms the wisdom of sinking the *Belgrano*.

International negotiation continued, led by the Americans, seeking a solution. As usual Margaret Thatcher would not accept compromise and instructed the preparation of our terms in the form of an ultimatum to Argentina.

The War Cabinet then met to sanction a landing on the Falkland Islands. An initial landing was achieved with no casualties and the Union Flag was soon flying over San Carlos. However, the fighting then became intense with fierce Exocet air attacks causing the loss of HMS *Ardent* and serious damage to HMS *Argonaut* and *Brilliant*, again with loss of life. Setbacks did not stop there as destroyer HMS *Coventry* and the Cunard container ship *Atlantic Conveyor* were also hit. Despite this the landing did not falter, with stores being landed at San Carlos to supply the battle to retake Darwin and Goose Green.

Suddenly the fighting came to a rapid end when Port Stanley was retaken with a heroic effort by British paratroops and commandos storming across the island in rapid order. However, this famous victory was not achieved before their commander Colonel Jones had lost his life.

The Argentines then surrendered. The war was won and the Falkland Islands were back in British hands, to the relief of the local population.

Prior to the conflict, government leaks and rifts were reflected in the polls which were not supportive. From an electoral viewpoint the government was clearly in difficulties and would not have survived a general election. I recall some commentators saying that taken purely on domestic issues Margaret Thatcher was somewhat lucky to have retained the leadership and hence her role as prime minister. She had achieved a great deal in becoming Britain's first woman prime minister but that alone would probably not have taken her away from the political hole she was heading towards prior to the Falklands War.

The conflict changed all that: her determination, resolution and decision-making turned her very quickly into a world leader with the deserved support of the nation. This short period transformed her in a very few weeks into one of the leading prime ministers of all time.

When the next general election came along the British public gave Mrs Thatcher a just reward, forgiving her initial problems within government and her economic and union difficulties. She had been the right person in the right place at the right time!

Margaret has to be admired for her tenacity in the face of opposition from all sides, best characterized by that statement to the 1980 Conservative Party conference which bears repetition here: 'You turn if you want to; the lady's not for turning.'

I have to acknowledge that her resolve took me to Westminster in 1983.

My View
As I have already noted, a retrospective evaluation of the performance of the first Thatcher government prior to the Falklands conflict was measured purely on domestic matters and could be considered less than satisfactory. True, they inherited a difficult and unstable Britain from the previous Labour government and then governed with a Conservative administration that was in itself unstable. It had taken a few attempts at Cabinet re-structuring to gather a cohesive team. I have already speculated on the reasons for these problems.

Chapter 5

General Election
1983

The Falklands War transformed the Thatcher project from a government in some difficulty into a major political success. Margaret Thatcher's status had been altered by her positive stance into that of an outstanding world leader. This achievement also transformed her style of politics into the philosophy subsequently known as Thatcherism.

This success of 1982 indicated that she would head for an early general election to consolidate her political position and to allow her to consolidate her philosophy into a real advance for Britain and its economy.

Like many others I speculated that there would be an election in the spring of 1983 and from my personal position it was now or never. I had been determined to get to Westminster for several years but hesitated because I believed my family were too young and that it would not be sensible to try to manage a young family and look after the interests of constituents.

By 1982 the position had changed: our eldest son Jonathan was heading to Oxford to read law and our youngest son Nicholas was beginning sixth form with the idea of also studying law but only if it did not interfere with playing rugby!

I therefore had the opportunity and was determined I would make the effort. I knew the political ropes reasonably well now as I had trained as a Conservative agent and had been involved in by-elections in Knutsford and Moss Side in Manchester and had also been the election agent for Peter Rost MP in Erewash for the 1979 general election. Additionally I had run my own campaign in North Yorkshire to become a North Yorkshire county councillor.

Regardless of this experience I needed to be placed on the Conservative Party candidates list to be allowed to fight for a Westminster seat. Here I ran straight into trouble when I attended the weekend candidate selection event. I was deemed unsuitable for Westminster, regardless of being a qualified election agent, a county councillor and someone who had run and developed businesses. I was obviously disappointed. I always knew that my formal education was a bit limited as I had left school early. However, what I did eventually discover was that I was considered to be 'politically unreliable' and this led to my rejection. My high-profile campaign against my own party's plan to scrap York grammar schools and my attack on the minister concerned had upset the party and I was 'blackballed'. I was told unceremoniously to learn to behave and toe the party line. This rejection did not temper my determination to succeed. It did make me determined that, should I succeed, I would apply an independent mind to issues and that I would never be swayed by political considerations. I would apply common sense, regardless of being considered politically unreliable; in other words a rebel. This is the philosophy I have followed ever since throughout my political career. I still subscribe to this today, now that I am on the fringe of the political scene. As we shall see, it has got me into plenty of difficulties and I believe I am still considered by some elements of the Conservative Party to be politically unreliable.

As I was not included on the candidates list I was not notified of the constituencies looking for suitable candidates. This was no problem as I had plenty of friends who were on the list and were happy to forward the details to me. As a consequence I applied for seats in the North of England including Blackburn and Grimsby, hoping something would turn up in Yorkshire that I wanted to represent. I got onto the short list for several seats but thankfully I did not succeed.

However, what I did discover was that it was difficult for a woman to get selected to fight a Westminster seat. The same questions always arose. What will you do with your family? Does your husband approve? Can he look after himself? What about your children? These things the selection panel would never ask the men!

Luckily in the spring of 1983 along came Batley and Spen, a new constituency looking for a candidate to fight the Conservative cause. The seat was then newly-formed and comprised parts of Batley and Morley which had been represented by Dr Alfred Broughton, a highly-respected Labour member. The Spen element was transferred from Brighouse and

Spenborough which had been represented from 1979 by Gary Waller MP and at a much earlier date by Michael Shaw (now Lord Shaw of Northstead). When I saw this opportunity I was determined that I should succeed. I did not know many of the people involved but I did know the area reasonably well and my husband had food industry connections in the patch.

I sent my application directly to Batley and Spen and I researched the area in detail because the constituency was one I really wanted to represent; it had a great industrial history together with plenty of challenges.

The political pundits measured it as a Labour seat with a majority of 6,000 but I thought it could possibly be won. Batley had not had anything other than a Labour Member of Parliament since the 1930s when one of the Wills tobacco family sat as a National Liberal. However, Spen had helped return a Tory member on several occasions for Brighouse and Spenborough.

From the initial interview to the final selection, the people involved in Batley and Spen were friendly, a friendship that has grown over the years. During this process I obviously met the president of the new Batley and Spen Conservative Association, a local solicitor the late Doug Brewer on whom I have relied on many occasions throughout the years. He remained a steadfast supporter, even when I got myself into difficulties due to my independent approach to politics. From day one in Batley and Spen I owed much to Doug Brewer and his wife Isabelle.

On 29 March 1983 I was selected by Batley and Spen as the Conservative candidate. We did not know when the election would be called but little did I realize that within two months I would be a Member of Parliament. After my selection trouble soon arose when Batley and Spen reported that they had selected me as their candidate. The party's response was 'You cannot have her; she's not on the candidates list', probably adding that I was a political liability.

I have always admired the stance taken by Doug Brewer and the Batley and Spen Executive: 'We have selected her; she's our candidate and we will get her elected.' They did and I was their member for fourteen years but the party never acknowledged me on their official candidates list! I was not disturbed by this position because I felt that during my fourteen years I could with the support of the president Doug Brewer, Sam Lyles our treasurer, the various chairmen and the Executive take an independent line on issues of special importance to the constituency.

As luck would have it I found out later that the three women on the Batley and Spen selection panel had decided that having a woman candidate would be good and this helped my cause. After an exciting selection meeting with other local candidates I won the contest and had jumped the first hurdle.

Getting elected

The euphoria of being selected to fight the general election as the Conservative candidate for Batley and Spen did not last long. I had work to do! I was confident that I could represent the area well and that I could win, even though it looked on paper to be Labour territory.

The constituency was new and it had no money on which to operate, never mind fight a general election. Any funds that it did have were still in the hands of the original constituencies Brighouse and Spenborough and Batley and Morley and would take time to sort out. There was a Brighouse and Spenborough constituency office in Cleckheaton but the lease had been terminated due to lack of funds. For the same reason there was no election agent but there was a constituency secretary, Mary Bentley, who proved to be a major asset. Mary was a straightforward down-to-earth Yorkshire woman who knew everybody, at least in Spenborough. Even more importantly, she had run election campaigns and had experience of handling constituency affairs for a sitting Member of Parliament, Gary Waller. Thankfully we had just enough money in the till to pay her salary as long as she moved the office to her spare bedroom in Scholes and we operated from her kitchen table and from the boot of my car.

The press at the end of March 1983 was full of speculation about an early general election so I decided to get stuck into the challenge of organizing a campaign for the early summer by taking as much time off as I could from my job as assistant director of the York Community Council.

My core team was small: Mary Bentley and my son Jonathan who was in a gap year between school and university and had been working in a pizza restaurant or on a turkey farm. As he had a great interest in politics he soon volunteered as my driver and assistant. We were joined in the first instance by President Doug Brewer who could not only give political advice but knew the area well and was respected everywhere. From that day forward Doug was my political mentor and supporter. Through the years I had good treasurers: initially Harold Morris and at a later date Sam Lyles who somehow found funds. In 1983 Harold found just enough funds to keep us campaigning. The chairman at the time, David Exley, knew the Spen area quite well but the Batley part of the constituency had little Conservative support. However, we managed to get a small team together when the election was called to cover the whole area. Batley, Staincliffe, Birstall and Heckmondwike had strong Conservative clubs; this may have been due to the superior quality of the snooker tables rather than an interest in politics! However, they became key points in subsequent campaigns.

Fortunately I had enough people to help develop a good campaign team: Noel Wadsworth in Heckmondwike; Charles Shaw in Batley; Malcolm McKennan in Gomersal; Alan Platts and Eileen Leach in Birstall; and the ever-present Peter O'Hara in Birkenshaw. In Eric Marshall I had a key supporter who had worked tirelessly among the Asian population in Batley to help with integration issues and who considered that a Conservative government was the best solution for the community.

One person who gave important help was someone who I had beaten for the seat during the selection procedure: Neill Crone, a local solicitor. Neill had attempted to get into Parliament before and had been a previous candidate in the area. His introductions and advice were invaluable in the early days and helped me design an effective campaign.

We were so certain there was going to be an early election that I talked my husband Brian into writing a draft election address and literature. As we had produced our own literature for my county council elections, we had some idea of what we wanted. Brian, who had been involved in marketing campaigns within the food industry, always contended that I was no different to a box of cornflakes; I just had to be advertised and sold! This has been a refreshing and somewhat controversial approach over the years and tended to clash with party policy, particularly when I wanted to follow an independent-minded line. Consequently at this early stage we took an individual approach. From day one in Batley I knew I had to be different. I was a woman fighting to get into a man's world, with only twenty-seven women in the House in 1982. I also knew I was not, nor would I wish to be, a traditional Conservative. Batley and Spen was likely to be marginal; it could be Labour or Conservative. I believed my politics had to be 'commonsense' and I wanted votes regardless of traditional party support. I had to attract the middle ground. Writing almost thirty years later I am certain this was the right approach and I know the trouble it has got me into over the years. I just had to be different and I was.

I had always been of the view that contact with local individuals, organizations and businesses was key to success as they provide the jobs and wellbeing for the community. So I put in place at once a programme of industrial visits to get to know the people running those businesses and those working there and, more importantly, get a briefing on their successes and problems. I had made some progress but not enough on this programme when the election was called. However, I made it plain that should I win, I would form a business association to bring businesses nearer to Parliament.

I also agreed with Doug Brewer that we should form a Conservative Patrons Club to attract more local finance to help provide funds to allow us to campaign properly. At long last after much speculation on a June or October date the election was called for 9 June 1983 and we were campaigning for real with four candidates in the field, the others being Ken (now Lord) Woolmer, the sitting member for Batley and Morley; Steve Woolley, SDP-Liberal Alliance; and the ever-present Clive Lord for the Green Party. Obviously as a sitting member Ken Woolmer, a sensible and academic socialist, was the front-runner and attracted press and party support attracting visits from Michael Foot, Gerald Kaufman and Denis Healey. Steve Woolley managed to get Roy Jenkins to visit to raise the SDP profile. I was lucky that I got Giles Shaw, Under Secretary of State Department for the Environment, to visit and received solid support from his namesake Michael (now Lord) Shaw, who was then MP for Scarborough and who had a home in Roberttown.

The big event for me was a surprise visit and support from Ted Heath, the former prime minister and Tory leader. He had a reputation of being grumpy and I was not sure what to ask him to do or how to handle him. In the end it worked well as he was perfectly happy walking about meeting shoppers in the Tesco store at Cleckheaton. In fact, ladies were queuing up to speak to him; I was so relieved. In the end we had a good campaign with the President getting our very limited army on the road canvassing. I did get some help from outside: June Drysdale from Wakefield; Joan Hall, former MP for Keighley; and my friend Carole Raylor from York who had helped with my County Council Election.

I have always believed that while politics and electioneering is a serious business, it has also to be fun and we should always have a lunch break at the pub and we should finish the evening back at the pub. One afternoon I was out canvassing with a team including Carole and my husband. Part way through the afternoon we lost them for a good hour. On their return they reported that they had decided to canvass the Liberal Club where they had stayed testing the gin and tonic and reporting to our dismay 'no Conservative votes there'!!

Jonathan and I used the boot of my car for the whole three-week campaign; canvassing, town walkabouts and business visits. We canvassed every street, if not every home in the constituency, including some estates never canvassed by Conservatives before. By election day I was just about out on my feet but thankfully we had rented a house in the middle of the constituency on a temporary basis which allowed some respite from the campaign.

Election day is always a bit of an anticlimax because all the candidates can do is check that the polling stations are working and that the supporters are getting pledged voters to the poll by whatever means. After some debate about image, Brian and I agreed to a tour of the constituency in the late Michael Brown's very impressive vintage car. As the day was fine it was great fun but it did get some interesting albeit good-natured shouts as we drove around. Who cares? We won in the end. During our tour we met my supporter Neill Crone who announced with some force: 'I've just been in the local bookmaker's office and they are tipping you to win so I have just invested £10 in you.' As a team we had always considered we could win with a bit of luck but this was the first time we had heard an outside opinion that we could overturn a projected Labour majority and win. It was quite worrying!!!

At last the fateful day came to an end, the polls closed and we headed to the count that was to provide the drama of the day. I have always preferred getting to the count reasonably early to see the boxes being emptied as this can give a measure of your support from particular polling stations. During our canvassing I had been told that there were certain housing estates that the Conservatives did not visit and did not canvass. My response had been 'Nonsense, we will visit these estates and we will canvass door-to-door', which we did. To my great satisfaction when seeing the voting boxes being emptied from the polling stations I realized we were getting good support. This gave some hope that we might do well.

As the count proceeded and the night drew on into the early hours it was obvious that the result was going to be very close. Eventually we could see that we had a few more bundles of votes than the Labour Party. This was confirmed when the returning officer brought the candidates and agents together to look at spoiled voting papers, stated that we were ahead by about 800 votes and asked whether the Labour candidate wanted a

The author – 1983 Election.

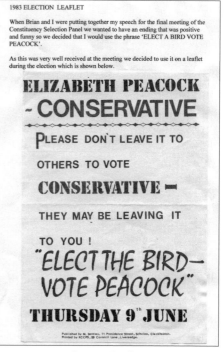

1983 ELECTION LEAFLET

When Brian and I were putting together my speech for the final meeting of the Constituency Selection Panel we wanted to have an ending that was positive and funny so we decided that I would use the phrase 'ELECT A BIRD VOTE PEACOCK'.

As this was very well received at the meeting we decided to use it on a leaflet during the election which is shown below.

ELIZABETH PEACOCK
– CONSERVATIVE
PLEASE DON'T LEAVE IT TO
OTHERS TO VOTE
CONSERVATIVE –
THEY MAY BE LEAVING IT
TO YOU !
"ELECT THE BIRD – VOTE PEACOCK"
THURSDAY 9ᵗʰ JUNE

Published by M. Bentley, 11 Providence Street, Scholes, Cleckheaton.
Printed by KCCPS, 89 Cornmill Lane, Liversedge.

Election leaflet.

Meeting local residents in Heckmondwike.

Meeting local people whilst shopping in Batley.

The winning team, 1983.

recount. Most certainly WE did not! We thought the Woolmer team would ask for a full recount but they just asked for a bundle check which confirmed the result. The official announcement confirmed we had won with a majority of 870 and I was the new Member of Parliament for Batley and Spen. How exciting!

Then came the speechmaking, thanking all supporters and the Conservative merriment which lasted until very early morning. It started with me being interviewed by an unbelievable number of press and TV people, and then carried shoulder-high around the town centre with a great deal of noise at two in the morning. My elections have always been closely fought so I made a habit of going to the count with notes for two speeches: a right-hand pocket (win) and left-hand pocket (lose). Thankfully I picked the correct pocket on this occasion.

One thing has always amazed me: having won a seat at three general elections, I have no official piece of paper to this day that confirms I was ever an MP, even though I was at Westminster for fourteen years. All a Member of Parliament gets is the official verbal statement: 'I the Returning Officer for the said election do hereby declare that the said Elizabeth Joan Peacock is duly elected to serve as the Member of Parliament for Batley and Spen.'

So we had won and I had achieved my ambition! I had a wonderful but small team of helpers and I will always be grateful to my agent Mary Bentley, my President Doug Brewer and my family with whose help and support I had succeeded.

On close analysis I have to admit I was lucky; I was in the right place at the right time. Margaret Thatcher had with her efforts in the Falklands made the Conservative Party electable on the back of her outstanding leadership. I have never been afraid to admit that I initially rode to Westminster on the tails of Margaret Thatcher's coat; however, staying there for fourteen years in a marginal constituency was a different matter as we shall see.

One of the issues that had driven me on was to succeed as a woman. I have long been an admirer of the Suffragette Movement and the struggle for votes for women. I had been driven on throughout my political life by the thought that these original women campaigned so long and hard to allow me to vote and I should make use of their efforts, which even today remain important. I had succeeded but by 1983 very few women had been elected to Westminster since Nancy Astor became the first to take her seat in 1919. We eventually calculated that I was the 115th woman to be elected in the intervening sixty-four years.

Chapter 6

I Made It

The election was on a Thursday and I needed the weekend to recover and had hardly started making plans for an obvious change in lifestyle and pattern when the telephone rang and a deep Yorkshire voice said: 'Donald Thompson here. Elizabeth, I see you won Batley and Spen, congratulations. I'm your whip, get yourself down to London and into Central Lobby by 10 o'clock on Tuesday and I will show you around', and down went the phone. It was the typical down-to-earth management style of my political friend and colleague, the Member of Parliament for Calder Valley. No slow start to the job, just get on with it!

If Donald said do something it was usually worth doing, so I spent Monday explaining to Mike Clemson, the Director of York Community Council who had given me one month's leave of absence to fight a hopeless election, that I would not be back. He was pleased for me but not too charmed that he would have to pick up the work I was doing in the City of York. I did indeed get to London and the House of Commons Central Lobby by 10 o'clock on Tuesday by a short head with a bag of clothes and a booking in the St Ermin's Hotel near Westminster; too expensive to stay there for long!

I had been to the House of Commons before but could not remember how to get to Central Lobby. As I arrived at the main entrance I presented myself to the policeman and said: 'I am the new Member of Parliament for Batley and Spen and have come to meet my whip, Donald Thompson MP.' The answer came, 'Don't worry Ma'am, I've already got a photograph of you here', and he opened an adjacent door and there was my photograph, 'but do you have any of your election addresses and photographs because my colleagues need to put your picture behind more doors?' From there I realized security was for real and my face was important.

At precisely 10.00am the 18-stone Donald Thompson appeared:

Congratulations Elizabeth, well done! You are now Member of Parliament for Batley and Spen. You had better get used to the idea, and get used to this place. By this time on Friday you'll have more post than you have ever seen and it all needs attention. I'll take you round the building so that you will know your way about and then you are on your own.

Off we went, up and down stairs, along corridors, through the Chamber, through the lobbies; I was thoroughly lost in no time. After about thirty minutes we emerged back in Central Lobby:

Right, Elizabeth, you now know your way around and you are on your own. You'll not get an office for weeks so you'd better bag a desk in the library to work from. You'll be sworn in and get paid from next week but don't rush back to Yorkshire without getting yourself organized.

And off he went, introductory policy fulfilled!

Just as he was going he spotted a lady he obviously knew so he introduced me to her. She was indeed the Member of Parliament for Mitcham and Morden, Angela Rumbold, who had entered the House at a by-election in 1982 and had just been re-elected. We got into conversation and went for coffee and soon established that we had similar ideas and outlook. She suddenly said: 'Do you smoke? Have you got the offer of an office?' 'No, I've just arrived and been here about two hours, why?'

There are about twenty women members of which probably ten are Conservative. We all have to share offices. I will not share with someone who smokes and I don't want to share with a man. Will you share with me if we can get something fixed up?

As the idea of a library table was not appealing I agreed at once and we arranged to meet in the Central Lobby the next day. By this simple introduction I came to share an office with someone who was to become a minister in the Thatcher and Major governments, and with who I was eventually to work as Parliamentary Private Secretary.

We did indeed meet the next day with the news that getting an office within the House of Commons building was hopeless; they had all been grabbed by ministers and more senior colleagues. However, we were told that there were offices waiting to be allocated in the Norman Shaw North Building along the Embankment but they required a ten-minute sprint from the office to the lobby for a vote, which was a big problem in the rain and with only eight minutes to get into the lobby.

We marched straight round to have a look and we picked what looked like a good-sized office and resolved to take squatters' rights there and then. Angela then set about acquiring desks etc and they were moved into the office the following day. Luckily we spotted the key in the door and locked up as we left. After a month of argument with the House authorities about our hijacking one of their offices, we had a happy five years of sharing. We soon discovered that former Prime Minister Ted Heath and Jim Spicer, MP for Dorset were neighbours.

So before I was sworn in I had an office, which was unheard of, albeit with squatters' rights but with nowhere to live during the week. To overcome this problem I rented a room at a hotel in Earls Court from Monday to Thursday at a cost I could just about afford.

On Friday of the first week someone said to me just before I headed back to Yorkshire: 'Elizabeth, have you been to the post office yet to collect your post?' I remember my reaction was: 'Why bother? We have not yet been sworn in as members; nobody will have written to me.' On second thoughts I decided I had better go and ask and get used to the system. I discovered that the House of Commons has its own internal Post Office and members or their staff go there and collect their post daily. I presented myself to the man at the office, saying: 'I'm the new member for Batley and Spen. I don't suppose you have anything for me yet but I need to check the system.' He gave me a funny look and went back into the office, saying as he went: 'Have you brought a bag? You are going to need one!' I thought he was joking. Suddenly there was an enormous bang and a rushing noise and the most enormous heap of post came down a chute into the office. I had never seen so much post for one person. He did lend me a bag but I could not carry it so I had to make two trips from the Post Office under Big Ben to the Norman Shaw Office across the road by Westminster Bridge and along the Embankment.

It took me the rest of the day to open the heap of post, so I missed my planned train northbound. Everybody seemed to have written to me. As soon as the election result was announced, the people of Batley must have grabbed their pens and written; many with congratulations and others disappointed that I was not a socialist!

I decided there and then that I would reply to every letter from the constituency, regardless of the content. I believe I always did, even though on occasions it put great pressure on me and my team.

From this first Friday and for the next fourteen years my post bag was of this size. It took most of every morning to collect and open the post before we started considering and replying. During the summer when the House was in recess and my secretary on holiday I had the post redirected to Yorkshire and a special van had to come out with it as it was at least half a sackful and was far too heavy for our local postman.

I soon learnt that the level of my post bag was relative to the things I said or did. If I picked a fight on an issue, the size of my post bag could double. When I complained, my husband used to say 'Serves you right; you'll eventually learn to keep quiet' but I never did!

By the second week as we were all being sworn in I realized that becoming a Member of Parliament was like setting up a business. I had to find a secretary and I then had to go out and buy all my own office equipment. Typewriter, copier and fax machine were bought and installed and put to work.

However, my tasks of organization in London were only half the problem. I had to get a system going in the constituency, which still had no money and no office. Thankfully Mary Bentley offered to help using her spare bedroom as an office plus her kitchen table if needed. This was invaluable because in 1983 while MPs did have an office allowance for a secretary it was a very small amount. Equipping an office in London and finding some things for a Yorkshire office with secretarial costs soon used up the funds. Members could claim an allowance for living in London during the week but it was tightly controlled and did not cover all costs. It could only be used to pay rent and not to buy a property.

I soon discovered that the real costs of carrying out my duties were not covered by the allowances, certainly for my first three years at Westminster. I had to cover operational costs from my own salary and family resources to ensure that my work was to the standard I required. It was obvious that MPs needed better allowances to cover their operational costs.

Writing now with hindsight, expenses allowances did not cover costs in 1983. In my view members' expenses allowances were subsequently driven in the other direction: much too high! So much so that with the generous allowances available by the turn of the century members could not find legitimate reasons for claiming the funds and the temptation of doubtful claims set in. The original tight and traditional Fees Office System fell apart with mismanagement, allowing the 'expenses scandal' to develop.

I discovered at an early date that I could not take part in the debates in the Chamber until I had made my maiden speech. The advice I was getting was: 'Do not rush into making your maiden speech; get used to listening to the proceedings.' Speaking in the Chamber is difficult and you have to get used to it! I took all this to heart and decided that as we were to have a short session in July I would not make my maiden speech until the autumn and did not give the matter much further thought.

Suddenly everything changed. John Whitfield, a local solicitor who had won the adjacent seat of Dewsbury came to me in the lobby saying: 'There's a debate tomorrow Friday (22 July) on Regional Industrial Policy and I'm going to make my maiden speech based on the wool and textile industry and its problems in Yorkshire. Will you support me?' Being somewhat taken aback, I spluttered: 'Yes, if I can get a speech together in time.' This was pressure but an opportunity not to be missed so a speech was prepared overnight and my turn in the debate arrived.

Making a maiden speech in the Chamber of the House of Commons is a pressure-driven nerve-wracking experience that I shall never forget. I managed to thank my predecessors as members for the constituency: the very well-liked and competent Ken Woolmer, the Labour MP for Batley and Morley who I had defeated in the election and my friend Gary Waller who had represented Spen as MP for Brighouse and Spenborough. I then pitched into the business of the day, a review of industrial policy. I attacked this from the textile industry position, noting how the industry was suffering, what needed to be done to help it and what should be done to encourage the development of replacement industries. This included a review of Regional Investment Grants and a demand for the extension of the Intermediate Grant Status, then covering the coal and steel areas of South Yorkshire to the West Riding. I followed this with a demand that the EEC provide a fair deal for the wool and textile industry. This took about ten minutes but it was an experience that I will never forget. It was more difficult than I imagined. At least I was now legitimate, an accepted Member of the House and could take part in the work of the House. If you make a decent job of a maiden speech you receive notes of congratulations. I got quite a few so it must have been satisfactory. One of the best congratulations came from Michael Meadowcroft (Leeds West), who followed me with his maiden speech when he recorded that even though he was a real Liberal and I was a Conservative, we were friends with the best interests of Yorkshire in mind. The one I treasure came from the Chief Whip John Wakeham.

I Made It

Mrs. Elizabeth Peacock (Batley and Spen): In my first address to this House it is appropriate for me to support what my hon. Friend the Member for Dewsbury (Mr. Whitfield) said today. However, at this point I pay tribute to the former Member for Batley and Morley, Mr. Ken Woolmer, who I know worked hard and long for the woollen industry in his role as trade spokesman on the Opposition Benches. I had the honour, good fortune, and sufficient votes to defeat Ken Woolmer for the Batley and Spen seat in June. I thank him again for the clean campaign that he fought, and I thank him sincerely on behalf of his former constituents in Batley for his hard work between 1979 and 1983. I also thank my hon. Friend the Member for Keighley (Mr. Waller) for the good stewardship of the Spen part of my constituency, in his former role as the Member for Brighouse and Spenborough.

Being the Member for the constituency that adjoins Dewsbury I find that many of the problems highlighted by my hon. Friend apply in my area also. That is hardly surprising, as the new constituency of Batley and Spen includes a small but important part of Dewsbury. I, with my hon. Friends the Members for Dewsbury and for Bradford, North (Mr. Lawler), have a special responsibility in this Parliament. We have been returned by parts of Yorkshire that have not returned Members of Parliament to these Benches for many years. In fact, Batley has not elected a Conservative Member of Parliament since 1931. There is a new mood in Yorkshire, looking for change, and there is a radical new approach to life and the problems of the county. I for one am determined to do all that I can to see that that is achieved.

The name Batley and Spen united Batley with such famous places as Cleckheaton, Heckmondwike and Liverseage. They are famous because of their deep-rooted involvement in the development of the Yorkshire woollen industry. They remain famous today for their down-to-earth reliance on Yorkshire thrift, grit and graft, which to those who live south of Watford means hard work. Perhaps the Minister will see this for himself when he visits the constituency, which I hope he will do in the not too distant future.

The Batley and Spen valley towns are medium-sized communities that grew up with the development of the woollen industry. They are fiercely independent, with a population that wants to work hard, utilising the skills of the textile industry, not only with wool but with fibreglass and other fibres. We have developed a mixed industry, from brake linings to biscuits and general engineering, with soundly based, progressive companies. Now we must move forward to attract, develop and extend the businesses of the 21st century—electronics, communications, and their satellite industries. That will be one of my priorities in this Parliament.

The textile industry in Batley and Spen, like Yorkshire cricket, has seen better times, much better times, and that is where we must offer help and support. The shoddy or heavy woollen industry based in Batley, has been particularly badly affected by the recession and can expect to be the last part of the woollen industry to recover as the industrial climate recovers. For that reason, I am looking for special Government help for that part of Yorkshire to aid recovery, put new life into existing industry, and attract new technology and new industry to this attractive part of the north.

I return to the immediate problems of my part of Yorkshire. I place certain demands upon the Government, and I shall continue to press those demands until I have the right response on the ground in my area. First, I am looking for a review of the regional investment grants. I may not be able to justify special development status for the whole of my constituency, but there is absolutely no reason why intermediate status should not be granted. In fact, with unemployment in Batley approaching 20 per cent., there is every reason for the establishment of an enterprise zone. If Wakefield and Rotherham can achieve that, I shall certainly seek it for my constituency.

We in Yorkshire will invest if we see a good thing, and I know that existing businesses in Batley and Spen will invest. What we want is a little help and encouragement to do so. Secondly, I have a deep-rooted suspicion that the British textile industry, in particular the woollen industry, is not getting a fair deal from Europe. I should like an assurance from the Secretary of State for Trade and Industry that we really do have a common market for woollens. It seems highly likely that certain member countries of the European Community are giving preferential treatment to their own woollen industries—whether by taxation advantage or by investment, I do not know, but they appear to be getting advantage from somewhere. Those advantages must either be stopped—a vain hope, I suggest, even if we took the case to the European Court—or we must provide similar assistance to our own industry. We must be in a position to compete. The Government cannot afford to let us down in this respect.

We in Yorkshire are proud—but not too proud, I hope, to accept some criticism, and at the risk of having much criticism heaped on my head, I must say that I am looking for new initiatives for the marketing of British textiles and clothes. Currently, it is to be hoped, the international tide of designer blue jeans is receding and there is a resurgence of suits, jackets and trousers for men and women. To grab any advantages that can be gained, we need to look at the styles of clothes that are demanded, checking whether the jackets are too long or too short, or whether the trousers are too baggy. I suggest that in many cases they are, and that the continental designers are stealing our markets from us. To overcome the problem, I am looking for assistance with hardware—buildings and machinery—and for Government assistance to develop markets by investment in a marketing programme, initially for the whole market, but one that will provide a new impetus for imports in the future.

Maiden Speech, 22 July 1983.

Results of the general election 9 June 1983

<u>Batley and Spen:</u>

Elizabeth Peacock	Conservative	21,433
Ken Woolmer	Labour	20,563
Steve Woolley	SDP Alliance	11,678
Clive Lord	Green	493
Conservative majority		870

<u>National Result</u>	<u>Seats</u>
Conservative	397
Labour	209
Liberal/SDP	23
Others	21
Total	650

Mrs Thatcher's overall Conservative majority	144

My View

Yes, I was lucky. I did get to Westminster on the tails of Margaret Thatcher's coat but I was in the right place at the right time and I was determined to succeed. In life you have to make your luck on occasions and hold on. I did, and won!

Thank you, Batley and Spen.

Chapter 7

The Positive Years
(1983–87)

Reshaping industrial policy

The Conservatives were back in government with a 144-seat majority and I was there.

As you would expect from 'the lady', this was not by chance. Mrs Thatcher had recognized the political advantage and moved positively to the general election. As you would equally expect, a detailed planning exercise had been in place for some time awaiting this political advantage. Geoffrey Howe had with the help of Cecil Parkinson, Keith Joseph, David Howell and Norman Tebbit provided a well-honed manifesto. Cecil Parkinson had reorganized Central Office so the party moved smoothly into electioneering mode with the advice of Tim Bell, the advertising guru. Like any other election campaign it had its ups and downs with such issues as the *Belgrano* affair and more remarks from Francis Pym trying to dent our firm 10–15 per cent lead in the polls by saying on BBC *Question Time* 'landslides on the whole do not produce successful governments', this indicating to the electors that we should not be allowed to win with a large majority. I believe Margaret Thatcher never forgave him for this remark, even though it made no measurable difference to the election result.

Mrs Thatcher did visit Yorkshire during the campaign for a business lunch at Harry Ramsden's fish and chip shop in Guiseley and a more considered speech in Harrogate. Not being expected to win, I could not expect a Prime Minister to visit Batley and Spen. I was not disappointed though, as we won without!

Lack of firm policy: the difficulties of hitting the ground running

Yes, we had won with a majority of 144 and Mrs Thatcher returned to govern the country. However, in contrast to her reaction in 1979 she found hitting the ground running more difficult this time. The well-planned and executed election campaign masterminded by Cecil Parkinson had been based on a manifesto weak in instantly actionable policies with the exception of the abolition of the London GLC and the Metropolitan Counties. It was too full of 'more of the same' issues.

Margaret did, however, realize that the axe had still to be applied to socialism and that a new team was needed for this objective. A major government reshuffle ensued with Francis Pym, David Howell and David Young disappearing and others moving. Geoffrey Howe went to the Foreign Office and Nigel Lawson and Leon Brittan came in as Chancellor and Home Secretary respectively. This allowed John Wakeham as Chief Whip to manage the large majority. Clearly Cecil Parkinson who went to Trade and Industry could have expected a more senior role, probably the Foreign Office, but it appears that Mrs Thatcher knew he had a potential personal problem. Within a short time it became clear he did indeed have a problem. Consequently he was forced to resign, being replaced by Norman Tebbit. With these changes the government was re-shaped to defeat socialism but possibly not with the team Mrs Thatcher would really have preferred.

The start of the second Thatcher term was taken up substantially with issues covering the economy, Europe and relations with the United States. However, these issues did not get into the public mind and soon gave the impression that the government was not in contact with 'real' issues.

I suppose I was too busy concentrating on Batley and Spen matters to appreciate the problem. Having got to Westminster and fulfilled my dream I was determined to make it work and hopefully get elected again. The pressure was on to serve the constituency. I had no ambition to be in government and become a minister. I just wanted to use caring, commonsense Conservatism to represent Batley and Spen and Yorkshire.

The 1983 economy
As we opened the new parliamentary session the economy was sound with the prospect of getting better as we got our programme of privatization moving forward. Inflation was low and industry was recording high output and productivity. There was one difficulty: unemployment was high and stubbornly refused to fall below 3 million. Interest rates were falling but because of the high demand for property ownership mortgage rates were rising. Regrettably government borrowing was rising due to lower revenues and some overspending in the economy. The Chancellor had

predicted that the borrowing could be balanced by public spending cuts and by privatization asset sales. We had a sound economy in the short term but in retrospect maybe there should have been a stronger reaction to the potential problems on the horizon. Maybe it was the beginning of the Thatcher government being too generous with its spending; an issue I will return to throughout this retrospective analysis of the Thatcher years. Margaret had gained a hard-nosed reputation as Education Minister in the Heath government as the 'milk snatcher' when she abolished school milk for more senior children. As we analyze her later decisions we can now conclude that on the contrary she was in some areas too generous, particularly in the area of social security funding.

There is a case for arguing that successive Thatcher governments allowed the development of excessive generosity in social security funding that has influenced policy throughout the past thirty years. While tough economic decisions had to be made during these years the original base for social security support was funded by cash flow from North Sea oil and from the extensive privatization programme. In this present era of austerity the current Cameron government is struggling to rationalize this spending. This is an area we will explore and analyze further as we summarize the Thatcher years.

As a lowly backbencher national financial strategy was not my initial challenge. I was at Westminster to represent Batley and Spen and so I got on with handling local issues.

Activities at Westminster

Yes, I had made it. I, one of the twenty-three women who had made it in 1983.

However, I was soon brought down to earth by the challenge of the task ahead. I had acquired a shared office by 'squatting' with Angela Rumbold but still needed a secretary. My post was arriving by the ton and the business of the House was starting. The pressure was on and little did I know it would last for fourteen years!

I soon realized that for many constituents who came to see me at my surgeries and during my many constituency visits local issues were almost more important than national issues. Yes, there was always someone who had a view on a national political issue and wanted to debate the matter but they were in the minority. So I concentrated on local issues.

Throughout my career I have often been asked where I stood politically. This has always been difficult to define as I am capable of moving across the political spectrum depending on the issue we are considering. In summary, mine is commonsense Conservatism which is caring when required but it can have a hard core. If we add the commonsense element I could subscribe to Andrew Roth's parliamentary profile of me and I quote:

> A community politician and active job defender, a warm-hearted socially conscious mainstream populist in a marginal constituency: gets emotional about abortion (critical) and hanging (pro). Disliked by ideologists of the hard Right for her rebellions (poll tax, dental and eye tests), although normally a right-wing loyalist. Initially took over her starring role in a misjudged 'Labour marginal'.

Andrew wrote this in 1990 so I suspect that the 'loyalist' description had worn thin by 1997 with my reservations about Europe and my major row on energy policy and the instant closure of coal mines and sacking of miners.

I had realized during the election campaign that Batley and Spen would not want a traditional Conservative as their Member of Parliament. In our part of Yorkshire we are down-to-earth and call a spade a spade, or even a shovel. When I was elected with a majority of 870 I acknowledged that I had to represent everyone in the constituency and that more people had voted against me than for me.

This presented no problem as I had always had an independent attitude to politics and would if necessary take a different view from the party line. This attitude got me into trouble early in my career and still does today. Indeed, some people in the Conservative Party have never forgiven me for some of the issues on which I fought my own government.

Indeed, very recently I met David (Lord) Waddington, the former Conservative Chief Whip who in conversation suddenly said: 'Elizabeth, you have not changed much. I remember the trouble we had with you fighting and rebelling against your own government during the time I was Chief Whip but you were often right.' I claimed then and still do that I was applying commonsense Conservatism. So what did I get up to in these early years? What was happening in Batley and Spen?

In retrospect some of the issues on which I fought my own government look trivial today but they were real issues in the 1980s. So just what were they and why did I rebel?

I had got my parliamentary career off to a conventional start in my maiden speech in early July 1983 by urging Intermediate Status for Batley and Spen, a review of Regional Grants and a fair deal from Europe for the local wool and textile industry.

This was followed rapidly in July by my first rebellion when I voted against the Matrimonial and Family Proceedings Bill on the basis that it would hurt children by breaking up marriages. I therefore gained an early reputation as a potential troublemaker as I had rebelled against my government within a month of arriving at Westminster. That rebellion was compounded by pressing for legislation to control 'video nasties' which the government did not, for some reason, want to do.

In my early days in the House I was somewhat appalled by the behaviour of some of my colleagues so that when the issue of televising Parliament came up for a free vote (i.e. without party whipping control), I voted against televising on the basis that I did not want the country to see this bad behaviour and on this occasion the Noes won. I was, however, wrong in retrospect and at a later date I changed my mind when the issue came up for another vote. In the meantime I had come to the view that if the proceedings were televised we would get better behaviour as my colleagues would not wish their constituents to see them playing the fool. This has proved to be true following the change of mind by the House and the introduction of controlled TV coverage of the proceedings. I put my hand up; I was wrong!

My opinion and resolve were tested at an early date at Westminster by a free vote on the restoration of capital punishment for certain categories of murder. Throughout my adult life I had been of the view, and remain so, that the death penalty should be available on the statute book for, at the very least, some categories of murder. It should be available as the ultimate punishment and as a deterrent, a policy which it seems the majority of Britain would support. For some reason this was not true of Members of Parliament as they had on several occasions in the past recorded a majority with the opposite view.

Several of us campaigned hard on the issue with plenty of support from around Britain and from Yorkshire but it was a lost cause and we lost the battle. My view has not changed. The death penalty should be available to the courts, even if only for some types of murder. Again taking a hardline approach to crime and discipline, I took a firm stance on the availability of 'video nasties'. At the time there was a spate of cases of young people getting into serious difficulties with violent behaviour. The view was that the availability of videos highlighting violence and horror was influencing some of these young people. Consequently I took the view that legislation should be available to control the content of these videos or their distribution and sales. For some reason which I have never understood, the government did not want legislation and I could not agree so I rebelled and I was not popular as a result.

In my first few months at Westminster in the summer of 1983 I do not think I have worked so hard before or since, even though the pressure continued for fourteen years. I had found an office and got used to the mountains of post. Early in 1984 I then discovered that I had been put onto a series of committees dealing with legislation that was heading into and through the House. The problem was that they sat at all sorts of hours and on several occasions right through the night. This just left me time to go home and take a shower before returning in time for the day job which usually included yet another committee. At this time I was also trying to keep my County Council affairs going and had to travel on the sleeper train to York, go home and shower, then drive to Northallerton for the meeting and subsequently get the train back to London in time for a 10 o'clock vote.

I had not been in the House long when I was put on the Employment Select Committee. I suspect it was another whip's strategy of giving me more work to do so that I could not get into mischief. The Select Committee was dominated by the Labour Party and because some of my Conservative colleagues failed to turn up, Chairman Ron Leighton (Labour) usually got his own way. He had previously chaired the committee so he was always keen to go somewhere overseas to collect evidence and look at employment issues. He had a budget and was determined to spend it. So off we went to Japan to look at engineering, shipbuilding and car assembly, visiting Tokyo and Osaka. One night in Tokyo we had an earthquake which nearly shook me out of bed. At breakfast I made the mistake of saying to my male colleagues: 'Did anyone feel the earth moving?' Everybody laughed and grinned at my expense and said 'NO'. I thought no more of the matter until reading the gossip column of the *Sunday Express* two weeks later which had a small headline: 'MP gets first earthmoving experience in Japan.' My colleagues at Westminster had a good laugh for days! Just who did pass that story to the press?

Sometime later the Select Committee had another outing to New Zealand and Australia with less comment afterwards but at a dramatic time. I travelled out with Gerry Neale from Heathrow as we had both been at the Conservative Party conference in Brighton the day before. Indeed, I did not leave the Grand Hotel in Brighton on that day until 7.00pm. During that night the bomb went off causing chaos, death and injury. The captain of the plane knew he was carrying two Conservative MPs and came back to give us the details as he received them over his radio. Obviously he was concerned for all involved, particularly Margaret Thatcher and her husband Denis. However, he was especially concerned about Norman Tebbit as they had worked together when Norman was a pilot and their friendship had continued.

The bombing of the Grand Hotel in Brighton during the Conservative Party conference in October 1984 was a blatant attempt on the lives of Margaret and Denis Thatcher and senior members of government. The explosion killed five people and thirty-four people were taken to hospital with injuries, some serious. Those killed were Roberta Wakeham, wife of Treasury Secretary John Wakeham; Sir Anthony Berry MP; Eric Taylor; Lady Jeanne Shattock; and Lady Muriel Maclean. Among those trapped in the building were Norman Tebbit and his wife Margaret, the latter sustaining serious crippling injuries.

I deal with the threat of Irish terrorism and the Brighton hotel bombing more fully in a separate chapter as it was a constant theme throughout the Thatcher and Major years. At this stage I would record the fact that a shaken and thankful Margaret Thatcher pulled the troops together by morning and in typical determined style announced that the conference would continue. I will also note the part played by an old friend Dr David Skidmore who entered the damaged building with the fire brigade to help the injured (see Chapter 24, The Irish Threat).

The work of the Employment Select Committee was interesting but I thought with its then chairman was not going to achieve much and as the work was not directly benefiting Batley and Spen I found a way of resigning to make better use of my time.

Private Member's Bill

In each parliament members can put their names into a ballot to allow them to take a Private Member's Bill through the House of Commons. Whip Donald Thompson suggested I should sign the book to go into the ballot. I was very reluctant to do so as I was not sure how I could handle such a bill. However, my name went into the ballot and out it came at number 20, the last one. Number 20 is usually considered to be too far down the list to get anywhere due to lack of parliamentary time.

Instantly I had a problem because the area I wanted to cover was already being handled by an earlier bill. I therefore opted for what I thought would be non-controversial: a bill establishing minimum standards for driving instructors before they could teach anyone else to drive. At that time unqualified, unlicensed trainee driving instructors were teaching people in some of the driving schools. A driving instructor did not need to display his certificates or qualifications when he was teaching. Many people thought this was not a good idea as it was therefore not possible to know if your instructor was a trainee or someone well-qualified.

Together with help from Lynda Chalker, a Minister in the Department of Transport, I got the bill through a first reading in the House before the summer recess. In doing so I was not confident I could get it onto the statute book, even though some of the earlier bills in the ballot had fallen due to drafting difficulties. At this stage little did I realize that politics would get in the way before the second/third reading in December. I soon discovered I had opposition to the measures in the bill and for a long time I did not know why. Eventually I discovered the Liberals who mounted the opposition had received a £188,000 contribution from their Treasurer who was the owner of the British School of Motoring and presumably he did not like the constraints of the bill on his business.

Private Members' Bills were at that time progressed in turn on Friday mornings and for weeks, Friday after Friday I was in the House ready to move the bill along with a debate as necessary. However, a Friday came along in the spring when I just had to be in Batley to deal with an issue there. I reported my dilemma to my Friday whip Tristan Garel-Jones (now Lord Garel-Jones). His reply was: 'We will never get to your bill this week and if by chance we do I will move it on for you.' As luck would have it, some more of the earlier bills failed to make progress and up came my bill. Now the Liberals had either lost interest in providing opposition or they failed to turn up. On this Friday without me being present no one opposed and Tristan moved my bill straight through all its stages and then to the House of Lords. The bill went through the House of Lords and received Royal Assent in April 1984. It is on the Statute Book in my name. Only one other person, Margaret Thatcher, had managed at that time to achieve such a bill in their first term at Westminster. Tristan always reminds me of this when we meet!

Women's issues
Being one of only twenty-three women in a House full of men I could not

avoid getting involved in any debate on women's issues in the House or often in the media. This was demonstrated when Jo Richardson launched a Sex Equality Bill. I have always made it clear that I am a firm advocate of women's rights across the board and an admirer of the Suffragette Movement. I have never been a so-called feminist but I believe the issues have to be fought one by one on a rational basis. To the annoyance of some of my fellow lady members I voted against Jo's bill as I considered it to be too wide-ranging and badly constructed.

In this general direction of women's issues I had the opportunity to visit Greenham Common where women picketed the American base for months in 1984 protesting under a CND banner about nuclear weapons and demanding their removal. While I could not support their cause which I considered misdirected, I had to recognize the dedication of the women concerned and their determination to see the end of nuclear weapons in Britain.

In 1984 I did press for women's rights by demanding legislation to control test-tube babies, surrogate mothers and similar experimental pregnancies, a topic I will discuss in greater depth under the Pro-Life banner.

Coal and energy

The year 1984 was one of dispute in the coal industry which first brought me into contact with miners' wives and introduced me to the problems of coal and the energy market; topics that were to get me into serious trouble in later years which I will explore separately.

My independent views

On looking back I realize that 1985 was the year in which I established my reputation for outspoken opposition on issues that affected my constituents and marked me down as 'unreliable'. I gained this label by voting against several government proposals: Sunday trading, increasing the Lord Chancellor's salary, and arguing against badly-structured tax cuts, saying people who are in work are not necessarily looking for tax cuts. I also annoyed the party by saying: 'We must have a new strategy for the presentation of Conservative policies as the present strategy is no good in Yorkshire.'

By 1986 I had gained a reputation of voting with the opposition or abstaining on issues when I believed the government was getting it wrong. This led to comments from my Conservative colleagues when I did vote for the government on routine matters, such as: 'Elizabeth, are you sure you are in the right lobby? Your usual friends are in the other lobby!'

The year 1985 was that of Mrs Thatcher's big bust-up with Michael Heseltine on the Westland helicopter issue which eventually led to his resignation. For once I was a good government supporter, even though I understood Michael's position on the matter. In this instance I said that Mrs Thatcher must not take my support for granted in the future. She must take not only her MPs with her but the people in the country as well.

While I had become a nuisance to the party, our leader kept an eye on the troops and was very thoughtful about her team, even the troublesome ones. One hot night in July I collapsed outside the lobby and was dispatched to Westminster Hospital for a check-up, even though I had recovered almost at once. By 8.00am the following day I had a handwritten note in my post from Margaret Thatcher wishing me well and hoping I had recovered. One of the newspapers had noticed the affair,

22 MAY 1986

10 DOWNING STREET

THE PRIME MINISTER

20th May, 1986

My dear Elizabeth,

I was so sorry that you were taken ill on Tuesday night.

I send you every good wish for your recovery, and hope you will soon be back in action.

Yours ever,

Margaret

Mrs Elizabeth Peacock JP MP

Letter from the Prime Minister following my collapse in the Commons.

62

Letter from the Speaker, Bernard Weatherill.

reporting: 'Elizabeth Peacock collapsed in the Commons last night but recovered immediately when she was told someone had gone for Dr Owen!' (David Owen, former Foreign Secretary); a very unkind comment as he was and still is a charming man.

Yes, Westminster can be a tough, ruthless place but when someone is ill or has a problem it can also be kind. Not only did I receive a message from the prime minister, I received a note from the government Chief Whip and a handwritten one from the Speaker Bernard Weatherill. At an earlier date, September 1985 Mrs Thatcher wrote to me in hospital when I had spinal surgery which put me out of action for several weeks. She really did keep an eye on her troops, even though the House was in summer recess at the time.

With these activities and the pressure of my post bag and only half a secretary I had little spare time but exceptions come to mind. In June 1984 I was invited, along with a small number of other new colleagues, to meet President Reagan and his wife Nancy. In truth when I went I was

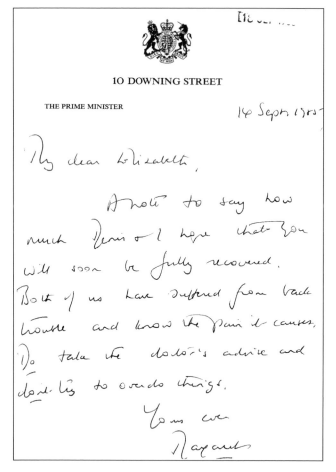

Letter from the Prime Minister following spinal surgery, 1985.

somewhat sceptical about meeting Ronnie Reagan the movie star. However, when I came away that all had gone; he was extremely charming! I was impressed that he seemed to be 'a man you could do business with' as Mrs Thatcher later said.

I was also invited one evening with my husband to have dinner with Mr Speaker Weatherill, again with colleagues and their wives. My husband sat next to a Mrs Anthony Blair of future fame. His comments later were: 'She's a hard left-wing determined lady going places and she'll take Tony Blair with her! But he will have to do as he is told!' How right he was! Cherie Blair I am convinced played a significant part in Blair governments and policy-making.

Foolishly I had made my first year at Westminster much too difficult and pressurized by hanging on to my North Yorkshire county council seat, as the Conservatives in County Hall knew they would lose the seat in a by-election and they only had a one-seat majority and assumed that the Liberals would win my seat. In retrospect this was misguided as I spent the year regularly travelling between Westminster and Northallerton which caused problems with my whips 'big time' when there was an important vote at Westminster. I should have resigned at once which was my original plan but had been persuaded not to as the County Hall Conservatives knew they would lose their majority. However, when I did resign they blamed me for hanging on to the seat!

22 MAY 1986

Government Chief Whip
12 Downing Street, London SW1

21st May, 1986

Dear Elizabeth

I was very sorry to hear that you were taken ill yesterday and I am so glad to hear that you are now recovered. I hope you will take your doctor's advice and take things easily for a day or two.

Yours ever

John Wakeham.

Mrs Elizabeth Peacock M.P.

Letter from John Wakeham, Chief Whip.

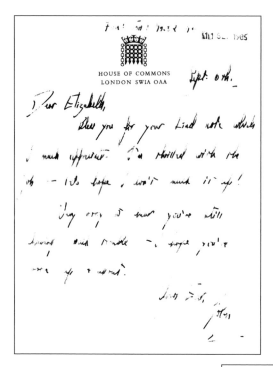

Letters from John Major as he took up his early ministerial appointments.

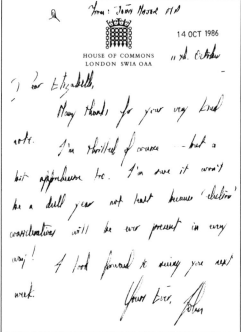

Chapter 8

Constituency Reflections

Throughout my fourteen years at Westminster my secretary kept a scrapbook of items from the press; mainly from Yorkshire but some from the national media. As I now write I realize how valuable this is as an aide-mémoire of past activities, particularly my column 'Westminster Note Book' which I penned for the local press on a weekly basis.

Soon after the election there was, as I have recorded, a vote in the House on the reintroduction of capital punishment for murder. I ran my colours straight to the top of the mast by voting for the reintroduction; something I supported then and still do for certain categories of murder. My press cuttings and the 'Note Book' clearly reflect my views and how I planned to vote.

The scrapbook indicates a continuous round of attending and opening community functions which I enjoyed. Issues of a more serious nature did receive attention, such as support for local industry and the creation of jobs allied with support for schools and young people especially the Scouts and Guides. I note that in 1985 I was able to invite a local Scout to attend the Speaker's tea party where he met our former Prime Minister Harold Wilson and discussed the fortunes of Huddersfield Town FC. The community activities, defending the future of post offices and my resolve to vote against the government on ill-conceived health reforms stimulated plenty of local interest, so much so that local Labour Party supporters 'invaded' my weekly surgery. These supporters overran my surgery with journalists and cameras to lobby me and to test my resolve. They got the answer very quickly: I reacted instantly by throwing them out and threatening to call the police. My firm reaction caused even more press comment but set the scene for the future; an important point as it established my position with an active local opposition.

By 1984 the miners' strike had begun to influence not only national but local thinking, thereby stimulating my interest in the coal industry that

The author meeting the President and Mrs Reagan at the US Embassy in London.

David Trippier MP, Minister Department Trade and Industry visiting Batley.

Industrial visit to Layezee, Batley by
James Clappison MP, Minister
Department of the Environment.

The author as
Chairman of the
House of Commons
Motor Club making
a presentation to
the Order of St
John, 1990.

Receiving Industry
and Parliament
Trust Fellowship
Certificate from
John Egan,
Chairman of Jaguar
cars, 1989.

was initially based on attempting to support local businesses who supplied goods to the industry. As the strike progressed, this interest extended to wives and families of working miners. This was in contrast to my Labour-controlled local authority, Kirklees, who were providing cash for strikers.

The scrapbook records that when I spoke in March 1984 at the AGM of the Batley and Spen Conservative Association I warned members that my early experience at Westminster confirmed that if I was going to truly represent the interests of all local people I would not always be able to vote with the government and that some issues I would have to openly oppose. I emphasized 'I work for all' and that this was the course I intended to follow but I would not abandon basic Conservative principles. My 'commonsense Conservatism' was born and for the fourteen years that followed, the Association loyally supported me and my position on issues. This local support was of great value in my battles at Westminster.

Surprisingly during these early years I had, despite my rebellions, great support from ministers, albeit those with similar northern seats. David Waddington, the then Immigration Minister, visited to discuss issues with my Asian constituents in Batley; followed by David Trippier picking up his business ministerial role to support my local textile businesses, all well recorded in the local press. Thankfully spending on the Staincliffe Hospital Batley, regrettably renamed Dewsbury, increased with good ministerial support for the then chairman of the local health authority and my Conservative Association treasurer the late Sam Lyles who played a significant part in developing the local health service.

My opposition to the government was recorded locally when I helped to initially defeat it on the introduction of Sunday trading. I continued to oppose the government until the issue was more clearly regulated. Sunday shopping has now become a way of life but it was an emotional matter for many in 1985 and their concerns had to be aired. I would still feel somewhat out of place in a supermarket on a Sunday and therefore very rarely go!

By the summer of 1985 I was recording that the government was flagging with a need for a Cabinet reshuffle to re-establish Mrs Thatcher's authority. These comments and my opposition to some proposed limited tax cuts thoroughly irritated my colleagues.

It was clearly not all work as I found time to raise money for charities by driving in the Lords versus Commons motor race at Brands Hatch with fellow MPs racing against their Lordships in identical red sponsored Ford cars. The race was won easily by Lord Strathcarron who had driven in

House of Commons' charity race at Brands Hatch.

'Ready for the off'.

races at Brooklands pre-war, followed by a certain Health Minister Ken Clarke. I was not last: I managed to beat the then Sports Minister Colin Moynihan (now Lord Moynihan) who managed to spin his car onto the grass and therefore did not finish. After the race he was clearly not too happy but being the good sportsman that he is he saw the funny side: 'Sports Minister last'!

During these early years I became progressively more involved with the activities of the Pro-Life movement and abortion with its related issues. These matters were well covered by the press and continued to be so during my years in the House.

Another cause that claimed my attention was a campaign to get Britain to tidy up under the 'Keep Britain Tidy' banner spearheaded by Richard Branson. I was convinced and remain so that 'green' issues to help save our planet are laudable but these are failing to save our planet unless we tidy up all the rubbish we throw around in our towns and cities or leave scattered across our countryside. Did we succeed? Well, in truth not much; the topic was put on the radar but little progress has been made since. I remain convinced that we have to tidy up our environment alongside working on green issues; one is no good without the other. In 1987 I received a Special Mention in the Keep Britain Tidy Queen Mother's 80th Birthday Awards.

I pushed hard during these years on housing and law and order matters. Housing has for many years been a matter for concern in Batley and Spen and required me to press the local council Kirklees on details of housing issues raised at my constituency surgeries. Eventually I got tired of chasing this no-win topic so I put pressure on government for a radical review of housing policy which did happen in later years. Where I did gain something of a reputation as a hardliner was on law and order. In my early weeks at Westminster I voted for the reintroduction of the death penalty and continued to do so at subsequent votes throughout my parliamentary career. I called for the death penalty for terrorists following the Brighton bombing in 1984 and took part in university and TV debates to make my case, although not always successfully! To my continuing amazement Westminster has always been out of step with public opinion on this issue. Many in our communities want it to be available as the ultimate deterrent but MPs do not always oblige. This was a regular discussion point locally at the time and will, I am sure, raise its profile again.

Where I did get myself into hot water was with my public position,

Brands Hatch race team with winner Roger King MP and Sports Minister Colin Moynihan MP.

Practice Day at Silverstone circuit for the Brands Hatch race.

clearly expressed in the press, on the unemployment issue. In an area that had been suffering from a steady decline in the wool textile industry, further increases in unemployment were unsatisfactory and it was happening as a consequence of the government's economic policy. I made a lot of noise at Westminster and within the press, especially locally by demanding economic Plan B that would require government spending to create employment. The Conservative government was not in the least happy with my outburst and I was sent a message to behave and follow the party line. Of course I 'did a Nelson', failing to recognize the signal and getting deeper into trouble. This incident clearly demonstrated to all concerned that I was determined to show independence to support the interests of Batley and Spen; importantly others, including the local press, recognized this fact.

By February 1987 it was obvious that a general election was coming and we were pleased when Mrs Thatcher agreed to visit Batley and Spen to support the Conservative cause. At the time the teachers there were unhappy with their terms and conditions and openly supported the opposition. During Mrs Thatcher's visit I called on teachers to stop playing politics and negotiate the issues. This promptly caused a local upset and I received a series of threatening telephone calls which Special Branch took seriously; so much so that at the election an officer followed my movements almost every day.

Yes, four years had gone by in a flash. It had been hard work but I had enjoyed it and was convinced that I had expressed the views of my constituency at Westminster.

My View

The Thatcher second term was in my view less of a success than has often been reported. Even with the huge Conservative majority, change was slow due to a lack of firm policy at the beginning of the parliament and problems with a flagging economy. It took Mrs Thatcher some time to get her team working on the lines she required and she was driven off course by events: the miners' strike, the dreadful Brighton bomb and her dispute with Michael Heseltine on the Westland affair.

A school report would have read: 'Worked hard but could have done better'! The team had not had the drive of the first term when it was aided by the outcome of the Falklands conflict. I have always questioned whether we made best use of our large majority. The party had plenty of reforming ideas and capable ministers but Mrs Thatcher was having difficulty driving

'Keep Britain Tidy' group with Richard Branson, House of Commons.

the team and some colleagues in Cabinet were less than co-operative on some issues.

The miners' strike had proved very disruptive to government and when eventually resolved in favour of the government was a significant step along the road to ensuring that the trade unions could not rule Britain. Mrs Thatcher's resolve to break the power of the unions was achieved but at the expense of other government initiatives.

As we approached the 1987 election I felt similarly about Batley and Spen. I could not have worked harder in representing my constituents' views and I had rebelled on issues that I considered not to be in the best interests of the people I represented. I had fulfilled my pledge to apply commonsense politics and hoped that the electors of Batley and Spen would re-elect me to carry on the cause.

Chapter 9

The Miners' Strike
(1984–85)

The miners' strike of 1984–85 played such a significant part in the affairs of government and Mrs Thatcher's second term that I consider it separately.

I seemed to have just settled down to the routine of Westminster and Batley and Spen when in 1984 the whole national scene erupted in disorder brought about by the miners' strike. This strike, the outstanding event during the 1983–87 parliament, was not just an industrial dispute; it was about the potential defeat of a democratically-elected government or the defeat of undemocratic socialism in Britain. This became a titanic struggle between the influence and power of Margaret Thatcher and Arthur Scargill, the president of the National Union of Mineworkers (NUM).

The historic reliance of Britain on coal as its major energy source had created an industry that believed it was pivotal to the nation's success. Militant miners had caused the General Strike of 1926, and the recent 1974 strike that resulted in the demise of the Heath government. Control of the NUM was firmly in the hands of militant left-wing leaders but other more democratic unions were forming. With the developing need for change and re-structure in what was becoming a declining industry in the face of competing gas and sustainable energy, conflict was inevitable. The Conservative landslide of 1983 and the Thatcher policy of eliminating the power and control of left-wing politics and socialism from British industry confirmed this. Inevitably, with Arthur Scargill leading the NUM there were bound to be conflicting positions.

The National Coal Board (NCB) had a problem: they were losing money rapidly and they were producing coal that they could not sell. They had too many pits producing expensive unwanted coal and something had to be done. The NCB needed a 500,000-tonne reduction in production, so twenty to thirty pits would have to be closed; an action the coal miners could not support. The NUM took a militant line with the objective of stopping the pit closures and at the same time bringing down the Thatcher government.

Thus the 'great strike for jobs', as it became known in the NUM, was initiated in Yorkshire on 1 March 1984 when the NCB told the NUM that Cortonwood Colliery, a pit in the Dearne Valley, was to close within a month. The area director of the NCB claimed that Yorkshire NUM leaders were looking for an excuse to trigger a strike by opposing this closure.

Some 500 miners voted within days to fight the closure and Cortonwood men picketed the NUM offices in Barnsley, from where the NUM's Jack Taylor announced an all-out strike of Yorkshire miners. This strike decision was based on the authority of a 1981 ballot that raised the question about the legal position of the strike and thus put the union in danger of sequestration of funds. Arthur Scargill recognized this danger and promptly moved his funds to the Isle of Man and Jersey. To make matters worse, many of the Yorkshire pits 'jumped the gun' and went out on strike before the planned date of 9 March 1984 with pits in Scotland following under the direction of Eric Clarke (later MP for Midlothian).

I believe that Arthur Scargill always knew he was not on safe ground as many of the 179 NCB pits and coking plants were woefully uneconomic. The unions and the miners were split with many NUM members wishing to work and the Union of Democratic Miners (UDM) not supporting the strike. However, by 14 March 133 pits were on strike or picketed out. Picketing caused huge unrest and violence, requiring a massive police operation in South Yorkshire and Nottinghamshire that allowed 40,000 miners to cross the picket lines and go to work.

The election of Arthur Scargill to the presidential role had created the likelihood of a strike in 1981 that was averted but he was looking for an opportunity to act. With the ongoing threat of a strike, Nigel Lawson as Secretary of State for Energy skilfully organized a progressive build-up of coal stocks at power stations throughout the country to forestall a miners' strike and the interference of pickets preventing coal movement; clearly an important strategy.

By 1983 Peter Walker, the ace communicator, had taken the Energy portfolio, recognizing that conflict was likely with any required re-structuring.

Ian MacGregor was appointed chairman of the National Coal Board with a remit to restructure the industry with some twenty pit closures to remove excess capacity and eliminate serious financial losses. With his plan in the public domain, it was not surprising that the miners would vote for a strike in their traditional ballot.

This was not good enough for my fellow Yorkshireman Arthur Scargill who planned to bring the government down. He forced the issue when the closure of Cortonwood Colliery was announced on 1 March 1984 by using his three-year-old local ballot as the confirmation of strike action. In response Ian MacGregor confirmed the closure of the twenty pits and all NUM members walked out in protest in Yorkshire and Scotland. This closed roughly half of the 160 NCB pits. Picketing of working pits in Lancashire, Nottinghamshire and Derbyshire rapidly became a problem for the police who were given the task to get those miners who wished to work into their pit.

The Nottinghamshire, Derbyshire and Lancashire miners, mainly members of the UDM, held separate ballots and voted against a strike, thus creating a lifelong split among miners, their families and whole mining communities that still exists today.

As a member for an industrial West Yorkshire constituency, albeit no longer with any working pits but with manufacturing companies supplying the mining industry, I took a daily interest in these developments as they could have had local implications.

In particular the phenomenon of 'flying pickets' who moved from pit to pit to deter working miners became a serious issue. This activity became progressively more violent in Nottinghamshire when the police intervened to uphold the law at the direction of the High Court.

In typical Thatcher style, what amounted to a 'war Cabinet' was set up to handle the implications. This included Mrs Thatcher, Willie Whitelaw (Deputy Prime Minister), Peter Walker (Energy), Leon Brittan (Home Office), Nigel Lawson (Chancellor), Norman Tebbit (Trade), Tom King (Employment) and Nicholas Ridley (Transport) with the objective of minimizing the effects of the strike and leaving the management of the NCB, CEGB (Central Electricity Generating Board) and British Rail to handle day-to-day strike issues. George Young was co-ordinating matters in Scotland.

Peter Walker's management
Some coal-mining had been carried out in Batley and Spen at an earlier date but had all disappeared well before my day. However, when the strike broke out Peter Walker, the Secretary of State, invited all northern

Conservative members to his briefings and so I developed an interest in energy matters and the coal industry in particular. Peter Walker with his business background handled the issue brilliantly, if to the annoyance of Mrs Thatcher on some occasions.

I made and kept some very rough notes from these meetings that I refer to here as a record of the events as I saw them. Peter Walker held face-to-face discussions with members but nothing was put on paper.

Mrs Thatcher had made it clear from government: 'There will be no surrender to the mob and the right to work will be upheld.'

As the strike progressed and violence grew, government and Home Office relations with the police and the courts became an important issue as large numbers of pickets had been arrested for intimidating those who wanted to work. It soon became clear that while there had been no formal ballot it was going to be a long strike with the NUM determined to prevent the movement of coal by rail, road or by sea while the CEGB was sitting with large coal stocks at all the power stations! So it proved, with no negotiations until May and the violence increasing week by week. This led to a major incident at Orgreave Coke Works on 29 May when over 5,000 pickets were attempting to prevent coal movement to the Scunthorpe steel works. The violent scenes at Orgreave turned public support away from the miners, particularly when it was realized that the pickets were receiving a daily allowance. Wisely the government, in the interests of minimizing the spread of the strike and to prevent alienation of working miners, did not resort to law to ban picketing. As the summer progressed miners began to drift back to work, allowing some pits to reopen albeit under picketing pressure.

The strike was causing significant human pressure on the mining communities with families being split in many cases between striking miners and working miners, sometimes with brother against brother or father against son. The striking miners' families were struggling to exist on savings as no NUM strike money was being paid. This put huge financial strain on families who could barely afford to eat. This in turn had a serious effect on tradesmen and service providers within these communities. Working miners' families, while not under financial constraints, were under human pressure for strike-breaking, regularly being labelled 'scabs'. Regrettably, intimidation of working miners and their families increased in the autumn in Yorkshire and especially in Derbyshire. These circumstances made the mining areas very unstable.

The working miners and their wives came under real personal attack within their communities and needed help to be provided by a support group. Being the only Conservative woman MP in Yorkshire and one who was in sympathy with working miners' wives, I was asked to arrange a meeting with several of the wives so that I could pass on their worries and concerns directly to the prime minister, at the same time advising how the wives might ensure that government understood their problems and also how they should get these covered in the media. This I agreed to do together with the Minister for Coal, David Hunt, arranging for a wives' delegation to come to see us and other sympathetic members at Westminster. From this both David and I were able to pass their concerns directly to the prime minister and arrange for a delegation from the miners' wives' 'Back to Work Campaign' to visit Downing Street to meet Mrs Thatcher in September.

Did this have any influence? I will never know but it did appraise government of the human aspects of the strike with my report going straight to 'the top'.

Margaret Thatcher was moved by the courage of these women whose families were subjected to abuse and intimidation. They told her a great deal and confirmed her suspicions that the NUM was out of control and the NCB was not handling the strike very well. They reported that the majority of the miners still did not understand the full implications of the NCB's pay offer and their plans for rationalization and investment. More needed to be done to get the NCB's message across to all the miners who wanted to work and those who were on strike. The women told Mrs Thatcher how small shops in the coal fields were being blackmailed into supplying food and goods for striking miners but withholding them from working miners. Margaret gave an undertaking that the government would not let working miners down.

In October a working miner's wife from Kent spoke at the Conservative Party conference, describing the harrowing experiences she and her family had suffered. Even her small children were targets for the vile tactics of the strikers. Regrettably after she had spoken the *Morning Star* published her address and a week later her home was attacked; a clear example of life in the mining villages!

To add to the problems a supporting dock strike was called that appeared to make matters worse but failed to have any real impact. From August onwards Arthur Scargill and his militants were on the back foot as picketing was not winning and Yorkshire miners took the NUM to court for striking without a ballot and won. This allowed sequestration of the assets of the NUM which changed the union scene. However, the strike struggled on for the remainder of the year with more miners returning to work and the violence and intimidation continuing. Throughout the strike the NCB with Ian MacGregor in charge had failed to handle the issues with efficiency, in particular links with the media. This was demonstrated by the stupid handling by the NCB of mine deputies. The working mines had been kept open throughout the strike by the co-operation of the mine deputies who are required by law to be present if coal is to be mined.

Suddenly the NCB proceeded to take issues with deputies' union the National Association of Colliery Overmen, Deputies and Shotfirers (NACODS); so much so that they threatened to join the strike just when Scargill & Co were beginning to crumble. Under government pressure the NCB and NACODS came to an agreement that just saved the day. The strike dragged on through the winter, albeit with almost 75,000 miners back at work by late December and with 2,500 returning each week. Other major trade unions had lost patience with Arthur Scargill so their leaders were working to bring matters to an end, despite a stubborn Scargill.

At the end of February with increasing numbers of miners returning to work due to hardship and family concerns, it was evident that the strike was over.

The strike was never just about the closure of pits: it was a pre-planned attack on the British way of life and elected government by a highly-militant union led by a dedicated Marxist. This attack was countered by an organized Conservative government led by an equally determined leader. Margaret Thatcher again demonstrated the world-class leadership that she had used to succeed in the Falklands campaign. Arthur Scargill misjudged her determination and in doing so allowed her to totally change the British industrial scene by removing the left-wing control of British industry.

Throughout the strike Scargill made it clear that his objective was the downfall of 'Thatcher' and he never accepted the concept of uneconomic pits. By the end of the strike he had lost control of the strategy and his members. The violence caused by a clash of 5,000 picketing miners led by Arthur Scargill and the police in May at Orgreave Coke Works turned the public against the strikers, clearly demonstrating that the NUM had lost control of the situation.

My View

With its many high and low points Margaret Thatcher's second term was a triumph but very different from the triumph of her first term, achieved by her leadership in the Falklands conflict. I have referred to it as the 'Positive Years' because it was in 1983 to 1987 that she truly put the 'Great' back into Great Britain, following on from her success in the Falklands and on the British industrial scene. The Falklands had placed Margaret Thatcher on the world stage as a major player and she shone, dealing positively and making real friendships with her counterparts around the globe. In addition the economy was sound, a major privatization programme was in place, North Sea oil was flowing and funds were available for the benefits system.

By reconstructing her government Mrs Thatcher had created a team she could work with, at least until the Westland affair. The dominating issue in Parliament was the miners' strike. The original strike issue was the financial performance of the UK coal industry but it was really about the question of who controls Britain, the unions or the government. Arthur Scargill got the answer and lost to a woman of steel and in so doing sacrificed the British coal industry.

Being prime minister is a daunting task and making a success of the role is an even greater challenge. Margaret Thatcher achieved all this and more. The 1983–87 years really were the 'Positive Years' and Margaret did deserve to be re-elected in 1987.

On a personal level I had found that I could not support the way some of the issues in the domestic arena were formulated and handled, so I rebelled. I was particularly unhappy with the way some welfare and benefit matters were structured. The government had funds available from oil and privatization which were used generously; in retrospect too generously in my view. The benefits system has in recent decades encouraged some to have a lazy approach to life. Too many people have become better off on benefits than while working; an unsustainable position that was compounded by this often unrecognized generosity of the Thatcher second term and a factor more easily recognized now than in the 1980s.

Chapter 10

Characters in the Commons
I

Introduction

As I began to write this book I resolved to make some comments on the interesting people on the Westminster scene during my years there. They include the following: my fellow Yorkshire MPs (the 'Yorkshire Mafia'), lady members, the Speakers of the House, media men, lawyers and whips.

As in all collections of people there is always a great cross-section: the good, the bad and the ugly, the friends and the potential enemies.

Interestingly, politics had very little to do with the outcome and my subsequent comments. I made many long-standing friendships across the political spectrum that last to the present day and have been strengthened by my ongoing role within the Association of Former Members of Parliament. Friendships in the House can be unpredictable. As mentioned earlier, for years I had an office next-door to Ted Heath but he would never pass the time of day. Suddenly he invited me to a cocktail party at his London home, during which he took me on a tour of the house to inspect his great collection of photographs of his sailing exploits. In later years I was the next-door neighbour of Winston Churchill (the younger), and he was just the opposite. His head regularly came round the door. Could he 'borrow' tea, sugar, paper-clips or even my secretary? Certainly I could work with him, even though he did 'jump off the bus' at the last minute when we were falling out with Michael Heseltine during his attack on the coal industry in 1991/2.

These differences in character were apparent almost daily during my time with an office on Parliament Street, with Labour Party members on the floor below the Tories. Obviously we all used the same lift but certain people would never ever say 'Good morning'. Those included Robin Cook and Gordon Brown; I do not remember them ever speaking. In contrast, Jack Straw had a friendly style but was easily outdone by Neil Kinnock who always had some cheery comment to add to the 'Good morning'. He often reminded me that I should stop wearing red jackets as I was not a member of his clan. More importantly, he did not take issue with me when in some debate I had intervened to tell him I believed that he 'could not run a whelk stall'.

Eccentric behaviour has some merit but not always. Alan Clark never spoke to me in my entire time at Westminster and ignored me totally but I still got some rough treatment in his diaries. Maybe I deserved some of his ire; he probably thought I was not a real Conservative. I, like Michael Heseltine, had bought my own furniture! I never did know why he disliked me. My husband took him to task in later years for his comments.

I should not give the impression that the House was full of miserable souls; nothing could be further from the truth. If you got into the swing of the place and did not take on 'airs and graces' the place was full of friendship and banter; even when dealing with sensitive issues someone would find an amusing twist. For example, one of the perennial cheery souls was the robust Nick Soames who always referred to me in a loud voice as Mrs P and took me to task on the sartorial colours of the day.

Women about the House
Until the late 1990s and the positive selection of women by the Labour Party led by Tony Blair, the number of women in the House was always small. Even today after the use of all-women short lists for the selection process the number of women who have served in the House since we got the vote, and since Nancy Astor became the first woman MP in 1919, is still no more than 300.

After the 1983 election only twenty-three of the 650 members elected were women and it was calculated that I was the 115th lady member since 1919. By 1984 the number had risen slightly to twenty-five and following the 1987 election reached a record thirty-seven, a fact recorded by the Guinness Book of Records with a collective photograph 'Lady Legislators'; a record-breaking picture of the largest assembly of British women MPs ever taken in one shot.

The continuing low representation of women in the House has always concerned me. Many fought hard with the Suffragette Movement to secure votes for women but we have failed to get sufficient women into the House to balance the decision-making process. Hence my long-standing efforts to promote women's issues and get more women involved in public life; an issue I will expand upon further.

I return to my theme of 'characters' in the House and in particular those talented women who were elected with me in 1983 and who have since made such a great contribution to the nation's affairs. Consequently I must acknowledge the part played by these women in the life of Britain for more than a quarter of a century: a prime minister, a Speaker of the House of Commons and ministers in various governments, all of whom influenced the way the country has developed. I had the experience of working with these accomplished women and I acknowledge their good humour and friendly spirit. It is worth summarizing the achievements of this highly-motivated group, noting that my comments are purely an outline of their successes; they achieved much more!

I must, of course, begin with the Prime Minister of the day; the first and as yet our only woman in the role.

Margaret Thatcher

A unique woman on whom much of this book is based so I do not need to go into detail at this stage. Love her or hate her, she has earned a place in the history of the world.

She has been leading the charge to involve many more women in politics for years, saying: 'When a woman becomes equal to men, she becomes superior,' a statement suitably upsetting to the men!

Margaret Beckett (Labour, Derby South)

Margaret has always been at the heart of Labour Party affairs, both in and out of government. She had influence with wide-ranging ministerial experience during the Blair premiership, serving as Foreign Secretary in his last term.

For a short time she was interim leader of the Labour Party as the organization changed direction and elected a new leader. At last her contribution to British politics has recently been recognized with her appointment as a Dame. One of her great assets during her career has been the support of her husband Leo, a very pleasant fellow.

Betty Boothroyd (Labour, West Bromwich West)

First elected for West Bromwich in 1973, Betty was a Member of the European Parliament 1975–77, Member of the Speaker's Panel of Chairmen and the Labour Party National Executive; a friendly former

Tiller Girl from Yorkshire with a steely but fair approach to politics, highly popular on all sides of the House, an attribute which propelled her to the Speaker's Chair. Betty got my support during the Speaker's election of 1992 despite my equally good friend Giles Shaw being in the running but unlikely to succeed due to a split Conservative vote. Betty proved to be a great success, becoming a star among those elected or re-elected in 1983.

Virginia Bottomley (Conservative, Surrey South West)
Virginia was the candidate for the Isle of Wight at the 1983 general election but was not successful. She was, however, elected for Surrey South West at a by-election in May 1984. Virginia was a highly-motivated politician who achieved ministerial office in various areas of government. She neither liked nor approved of independent-minded members who had the 'balls' to rebel against their government on issues affecting their own constituencies. This I discovered when I led the charge against the government's plans in 1992 to close coal mines. The night on which the Tory rebels very nearly sank the plan, with Labour support, Virginia spotted me in the Members' Lobby and described me to the whole collective gathering as 'an undisciplined rebel' and a 'total disgrace to the Conservative Party'. Many of those listening thought she was high-handed and had overreacted!

I don't recall that we have yet settled the matter some twenty years later!! I still believe we were right to challenge the government's energy policy and in the same circumstances I would do the same again.

Lynda Chalker (Conservative, Wallasey)
Elected in 1974 becoming opposition spokesman on social services during the Thatcher era, Lynda played a key role in the Conservative Party during the 1980s and 1990s, firstly as a transport minister and later as a highly-regarded international development minister and eventually chairman of the party.

Ann Clwyd (Welsh Labour, Cynon Valley)
Ann has been a leading Labour figure since 1984 when she won a by-election. During the Blair years she had a direct link to Downing Street on international affairs and was influential. I had some good debates with Ann during the 1980s and 1990s on a range of issues when she was always fair and frank, even when we were disagreeing.

Edwina Currie (Conservative, Derbyshire South)
A former teacher and Birmingham city councillor, Edwina, with a live-wire personality, joined the Commons in 1983 with a plan for change and who could blame her! However, she found it more difficult than she thought and met plenty of opposition. Understandably with her energy she soon became a minister but she made some infamous statements on 'woolly hats and long johns' (to combat hypothermia) and salmonella in eggs which got her into trouble, probably unfairly as the media belittled her views. She was always lively enough to attract the opposite sex and had a famously reported affair on which I will make no comment. Edwina remains a successful author and communicator.

Gwyneth Dunwoody (Labour, Crewe and Nantwich)
Gwyneth had a long and distinguished career at Westminster serving in many senior capacities in the House, including the Shadow Cabinet and spokesman on health and foreign affairs. During her tenure Gwyneth gained admiration in all parts of the political spectrum. She had become a renowned expert on transport matters and was consulted by most governments for her views, regardless of party politics. She was one of the real political successes of the era, not only at Westminster but also in Crewe and Nantwich, holding this seat with her strong personal support.

Peggy Fenner (Conservative, Medway)
Formerly MP for Rochester and Chatham 1970–74 and 1979–83, Peggy appeared on several select committees and became parliamentary Under Secretary of State in agriculture where she knew the business and impressed the industry, which is no mean feat. Her reputation lives on in agricultural circles.

Janet Fookes (Conservative, Plymouth Drake)
First elected in 1970 for Merton and Morden and to her Plymouth seat in 1974, Janet served on several influential committees. Not only a superb MP, she got involved in the running of the House, firstly as a member of the Speaker's Panel of Chairmen and later as a Deputy Speaker. As Baroness Fookes, she is now in the House of Lords.

Harriet Harman (Labour, Peckham)
Harriet was, and still is, a well-organized ambitious lawyer always destined to shine in the Labour Party. This she has done, holding a range of

ministerial posts in the Blair and Brown governments. She is often somewhat unkindly referred to as Harriet 'Harperson' by the media but she has become deputy leader of the Labour Party and holds the position with distinction. Harriet's success is a clear example of what women can achieve at Westminster.

Dame Judith Hart (Labour, Clydesdale)

A long-standing and leading member of the Labour Party, Judith was first elected for Lanark in 1959, holding many government positions including Paymaster General and chairman of the Labour Party in 1981–82. She held a seat in the Cabinet in 1967–68, something very few women had achieved at that time.

Elaine Kellett-Bowman (Conservative, Lancaster)

A former MEP for Cumbria, Elaine was one of the real characters in the House, being a good if somewhat eccentric member with the well-known ability to totally disrupt the Ladies Room in the House of Commons by using all the chairs as her filing system. If Elaine was around there was nowhere to sit and little room to stand as she used every inch of the room. However, her knowledge of the political scene in Britain and Europe was impressive, as were her widespread interests as barrister, farmer and social worker.

Jill Knight (Conservative, Birmingham Edgbaston)

A long-serving member who was deeply involved in the work of the House and the Conservative Party, Jill was renowned for being outspoken against the permissive society and easier divorce. First elected in 1966, she had been a member of the Council of Europe and was a popular backbencher. She was also a member of and then secretary to the influential Executive of the Conservative 1922 Committee.

Joan Maynard (Labour, Sheffield Brightside)

Joan was a sound Yorkshire MP who could pass the time of day with anyone, even a Conservative! This could be considered unusual as she was often unkindly referred to as 'Stalin's Granny' because of her early communist sympathies; she was a great character. As a girl educated in rural North Yorkshire Joan's great interest was in agriculture, being area secretary of the Agricultural Workers' Union. In the House she played an important part in the agriculture select committee.

Anna McCurley (Conservative, Renfrew West and Inverclyde)

A new member in 1983, Anna was one of the few Scottish women ever to be elected to the House of Commons. She charmed her way through the jungle of Scottish politics only to lose her seat in the 1987 election which was a great shame.

Oonagh McDonald (Labour, Thurrock)

Oonagh first won the seat in 1976 and rapidly became opposition spokesman on defence and treasury affairs, having been a member of the select committee on employment and PPS (Parliamentary Private Secretary) to the Chief Secretary of the Treasury. She lost her seat in 1987 and was a loss to the Labour Party at Westminster.

Sally Oppenheim (Conservative, Gloucester)

Sally won her seat in 1970 and became a Shadow Minister and the Consumer Affairs Minister in 1979; a very positive lady in the House. She retired from the Commons in 1987 to become Baroness Oppenheim-Barnes.

Jo Richardson (Labour, Barking)

An important member of the Labour Party National Executive Committee first elected to the House in 1974. I could never agree with Jo's politics but I recognized her dedication as the Labour front-bench spokesman on women's issues. During the 1983 parliament she brought forward a bill to help women but it had so many clauses it could not possibly succeed as it was not easily understood. For this reason I had to oppose her bill; much to my disappointment as had it been presented in a simpler form it would have had some merit.

Marion Roe (Conservative, Broxbourne)

Elected in 1983, Marion became a long-serving backbencher widely respected in the House as chairman of a whole series of important committees. In 1987–88 she was Under Secretary of State at the Department of the Environment. She remains active as a City of London Liveryman.

Angela Rumbold (Conservative, Mitcham and Morden)

Entered the House in June 1982 as victor of a by-election; one of the few Conservative by-election victories of the Thatcher era. Angela was a long-standing colleague and friend with whom I shared an office for five years, having met her on my first day at Westminster. I soon discovered that Angela was a special person: not only was she full of life and ideas, she was a woman of style and adventure. This was typified by her choice in cars; these being fearsome left-hand-drive American muscle cars which had to be driven at her appropriate pace: fast!

Her achievements in the fields of politics and education are well-known: Minister, Party Vice-Chairman, Privy Councillor and Chairman of Education Trusts. I recognized these talents when I served as her PPS in the Home Office. Angela had a wicked wit but could become frustrated and one day early in 1984 she declared in a loud voice: 'This bloody place runs on the old boys' network and we are not members. Elizabeth, we are going to do something about it!'

This we did, setting up the non-party old girls' network the Westminster Dining Club in 1984.

Clare Short (Labour, Birmingham Ladywood)

New to the House in 1983, Clare had a very positive and independent attitude to politics that kept her on the back benches for many years. She eventually became a successful International Development Minister in the Blair government. Regrettably, her independent-minded approach eventually did not conform to the Labour Party direction of travel later in her career and she resigned the Labour whip, becoming a respected independent member. Maybe I could not agree with her political outlook but I always admired her independent approach to issues; a style and attitude I recognized.

Rene Short (Labour, Wolverhampton North East)

A hard-working left-winger first elected in 1964 who applied herself tirelessly on health, children and pensions committees and was Chairman of the Select Committee on social services. She retired in 1987.

Ann Winterton (Conservative, Congleton)

Wife of my good friend and MP for Macclesfield Nicholas Winterton, Ann was elected in 1983 so we were new members together. Ann was to become a very experienced member with wide-ranging interests including agriculture, the countryside and Pro-Life issues. She was to remain in the Commons until 2008, having achieved a distinguished parliamentary career.

Others to enter the House between 1983 and 1987 were Elizabeth Shields, Rydale, Liberal/SDP; Rosie Barnes, Greenwich, Liberal/SDP; and Lin Golding, Newcastle-under-Lyme, Labour.

After the election of 1987 the number of women in the House increased to thirty-seven, the highest number since Nancy Astor arrived in 1919, hence the Guinness Book of Records' interest. There had been four retirements and three defeats: Anna McCurley, Oonagh McDonald and Elizabeth Shields. Sixteen new women MPs entered the House.

The Westminster Dining Club

Following Angela Rumbold's outburst in our office in 1984 we resolved there and then that we would set up an 'old girls" network to counter the domination of men in British politics and in particular in the House of Commons.

We decided to pull together a group of influential women to get them interested in the Westminster scene so that they personally could pick up the challenge of a political life or that they would encourage other women to do so. We decided to arrange a series of dinners or receptions with leading figures from government and the political scene to speak or to be present to hear discussion on points of concern. We concluded that we would be Joint Chairmen with Angela concentrating on her contacts in the London area and I would attempt to attract members from 'the rest of the world' and would organize the functions. We were successful from the beginning and continue to be so twenty-eight years on. We have maintained a changing but continuing influential group of women and remain, as we started, strictly non-political within structured aims and objectives.

The aims and objectives are:

1. To bring together women holding responsible positions in industry, commerce, the arts and from the academic world to promote a better interchange of opinions on current issues.
2. To create, with opinion-forming women, a clearer understanding of the work of Westminster and Whitehall.
3. To provide a more permanent link between women of influence who can help to promote new ideas.
4. To provide an opportunity for women from all areas of the United Kingdom to network with those with whom they may not have contact in their normal working environment.

The club will meet two or three times a year, either at a reception or dinner, with one of the Joint Chairmen and sponsors in the chair. For some functions numbers may be limited, in which case a ballot may be held.

Canapés or dinner will be served, for which those present will be expected to pay. Normally a prominent person will speak on a topic of current importance and this will be followed by questions and, if time permits, a discussion. It is hoped that all those present will make new and lasting contacts.

Over the years we have organized a regular series of dinners in the House of Commons and receptions in the Foreign Office, the Banqueting House, Carlton House Terrace (the home of the Foreign Secretary) and at 10 Downing Street. A similar programme is envisaged for the future.

As both Joint Chairmen lost their seats in 1997 and with the death of Angela Rumbold there had to be changes to maintain a link with the House of Commons. To this end the Rt Hon. Cheryl Gillan MP (until recently Secretary of State for Wales) agreed to be our President.

The Westminster Dining Club is now chaired jointly by the author and Margaret M. Miller FRSA, chairman of a company of Yorkshire furniture-makers. It should be emphasized that while one of the Joint Chairmen is a former Conservative Member of Parliament and the President is presently a Conservative Member of Parliament, the club and its membership reflect the whole political spectrum and more importantly will include women who have no permanent political allegiance but who can contribute to contemporary thinking.

My View
Elizabeth Peacock (Conservative, Batley and Spen)
I have always been honoured to be one of the twenty-three members of this elite group of political women brought together by the General Election of 1983 and subsequently increased to twenty-eight in by-elections up to 1987.

My contribution to the group's achievements may be considered somewhat differently from the majority. I got myself elected in 1983 as the Conservative Member of Parliament for Batley and Spen which many said could not be done. However, I did it and managed to stay for fourteen years. In this period I served on the Employment Select Committee, the House Administration Committee and was elected twice to the powerful Executive of the 1922 Conservative Back Bench Committee which advises the Party Leader/Prime Minister on back-bench concerns.

Women at Westminster with Mrs Thatcher, 1987.

Westminster Dining Club conference and dinner at the Belfry Hotel.

I did start up the ministerial ladder as PPS to ministers in Social Security and the Home Office but was fired for rebelling against my government on the reorganization of the coal industry. During my career I gained something of a reputation as a rebel but I have always defended my actions as an 'independent-minded Yorkshire woman' who was determined to represent all my electors and this I did for fourteen years!

In my view this group was unique as it included a Prime Minister and a Speaker of the House and it does show what determined women can achieve and is surely a role model for others to follow.

Votes for women

One of the drives behind my endeavours to get more women into public life and especially into the House of Commons is an understanding of and sympathy for the band of women who struggled for years to achieve suffrage for women. I greatly admire these gallant ladies and believe I could have been tempted to join their ranks if I had been around at the time.

I, of course, have studied the activities of the Pankhursts and their fellow Suffragettes. Indeed, shortly before her death in 1992 at the age of 102 I had the pleasure and honour of meeting the last of the true Suffragettes, Victoria Lidiard. Victoria, one of the first women opticians, on 4 March 1912 took part in the window-smashing raid in Whitehall, breaking a window at the War Office. She and 200 other Suffragettes were jailed.

Over the years I have undertaken many speaking engagements under the 'votes for women' banner where I usually concentrate on Nancy Astor, her activities in Plymouth and Westminster and her spats with Winston Churchill. I link this to Countess Markievicz (Eva Gore-Booth), the charismatic and rebellious daughter of a wealthy Irish landowner who was the first woman to be elected to the House of Commons but never took her seat because she was in prison for her part in Sinn Fein Easter Rising in Dublin.

Women have now got the vote and they must use it!

Chapter 11

General Election
1987

As I have already described, the government had suffered plenty of setbacks and challenges leading up to 1987, often looking as though the next crisis would bring it down. The Westland affair in 1986, causing two ministers to resign, was an example. Even with a majority of 144, Margaret and her team often found life at Westminster troublesome due to a sizeable group of Conservative members who were prepared to argue and rebel.

The really dramatic happening was the bombing of the Grand Hotel Brighton in 1984 during the Conservative Party Conference as an attempt on the life of the Prime Minister and her Cabinet, killing five people and inflicting lifelong injury on others.

The government had, however, after years of careful management found some funds that could be used for investment in health, education and housing. The privatization of state bodies such as British Gas and British Telecom was on the stocks and people were receiving shares, and council-house tenants were allowed to buy their houses. By design or good luck the economy was showing steady growth, inflation was under control and unemployment was falling. This all seemed very positive and reflected the opinion polls which gave the Conservatives 44 per cent, Labour 33 per cent and the SDP/Liberal Alliance 21 per cent; a useful position for a Conservative victory. However, the Labour Party was much better organized than it had been in 1983. They had a new leader in Neil Kinnock, with a sound organization run by their General Secretary Larry Whitty and communication in the hands of Peter Mandelson; a much more formidable team with impressive presentation of their plans for health, education and job creation. Norman Tebbit was appointed Conservative

Election leaflet, 1987.

Meeting local shopkeepers in Batley.

Party Chairman to give the campaign some bite with manifesto plans for schools to opt out of local authority control and for much more privatization.

The party was keen to demonstrate that after two terms of Conservative government Mrs Thatcher and her colleagues had not run out of ideas and had the determination to succeed with strong radical initiatives. The party leaders, as they always do, launched their campaign and then rushed around the country making regionally acceptable speeches.

In Batley and Spen we had a good election as I had a very enthusiastic team wanting me to be elected again. The team was once again led by my president Doug Brewer with a strong team of canvassers and supporters. Mary Bentley was again my agent and kept us within the election law. My London secretary Lorna Humphreys, who had become well known and knew the constituency well, decided she must get involved in the detail and excitement of an election campaign and would operate in our Cleckheaton office rather than at Westminster. She always proved invaluable, taking detailed control of the canvassing campaign and the production of election literature. Of course, during this period she was on holiday from Westminster.

Our choice of design and style of election posters and literature proved somewhat controversial. As the election approached I had a detailed discussion with my husband Brian on the issue as he usually did the design work. We rationalized that as I had become a rather 'different' Conservative I should not use the standard party posters and literature as they did not adequately reflect my approach of representing all electors and we wanted a more striking presentation. I suddenly remembered that my mother, who came from the North East of England, had once said that Harold Macmillan used literature printed in red in the 1920s. We could not use red on its own as it would cause confusion with Labour, so we decided on red, white and blue with a firm strapline of 'Peacock for Parliament – please'. The word 'please' caused as much comment during the campaign as the 'Peacock for Parliament'.

We had also taken one other radical decision: we would not include the word 'Conservative'. Throughout the year before the election I had been regularly approached by constituents saying: 'I am not a Conservative voter but I do like what you are doing for everyone in the area and I would like to vote for you but I am not sure I can bring myself to vote Tory.' This began to happen so regularly that we decided although we could not deflect from sound Conservative principles, we did not have to use

VOTE CONSERVATIVE
PEACOCK
FOR PARLIAMENT...."PLEASE"

Election leaflet, 1987.

At the launch of a foam tender for Hong Kong Airport at Angloco, Batley.

Minister Paddy Mayhew visiting BBA in Cleckheaton.

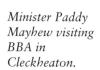

'Conservative' on our posters and in the literature. All this caused the Labour Party and others to get excited, with press comment and headline: 'Mrs Peacock's election leaflet makes Labour see red.' At my adoption meeting to start the campaign I warned it would be a tough fight but we could win again with the help of our team and hopefully with some help from government ministers.

At the time I rather wondered how much support I would get from ministers as the *Yorkshire Post* had run a long article on me and my activities titled 'Feather in her cap', saying: 'When someone stood up in the House of Commons and accused Elizabeth Peacock of being "a bloody nuisance" on behalf of her constituents, she knew she was getting it right!' The article went on to discuss some of my activities: 'All perfect ammunition to help her continue, she hopes, to be "a bloody nuisance" again when Parliament resumes.' I thought: 'Now I will not see a minister for the whole election!' but the reverse was true. I had a lot of good support.

David Waddington Home Office Minister, a good friend, arrived to meet the Asian community in Batley and Heckmondwike, visiting Zakaria Muslim Girls' High School and Heckmondwike Grammar School. Cecil Parkinson visited Birstall, going walkabout in the market and into shops to speak to electors. Education Secretary Kenneth Baker visited Batley Grammar School, using the occasion to make a widely-reported speech in which he attacked the Labour Party's defence policy, nuclear defence and the Polaris submarine. Moving on to education, he said he would introduce a whole series of radical proposals aimed at increasing basic standards in schools.

The star turn for local businessmen was Nigel Lawson Chancellor of the Exchequer who arrived for a lunch meeting so they could give him details of their problems and what he should be doing to help. He was followed by Home Secretary Douglas Hurd who came to a lunchtime meeting in Heckmondwike. I then had a barnstorming Deputy Prime Minister Willie Whitelaw arriving so I took him to Bysel's sweet factory where he was a great success; you just knew he had been electioneering before!

My final senior visitor before the election was my friend and at a later date my sparring partner the former Defence Secretary Michael Heseltine, who caused plenty of surprise by going walkabout in Batley and Heckmondwike.

Suddenly election day arrived with no more canvassing, no more visits, just a tour of the polling stations and then to the count, again with speech A (win) in one pocket and B (lose) in the other!

The outcome? We won again with a slightly increased majority. This was very pleasing as I believed it was due to my hard work and the stance I had taken on issues. I had not just ridden along on the tail of Margaret Thatcher's coat.

The result was:

Elizabeth Peacock	Conservative	25,512
Ken Woolmer	Labour	24,150
Keith Burke	SDP Alliance	8,372
Allan Harrison	Moderate Lab.	689
Conservative majority		1,362

Our election locally had been civilized. I suspect Ken Woolmer, a sensible Labour Party member, thought he could gain revenge for his defeat in 1983. He was opposed for some reason that I cannot now remember by Allan Harrison (Moderate Labour), but this intervention did not influence the final result. Keith Burke was to record a 7 per cent reduction in the SDP/Liberal Alliance vote.

After the election on 11 June 1987 the state of the parties was:

Conservatives	376 including Speaker
Labour	229
SDP Alliance	22
Others	23
Conservative majority	102

Chapter 12

Difficulties Begin
(1987–90)

Margaret Thatcher returned to Downing Street in June 1987 with a 102-seat majority, and I was returned by Batley and Spen with a slightly increased although still very slim majority of 1,362.

Margaret's initial pledge was to attack the problems of the inner cities which were widespread. The first responsibility of this Parliament, like all others, was to hold the government to account for its management of the country's affairs, particularly the economy which for this Parliament was linked to the financing of local government.

The Conservative Party had included reform of local government tax collection in its manifesto and now proposed legislation introducing the Community Charge, which became known as the Poll Tax, as a replacement for rates, originally to be phased in over four years. A badly-managed debate at the Conservative Conference urged the government to make the change all in one go. This proposition was then taken to the Cabinet by Nicholas Ridley Environment Secretary and a decision was made to implement the change in a crazy one-step move.

I was never happy about the Poll Tax and the manner in which it was introduced. Clearly the traditional Rate System needed to be reformed as it had not been updated for many years and its relevance had been lost. The idea of collecting local taxes from a wider proportion of the population always had merit, and I believe could have been made to work within a phased sensible time scale. The idea of a one-step introduction was doomed from the start. It gave all local authorities, particularly Labour-controlled ones, the opportunity to raise very high rates of community charge. The Prime Minister was badly advised on this project. Nicholas Ridley should have been more analytical.

As the bill worked its way through the House I abstained in the votes on the premise that the theory of change was right but the method of introduction and implementation was wrong. I was not popular in government circles for my stance because abstaining is considered by the whips to be a vote against and therefore an act of rebellion. Michael Heseltine, who was then in the political wilderness, led the revolt against the bill which reduced the government's majority to seventy-two but still allowed the government and Nicholas Ridley to plough on. By April the following year, the government majority slumped to twenty-five as the rebels attempted to change the bill with an amendment relating to ability to pay. Again I was in trouble with an abstention.

Poll tax worries dominated the start of 1990 as local authorities drew up their budgets with the prospect of huge increases funded by poll tax bills. This stimulated violent Town Hall protests and an eventual warning from the 1922 Back Bench Committee including me to the prime minister that the issue was becoming a poison pill for the Conservative Party. Regardless of this warning the Thatcher government continued on its course, creating in my view one of the reasons for Mrs Thatcher's eventual demise.

My second term at Westminster was characterized by me fighting tooth and nail on problems as the local MP should, with me picking a fight on a whole series of issues with local and national government. It seems it was from this activity that I gained the reputation of a rebel. Indeed, the *Telegraph and Argus* referred to me in an article in April 1987 as a 'Tory rare bird whose wings they can't clip'! This article recorded that I was only the second woman to get a Private Member's Bill through all its stages in one parliamentary session (as mentioned before). Margaret Thatcher was the first to achieve this with her Private Member's Bill on the opening of local authority meetings to the press. I did it on driving instruction. The article went on to note that I had ruffled the feathers of my government on numerous occasions by voting against part of the housing benefit bill, helping to amend the Sunday trading proposals and attacking the charges for dental and eye tests. As I review my scrapbooks of the period I see that I spent as much time and effort trying to attract and maintain businesses and jobs in the constituency as picking fights with government.

Following my surprise win in 1983 I had been re-elected with a still small but workable majority of 1,362 that allowed me to get on and attempt to change things. For example, I took issue with Labour-controlled Kirklees Council on the state of its ageing council estates and pressed government in London to find funds to allow refurbishment. This I eventually achieved in 1988 with a grant of £4.8 million to upgrade the Wilton Estate!

Equally I was engaged in attempting to bring business to the area, either directly or through the Trans-Pennine Group, a body I helped found to attract business along the M62 corridor. Eventually we attracted Petcraft, a Mars company, who built a huge new multi-million pound factory near Junction 27 on the M62, together with a new factory for Spring Ram who were manufacturing kitchen sinks.

My support for the textile industry, particularly wool, was and is long-standing to ensure a level playing field for products on the international market and to attract funds for investment. I was helped in this endeavour when I was elected Chairman of the All-Party Wool Textile Committee in the House. By contrast I was involved in trying to save jobs with proposed factory closures in the area such as the transfer of Coats Viyella carpets to Northern Ireland in 1989.

It was during this period that I truly gained my reputation as a rebel. Looking back I probably deserved it as I became something of a nuisance to my whips for the rest of my parliamentary career. Attempts were made to place me politically that failed because I could be a 'wet' on one issue and a right-wing hardliner on another. Maybe I did warrant the title of 'rare bird' with a conscience and a motto of 'caring Conservatism'. I said at the time: 'I agree with the basic principles of much of the legislation we have brought forward but far too often we get the small print and the implementation wrong. If I disagree with the detail it is my job and duty to say "No" on behalf of my constituents.' I did say 'No' on many occasions in the 1980s.

As already recorded, I was fundamentally opposed to the structure and mode of implementation of the community charge (poll tax). The idea had some merit but it was never going to work from day one so I abstained, despite having heated discussions on two occasions over dinner with Mrs Thatcher and her minister Nicholas Ridley. I got so uptight over the issue that I called for Nicholas Ridley to resign as he was getting the matter totally wrong. Thankfully I was eventually proved right.

The trouble was that this was only one of many matters with which I took issue. I voted against the government on the benefits bill not linking child benefit to inflation; the health bill in imposing charges for dental and eye tests; and argued about terms of privatization of the water industry. I initially voted against the televising of Parliament as I was of the view that members would 'play up' for the cameras. Fortunately this did not happen and I was wrong; television has opened up politics to the nation.

Chapter 13

Westminster Activities
(1987–90)

Clearly I had become 'trouble' to the whips so somebody looked around to find me a job so that I had less time to annoy the government. Obviously too unreliable to be given a government position, I was appointed to the BBC General Advisory Committee to use my energy in looking at the BBC which awakened my interest in broadcasting and I will report on this later.

The 1922 Executive Committee

Interestingly, you would have thought that my fellow members would be fed up with my fairly regular attacks on government policy and with my rebellions. However, it appears that my feisty approach to politics and my tendency to tell the government where they were getting it wrong had not gone unnoticed by my colleagues. I was approached by Donald Kaberry in 1987 after the election, who said: 'Elizabeth, you take a positive view of politics and tell the government straight from the shoulder where they are getting it wrong. You should put your name forward for election to the Executive of the Back Bench 1922 Committee to represent back-bench views.' So I did and to my surprise I was elected to join this influential body. The Executive of the 1922 Committee has the historic remit of directly informing the Prime Minister/leader of the party on issues and concerns of back-bench members. Traditionally the Executive had been 'staffed' by the 'Knights of the Shires' with very few lady members ever being elected. Times were changing and there were now two women, myself and Dame Jill Knight, and the gentlemen from the Shires were disappearing. This new appointment did give me the opportunity to express back-bench views more easily to ministers and from time to time directly to the prime minister. I learnt how to have a discussion with Margaret Thatcher without getting a good 'handbagging'. The answer was

Lunch for Prime Minister John Major at Fishmongers' Livery Hall given by the 1922 Executive Committee.

to stand up to her and make your point as forcibly as she did; she often became cross but usually left in friendship.

I have always thought that one of the contributing factors in her eventual downfall was the inability of her advisors to stand up to her on issues and say: 'No Margaret, you are wrong.' This was particularly apparent after she lost Willie Whitelaw from the team due to ill health. At home husband Denis I know fulfilled this role but he could not be everywhere. It is true that the tactic of 'standing up' to the Prime Minister's bowling did lead to some heated argument that on occasion earned me a rebuke from the chairman: 'Elizabeth, you should not be so direct with the Prime Minister.' My answer was always: 'Chairman, our remit is to inform the Prime Minister on party concerns. There is no point in pussyfooting around. We must tell it straight.'

As I continued to serve on the Executive for several years I will refer to its activities which were not all political.

Being one of only two lady members at the time I got some interesting tasks that gave me a relief from politics. When Mrs Thatcher had been prime minister for ten years the 1922 Executive decided we should mark this milestone with a gift of a piece of silverware to mark the occasion, preferably a newly-designed piece. I, with Winston Churchill and Sir Charles Morrison, was deputed to find something suitable. With the help of Rosemary Ransome Wallis, Curator of Collections at the Goldsmiths' Company, we held a limited design competition, the winner of which was the talented designer Lexi Dick to whom we gave the commission to design a suitable rose bowl that could be engraved. When it was presented to Mrs Thatcher it appeared to be a success and was put on her own dining table.

In the early 1990s the Executive decided that there should be a special lunch to entertain our new Prime Minister John Major and this would give us an opportunity to discuss issues that were worrying to backbenchers. We decided that it should be away from Westminster and this was achieved by holding a special lunch at the Fishmongers' Livery Hall. A photograph was taken to mark the occasion and we were all seated in front of the famous Annigoni portrait of HM The Queen (famous because it was used as a design on our stamps). Even today the photograph cannot be reproduced in its entirety as the copyright on the painting ensures it is never published.

Suddenly I was respectable and I was elected to the Executive of the Parliamentary Commonwealth Association which cements links with other Commonwealth parliaments, opening up a whole new level of interest. I reserved time within these new activities to fulfil my ongoing responsibilities as secretary to the Yorkshire MPs group. This I combined with the role of vice president of Yorkshire Young Conservatives and president of Yorkshire Area Conservative Trade Unionists which kept my feet on the ground.

As I reviewed my scrapbook to research this book I did spot one rather amusing press cutting which read: 'MP calls on SAS to save elephants.' In the summer of 1989 I was asked during the recess to join a delegation to visit Kenya to inspect some overseas aid programmes financed by the UK government, to check on tax-payer value for money. At that time there was a real problem in Kenya with poachers killing elephants for their tusks and aid was being provided to help resolve this problem. We visited Daphne Sheldrick's elephant orphanage near Nairobi and met Dr Richard Leakey, head of the Kenya Wildlife Service. We were able to discuss the military action that was ongoing to stop the killing of elephants and the international trade in ivory. I must have said to some of the African press, rather as a joke: 'What you need to stop this is our SAS.' This comment was passed to the international press and widely circulated; a lesson for me to watch what you say to journalists! As a penance I joined the Nellie the Elephant Club.

My View

I had built a reputation for straight talking on behalf of all my constituents and had been elected to the 1922 Committee to do the same for my fellow backbenchers.

On this point I had regular feedback from my weekend surgeries in Batley and Cleckheaton town halls and in Heckmondwike and Birstall libraries. By this time we had started a non-political Batley and Spen Business Club that held an annual lunch or dinner in the House of Commons and I visited members' businesses during the recess. Business people in Yorkshire give you their view straight from the shoulder and our members did just that! This was supplemented by views gained during the many visits I made to churches, chapels, mosques, galas, youth events, Scouts and Guides etc. These contacts kept me on my toes and briefed me well on local needs and views. My weekend programme normally comprised leaving London very late on Thursday night or Friday midday; speech at some organization and dinner/supper almost every Friday evening; surgeries on Saturday morning followed by an afternoon local event; another local event on Sunday afternoon and back in London by midday Monday, breathless and hopefully with clean clothes for the week! By this means I kept my feet firmly on the ground and responsive to local concerns; I could do no more.

The economy

The final years of the Thatcher era were dominated by economic issues, often of a dramatic nature and shown at a later date to have been progressed with considerable personal disagreement at Cabinet level that was not apparent at the time. These disagreements raise the question of Cabinet unity and whether action to change the players was taken early enough. Would earlier changes in the team have brought a different result and extended the life of the Thatcher regime? We will now never know. I suspect so but a bigger question arises regarding the suitability and resolve of Mrs Thatcher's close advisors.

The autumn of 1987 brought shock waves to the government with the collapse of world stock markets on 19 October (known as Black Monday), when some £50 billion was wiped off London shares with a further drop of £40 billion the following day. Chancellor Nigel Lawson responded by cutting back interest rates to help stabilize the markets. From this point disagreements on policy between Prime Minister and Chancellor seem to become routine.

By the Budget in March 1988 further remedial action was needed to help the economy, so Nigel Lawson cut the basic rate of tax to 25p and the top rate to 40p and also cut interest rates which then allowed the economy to overheat and move on to an inflationary boom. It eventually emerged that Margaret was unhappy with Nigel's policy of shadowing the German Deutschmark and did not like his policy of holding down the pound by selling on the foreign exchanges. She sensibly took the view that you cannot buck the market and did not approve of Nigel's approach to the European Exchange Rate Mechanism. Why Mrs Thatcher did not take her usual positive action on something she did not like we will probably never know but she had respect for Nigel's abilities in managing earlier problems. The position became serious in May as interest rates were cut to their lowest for ten years and then panic set in with rates being increased eight times by November, reaching 13 per cent to curb a consumer boom.

By the spring of 1989 with inflation worsening Mrs Thatcher decided something different had to be done. Lawson had by now been dubbed a 'one-club golfer' and as his interest policy was not working, she re-called her own economic advisor Sir Alan Walters to Downing Street. I recall this caused plenty of Westminster and press comment. Walters criticized Lawson in the City and Mrs Thatcher clearly blamed Nigel for letting inflation hit 8 per cent but had to back him to maintain stability. Interest rates were further increased in October to 15 per cent to cool the economy. Nigel complained that he was being undermined by Walters' statement; disagreement was public and as Margaret would not dispense with Walters, her Chancellor resigned. Nigel was immediately replaced by John Major with Sir Alan suddenly deciding to go.

Opposition activities
This would be a good point at which to take a look at opposition activity.

With Margaret Thatcher returning to Westminster with her 102-seat majority, the opposition parties realized that there had to be change and that they needed new policies; consequently they made re-appraisals and decisions. David Steel tabled a proposal for the Liberals to merge with the

Social Democratic Party that was agreed in a vote 57 to 42 per cent. However, SDP leader David Owen decided to go it alone with two colleagues, Rosie Barnes and John Cartwright.

The Labour Party reviewed the policies that they had followed for recent elections and decided to indulge in leadership contests. As the left of the party objected to the direction being taken by Neil Kinnock, he was challenged by Tony Benn and his deputy Roy Hattersley was challenged by Eric Heifer and John Prescott. The policy reviews clearly caused problems; the nationalization of British industry without compensation was abandoned, as was unilateral disarmament; all previous sacred plans. Kinnock and Hattersley were the victors but remained determined to change the policy. This stance was confirmed in the spring of 1989 with backing from the National Executive of the party.

In my opinion Mrs Thatcher's influence had become apparent within the opposition parties and they had to amend their structures and policies to remain relevant to the British people in the light of Thatcher policy changes.

Europe: a developing storm

Europe and our membership of the European Union that had been a challenge in the early 1970s became a progressively more emotive issue in the mid-1980s and through to the 1990s for the Conservative Party, the government and Mrs Thatcher in particular.

Ted Heath, our former prime minister and architect of our entry into the Union and a committed Europe enthusiast, remained in the Commons acting as a critic of all things Thatcher. Mrs Thatcher had beaten him to the leadership of the party, which he could neither forgive nor forget.

Europe was an issue that could be used to attack both the government and the party. The Conservative Party was split, not only into pro- and anti-Europe factions but by shades of opinion within these. With her earlier difficulties and eventual success in achieving the budget opt-out for Britain, Mrs Thatcher had alienated her fellow European leaders with her style and inflexibility. In her view and mine, Europe was heading in the wrong direction towards becoming a federal state with a central government, a central tax and spend control. This just had to be wrong and the historic speech she made in 1988 in Bruges where she set her face positively against European political and economic union laid down the basis of the issue and became the focus for anti-federalist views. It equally became a source of discontent to Euro-enthusiasts that in the end contributed to her demise.

Party unhappiness continued in 1989 following this hard-line speech, with Ted Heath adding to the opposition by saying that Mrs Thatcher would leave Britain as a 'second-rate power in a second-tier community'. However, to the surprise of many including myself, she suddenly agreed at the June 1989 Madrid council meeting that Britain would one day join the European ERM (Exchange Rate Mechanism). It later transpired that Mrs Thatcher had done this under the threat of resignation of Sir Geoffrey Howe Foreign Secretary, a committed European, and Nigel Lawson, her chancellor. Little did we know of the widespread disagreements within Cabinet on economic issues with Nigel Lawson and on Europe with Geoffrey Howe where Mrs Thatcher disliked his stance on more rapid integration.

This led to a major Cabinet re-shuffle in July with Sir Geoffrey moving reluctantly to Deputy Prime Minister, being replaced by John Major as Foreign Secretary (a position he was to hold for a very short time before the move to Chancellor). In my view, Margaret had clearly run into trouble around the Cabinet table that she did not deal with early enough due to loyalty or due to lack of independent positive advice, an issue I will return to later.

Local concerns

Throughout this parliament there were issues within a Yorkshire context that I had to consider and act upon.

The matter concerning us in Yorkshire was the serious problem being faced by the textile industry. The others were national issues but with Yorkshire implications, namely the poll tax and where Mrs Thatcher was going as leader of the Conservative Party and in leading the country. Dealing first with textiles in which I had always had an interest with special emphasis on wool, I had been elected chairman of the All-Party Wool Textile Committee in the House of Commons just at a time when the industry was having trouble under threats of imports from around the world that were undermining our markets and prohibitive tariffs restraining our exports. Our textile industry needed help so in my chairman's role I was in the debate right up to my neck. Some sort of global import quotas were necessary to prevent the import of underpriced yarns from Turkey and elsewhere as thousands of jobs in the British textile industry were at risk including many in Batley and Spen.

The government was aware of these difficulties and was deeply involved at the international level with negotiation through the Multi Fibre Agreement to get fair trading agreements for all textile products including finished clothes. This became time-consuming, requiring taking wool-men to meet ministers and arranging visits by ministers to Yorkshire. Lord Trefgarne who had responsibility for the textile industry at that time was a most welcome visitor. To add to the pressure, textile questions came up almost daily in the House and we had several long debates on the detail. I was expected to speak which took much research time to cover ever-changing industry developments. I correctly concluded that it would be a long-running problem because of its international context and therefore slow-moving. So it proved, going on well into the Major era before any progress was made. We managed to deter imports, made progress with exports and did indeed save some jobs in Yorkshire.

The other two pressing matters were linked: the Poll Tax and Margaret Thatcher's leadership. However, before I got into the thick of these issues I became involved in a spat with the government on the detail in the NHS and community care bill relating to the costs to elderly people paying for care in private care homes. I rebelled once again to the annoyance of my whip because the government lost by three votes.

The issue may not now seem important but the government would not listen to backbenchers and apply some sensible amendments. Just who was advising Mrs Thatcher? This was possibly the beginning of her slide from power; however, we did not recognize this until much later but it was downhill from here.

The big issue was the Poll Tax and the proposals created riots in many of our cities and it caused unhappiness almost everywhere, not least in Batley and Spen. People quickly understood that I did not like the way it was being introduced and that I was unhappy with the way it would affect many households in the constituency. Basically I was in favour of a local tax system collected from wider groups of people within the community as the historical property rates system was outdated and no longer 'fit for purpose'. It was clear to me that the change had to be implemented over a number of years and carefully staged from the old system to the new. However, minister Nicholas Ridley decided the change had to be made in one step and Mrs Thatcher approved.

The problem was caused locally in Yorkshire and other parts of the North by the number of relatively low-rated street houses with suitably low payments. When the occupiers were asked to pay a poll tax, the payment demanded often more than doubled or quadrupled for the household. This problem was compounded by the idiotic decision to make the change in one step and by local Labour-controlled authorities who dramatically increased these charges. It was never going to work in this format.

The British people decided that the project was doomed from the beginning and so was Mrs Thatcher, though we did not realize it at the time. She just did not listen, as I discovered in the two rather heated meetings I had with her. Her immediate team did not help as they seemed incapable of giving her the message from the 'grass roots'. During this period I had almost daily press comment on my position in which I said I was looking for change but it must be sensible change. I got plenty of wild headlines that can be summarized by this one: 'Tory rebel Elizabeth Peacock Conservative MP for Batley and Spen – who has clashed with the government over the implementation of the Community Charge – says the new system being used is unfair as it does not reflect the ability to pay. She is therefore campaigning for radical changes and urging local people to apply for Community Charge rebates.' I recall that we put down an amendment to the bill requesting a banding system but it was defeated.

My View
No wonder there was rioting in the streets. Local taxation needed change but we had got it wrong. So had Mrs Thatcher and Nicholas Ridley and it looked as though the British public were withdrawing their support from her. She was moving from being a political asset to a political liability, due to a combination of her refusal to listen and her inner circle's failure to advise appropriately.

Other activities at Westminster
After I was re-elected in 1987 I decided that I should widen my interests and experience and take advantage of some of the activities available to Members of Parliament. I was now a member of the Executive of the 1922 Committee and I had the work of the Westminster Dining Club but I wanted something different. Many of my colleagues had become linked to the armed forces and I thought this would be a good idea. I was offered a commando training trip in Norway or a long-term link with the RAF on Harrier jets. I picked the latter and all was set until the RAF discovered I had undergone back surgery and they pulled the rug as they could not risk seat ejection! I was disappointed but concluded I had better do something more sensible so I opted for a Parliament-Industry link with the Industry and Parliament Trust.

Industry and Parliament Trust

With my interest in industry, particularly that of importance to Yorkshire, I was pleased to be offered a place on the Industry and Parliament scheme to get involved in a link with an industrial company to study their operations from raw material to finished product. The Trust, sponsored by industry, allows MPs to link with their chosen company and spend some time gaining experience of its day-to-day commercial activities.

I was pleased to be offered a link with Jaguar cars, being monitored by the Chairman's office and the chairman himself, John Egan. Subsequently I spent one day per week for some weeks mainly at Brown's Lane in Coventry looking at all aspects of car production and marketing. I started with component purchasing, assembly-line production and product distribution, then moved on to marketing and advertising followed by time with a Jaguar agent to do a bit of selling from the showroom floor. I was even allowed to visit the secret research department designing the next models that I later saw on the road. The whole programme took several months and was a fascinating look at an important integrated British business. My programme ended in style with an invitation to the Le Mans 24-hour motor race to see the Jaguar cars in action and what a performance it was! Jaguar won with a very impressive conclusion when the three Jaguar cars crossed the finishing line together to win. I thoroughly enjoyed the experience of my time spent with Jaguar. I admired the input of the Jaguar people from the assembly-line staff to the then chairman Sir John Egan. A worthwhile industry-parliament link and I gained a certificate to prove it.

House of Commons Motor Club

I have always had an interest in motoring as a hobby so when I got to Westminster I rather casually joined the Motor Club; although I was initially a poor meeting-attender, this changed after my spell with Jaguar. The House of Commons Motor Club was a different sort of club in that it was the point of liaison between MPs at Westminster and the motoring organizations like the RAC and others associated with road driving and motor sport. Hence it had a never-ending range of interests but also became involved in fund-raising for charities.

Initially being the only woman present I got the job of taking the meeting minutes. Suddenly the present chairman went and the committee decided that with my minute-taking I knew most about the activities and therefore I should become Chairman, which I remained until 1997!

Over the years we had a very busy agenda, often helping to raise funds for various motoring charities. We had celebrity races such as 'Lords v Commons' at Brands Hatch with on one occasion the then Chancellor of the Exchequer Ken Clarke, the Sports Minister and Olympic oarsman Colin Moynihan and Lord Strathcarron taking part; Roger King MP or Lord Strathcarron who had driven at Brooklands in the 1930s usually winning. As mentioned before, on the occasion that I was allowed to race at Brands Hatch I was not last as Colin Moynihan spun off the track! We also raised funds by MPs driving from their constituencies to Westminster in a classic car rally. I went from Cleckheaton to London in a beautiful red MG accompanied by my original Pudsey Bear.

As President each year Mr Speaker held a Motor Club dinner to bring together motoring interests and MPs, often with an outside speaker. On one occasion Ron Dennis, the McLaren boss, filled the bill. Another more difficult task for the chairman was to resolve car-parking problems in the House of Commons multi-storey car park under Big Ben. Several members tried to store their classic cars in the car park, the main culprit being Alan Clark. Maybe that was why Alan had rude things to say about me in his diaries as I had to tell him from time to time to move his car, which he usually did but just to a different parking bay!

Chapter 14

Europe and the World

The world

It could easily be said that I am the wrong person to comment on Mrs Thatcher's involvement on the world stage. This is probably true as I certainly concentrated my own efforts on domestic issues and Batley and Spen in particular. By joining the Executive of the Commonwealth Parliamentary Association I did widen my horizons and became knowledgeable about Commonwealth matters which gave me an understanding of Margaret Thatcher's impact and standing. I also gained a measure of her standing elsewhere around the world from various visits I made. I can say at the beginning of this review that Margaret had, and still has, a higher standing in much of the world than she had or has in Britain. The big question is why?

She initially became known as the first woman Prime Minister of Great Britain; still a unique position to hold. She was, however, propelled to the front of the world stage by the Falklands War. This was achieved by her rapid and positive decision-making to back up her absolute determination to kick the Argentinians out and regain the Falkland Islands for Great Britain. In this episode she was involved in discussions and negotiations with President Reagan and many of the European leaders who discovered she was not only an 'Iron Lady' but a formidable and determined woman who would not accept 'No' for an answer. During my fourteen years in the House I was able to get a measure of things when travelling privately in Brazil, the USA, Russia, South Africa and the Far East and always during the summer recess. We easily underestimated her standing in these countries. As in everything, she acted with style and panache, looking at the issues in detail and responding with energy and speed.

The 1979–83 Parliament was a period of review of our defence capabilities that proved controversial in Britain as we had to make decisions on our nuclear involvement. Britain together with our NATO allies had to ensure a nuclear strategy balance with the Warsaw Pact countries; therefore Margaret Thatcher's friendship with President Reagan was instrumental in making the decision to acquire the Trident II missile.

A trip to see the Berlin Wall in 1982 with Chancellor Kohl was a foretaste of things to come. Margaret's ongoing strategy of achieving close relationships had an early payback in 1983, requiring her to work with President Reagan on issues in Lebanon and Grenada. Having met President Reagan I can understand how this could be done! Her early development of a relationship with President Gorbachev was to pay off later but it put her in a position to act as the go-between with the USA and Russia on Reagan's Strategic Defense Initiative (SDI). She noted at this point that Mr Gorbachev was 'a man with whom I could do business'. Her strategy of relationship-building was put to the test in early discussions with Chinese leaders on the possible transfer of Hong Kong back to China, and also by her bridge-building for the future with the apartheid regime of P.W. Botha in South Africa. Having visited South Africa during this period I recognized the balance she had achieved between the need for long-term change to majority rule and the requirements of the Afrikaners within the population. Like many others before and since, Mrs Thatcher also took an interest in the Arab/Israeli problem but understandably made no progress in that sphere.

Progress was, however, looking possible in Eastern Europe where Gorbachev was making reforms in the Soviet Union that would lead to change throughout the region and the eventual re-unification of East and West Germany. As always Mrs Thatcher spotted the opportunity and helped it on its way by pulling the USA and Russia together on the long-standing issue of nuclear weapons and security. To the surprise of many, by the summer of 1989 there were signs of the collapse of communism in Eastern Europe and by the autumn the Berlin Wall was being demolished under German unification.

Undoubtedly Margaret Thatcher had become a towering figure on the world stage and played a part in the demise of Soviet communism. The big question is whether it would have happened without her. The probable answer is 'Yes' because Presidents Reagan and Gorbachev had sufficient understanding to make progress but her drive to see change moved the matter along more quickly.

Throughout these endeavours the world stage had a further wing: Europe. Europe and the European Union was of more importance to us in Batley and Spen as it meant 'business', 'jobs' and 'livelihood'.

*Meeting Benazir
Bhutto in the
House of
Commons, 1994.*

*With President
Gorbachev in the
House of Commons,
1991.*

*Meeting President Daniel
Arap Moi in Kenya,
1990.*

Europe

Throughout my time at Westminster I was never fully convinced about Mrs Thatcher's real position on Europe, despite her many speeches on the subject. After the earlier De Gaulle challenges to our entry, Edward Heath considered that it was his greatest achievement when he took Britain into the EEC. When the 1975 referendum on our continued membership came along there was some suspicion that Margaret Thatcher was less supportive. At the same time she claimed, however, that she thought it would be foolish to leave the community. The referendum result, 69 per cent in favour of remaining in the community, confirmed the people's wishes and the stance that politicians had to follow.

Mrs Thatcher recognizes in her book *The Path to Power* that once a politician is given a public image by the media it is almost impossible to shed that image. She became labelled as the 'Iron Lady', quite capable of 'handbagging' those who opposed her. It is true that she was single-minded on European issues and she did not back down in an argument. She was totally sceptical about European federalism and considered by many to be backward-looking. In retrospect it may be that this was a good thing, considering the problems experienced by Europe in the last few years.

Margaret was obviously well briefed with wide-ranging European knowledge when she took the leadership of the Conservative Party and became leader of the opposition in 1975. Equally in the years 1975 to 1979 until she became prime minister she obviously took a serious interest in European affairs. Clearly she had plenty of problems with the other European leaders during her premiership.

Consequently, I still remain to be convinced that she was a true European at heart; this may be unfair but I think not! Certainly she always had Britain's interests at the forefront of her mind and said so, which automatically made it difficult to make progress with other leaders. For this reason alone her record on success in Europe has been and remains difficult to measure. Her success with the budget 'opt-out' was immense and long-lasting to the present day. Her progress on other European issues was patchy but would anyone else have done better in the circumstances?

All we can do at this point in time is review the issues that confronted Mrs Thatcher and take a view on how she reacted. In this analysis I must declare an interest as I may well be more sceptical of Europe than Mrs Thatcher ever was and this may cloud my vision.

I have always taken a simplistic view of Europe and our involvement. We are in the European Union for trade and we will work together with our partners in this area. All other non-trading matters are British and the responsibility of the British Parliament; Europe has no part to play. Many may not agree with this simplistic approach; however, I suspect the majority of people in Britain support this basic thinking. During my first session at Westminster I took an interest in European affairs but was just too busy with Batley and Spen to take an active part.

Like all recent prime ministers who have moved into 10 Downing Street, Margaret Thatcher was faced with European matters that could be a distraction from the real business of running Britain. Soon after she was elected in 1979 the first direct elections were held for the European Parliament. Margaret had at an earlier date recognized the control over European affairs maintained by France and Germany that limited Britain's ability to influence European thinking. France had historically feared the military and now the economic strength of Germany. This French/German axis has been maintained by a close relationship between the French President and the German Chancellor, regardless of who occupies those seats.

As soon as she was elected in 1979 Margaret Thatcher launched her argument about the European budget and Britain's contribution. She had pre-warned Chancellor Schmidt of her intention to raise the issue. Britain, despite North Sea oil, was at risk of becoming one of the least prosperous members of the EU, yet would be expected to become the largest net contributor due to the distortion from the Common Agricultural Policy. Mrs Thatcher's demands on the matter were certainly noted, though the decision-making process was pushed forward from meeting to meeting. In the intervening months Margaret drove home the argument that Britain must have a budget rebate. This was a realistic strategy but made many of the members decide to test her willingness to stand up to them. Was it an anti-woman stance on their part? If so, they misjudged the woman!

By mid-year we had an initial three-year deal that has since been extended to the present day; a successful Thatcher legacy. This 'standing up to the boys' clearly irritated Valéry Giscard d'Estaing and Helmut Schmidt among others, earning Margaret the title of the 'Iron Lady' with a tendency to 'handbag the troops'; a perception she never overcame. With the budget argument settled and the arrival of the Falklands War, her major contacts abroad were more related to military issues than economic matters.

The 1983 election was followed at once by a European Council meeting at which the original rebate deal had to be extended, requiring long-term change to the EU finance structure. By this time, however, the players had changed with Messrs Kohl and Mitterand in the driving seats when the 'temporary' 1983 British rebate was extended. A meeting at the end of the year made no progress as Britain could not agree to an increase in the EU budget until the Common Agricultural Policy costs were constrained.

March 1984 saw Chancellor Kohl trying to 'horse deal' a settlement; again Mrs Thatcher's response was 'Non'!

Foreign Ministers were given the task at the next council meeting to see what they could achieve. As an MP with an all-consuming constituency I followed these discussions at the top level and did not get involved in the detail; the discussion was at a level well above a new backbench member. By now Mrs Thatcher had lost patience and put pressure on Messrs Mitterrand and Kohl and with some difficulty got a workable deal that lasted. History indicates that this success was probably the high point of her dealings with Europe because widening community membership and creating a single market became more important. Two competing visions of Europe had developed: a free enterprise 'Common Market' version or a federal European state with ever-closer integration of political and economic matters.

As this latter concept was favoured by the French/German axis, the continual pressure to go down this route caused much debate and tension because Margaret Thatcher was in the free enterprise camp. The discussion on the two versions of Europe continued well into the Thatcher third term when she ran into opposing views from President of the EU Commission Jacques Delors. This clearly stimulated her to set out her vision of free enterprise in the now-famous Bruges speech that encouraged opposition to her across Europe.

The federal approach to Europe and ever-closer integration was demonstrated in the proposed move to the Economic and Monetary Union (EMU) that was to bedevil not only the Thatcher government but also her successor John Major, causing great political and economic upset.

My View

So how do we sum up Mrs Thatcher on the world stage and in Europe? Following the Falklands conflict she really was a world leader who had to be recognized and listened to. She had positively put the 'Great' back into Great Britain. With Presidents Gorbachev and Reagan she can claim to have been responsible for changing the world order, an achievement for which many of the British people do not give her credit. As for Europe, the negotiation of a rebate on Britain's contribution to the EU budget that has lasted to the present time was a masterstroke that others may well not have achieved.

As for the other activities in Europe, I suspect Mrs Thatcher became frustrated with the never-ending arguments. Her efforts to make progress took too much of her valuable time and this reflected on her ability to drive domestic issues such as the poll tax.

This is a trap that prime ministers have fallen into before and since (e.g. Blair and Iraq). Throughout this period there was considerable discussion about Britain joining the ERM, the Exchange Rate Mechanism. Margaret Thatcher initially opposed such a move but was eventually persuaded to change her mind and agreed; a pity that she did not stick to her original position.

Her Bruges speech remains the basis of anti-federalism, and she was right.

Chapter 15

Loss of Confidence

Change at the top

Despite the great success of the Thatcher government in early years, the Conservative Party was suddenly suffering from a loss of confidence; not only in itself, its policies, but also in its leader. Sir Anthony Meyer announced that he would be a 'stalking-horse' candidate in a challenge to Mrs Thatcher's leadership; the first time she had been challenged since her original election in 1975.

The comments in the tea room were that this was just a joke; he was not serious. Margaret got my vote and secured a convincing victory but sixty Tory MPs voted against her or abstained, with many warning publicly that they would not back her again. This was the real beginning of the end of the Thatcher regime but it did not seem so at the time. Having re-shuffled the Cabinet in the autumn of 1989, there were still problems on most political fronts. The frustrating thing as a backbencher was that no one at the centre of the party, particularly those directly around the leader, wanted to hear about the problems we were all experiencing. These people were certainly not prepared to pass the message on to Margaret Thatcher.

As a member of the Executive 1922 Back Bench Committee I realized this problem in the party structure. Chairman and members of the 1922 Committee must also tell the leader exactly what the back bench and constituents are thinking and we struggled with this on occasions as the Chairman Cranley Onslow did not like me giving the true message to Mrs Thatcher.

By 1989 Margaret Thatcher had surrounded herself with 'yes men' who did not communicate within the party or apparently give messages to the leader. Her PPS Peter Morrison and others had much to answer for in this direction.

However, Margaret herself was not blameless. She had, I believe, realized that there was a problem within the party and that maybe she was not getting the direct message. Consequently she organized a series of lunch and supper 'get-togethers' with six to eight members to talk over the issues. I went to several but they did not work well. Margaret in her true style dominated the conversation and many of my colleagues would not say the things to her that they had been saying before the meeting. I found the secret was to wait until Margaret herself started to eat and then tell her exactly what you wanted to say and outline the problems in your area. She would then have to either listen or spoil her food by arguing. This was one way of having a balanced discussion. Each time I had a discussion with her she was happy to listen and argue her corner but did not often change her view. I continued to support her as our leader but became progressively less convinced that she would continue to take the party much further forward. What a pity, I thought; a great lady but not one who is likely to move us forward into the future.

At the start of 1990 the poll tax was the problem issue and we lost the by-election in Mid Staffordshire when a Conservative majority of 14,000 was overturned by Labour. We were clearly in trouble and Mrs Thatcher's continued leadership was in doubt. Suddenly things were going wrong; the British public recognized it and was beginning to defect from Thatcher support.

The economy was not helpful either as I have already discussed; the Prime Minister and her Chancellor (Nigel Lawson) having fallen out leading to his departure. A leading Conservative Party player 'big beast' Michael Heseltine was still out of government but making hints that he was available if the party needed him.

The poll tax introduction had incensed the nation and gone totally wrong, causing rioting in the streets and a serious loss of confidence in the government.

Many Conservative Members of Parliament had come to the conclusion that Margaret Thatcher could not lead the party to victory at the next general election. Some panic set in as they considered the loss of their seat, realizing that we needed a new leader. I was not in the panicking group but considered change was necessary. This was all very upsetting for party supporters who were welded to the Thatcher bandwagon. However, political parties have little or no conscience even for world statesmen or women and so change was in the air.

Michael Heseltine then indicated subtly that if Margaret stood down, he would be a candidate. This stimulated Norman Tebbit, who wanted to prevent the Heseltine candidate. The writing was on the wall.

Mrs Thatcher at the opening of the Dewsbury District Hospital, 1990.

On 4 October the government announced entry to the ERM to which John Major and Douglas Hurd had persuaded Mrs Thatcher to reluctantly agree. This decision provoked furious discussion at the following Tory Party conference that, together with the loss of a further by-election at Eastbourne, led to serious party differences regarding the speed of progress towards economic union and the single currency. I had then, and still have to this day, total opposition to the single currency and therefore was in serious difficulties with my support for the party.

In balance, Mrs Thatcher was clearly unhappy with the speed of change agreed by the European Council with a 1994 deadline for the second ERM stage; a fact she attacked in the Commons, naming it the 'back door to a federal Europe'.

Her rejection of this European move was all too much for Sir Geoffrey Howe who promptly resigned as deputy prime minister, a position he had reluctantly occupied. Within days he made a regime-changing speech in the House of Commons confirming his resignation and laying down a challenge to Mrs Thatcher's leadership, saying that she was risking Britain's future by her attitude to Europe and that others should consider their loyalties to the leader. I sat in the Chamber and listened to his speech. It was devastating; knocking the heart out of the Thatcher government and regime, and from which it could not recover.

Mrs Thatcher's days as Prime Minister were now numbered. She faced a serious party challenge and I have never been convinced that her surrounding 'yes men' realized that her leadership was in such danger: she was in trouble in the country due to the handling of the Poll Tax; she was in trouble with some in the party due to her attitude on Europe; and in my view she was in trouble as they did not support her as they should have done. She had lost Willie Whitelaw and no one else could or would put her right. I had always greatly admired the way her husband Denis supported her throughout her career but I recognize it is difficult for a spouse to interfere in what are issues of state as they too have become too close to the problem. Regrettably Denis could not get Margaret out of this situation; it was just too big for him.

The Howe speech dramatically changed the scene, so Michael Heseltine decided to throw down the gauntlet on 14 November and challenge Mrs Thatcher's leadership.

I now digress slightly before I move on.

Of all the speakers I listened to in fourteen years in the House there are only two that stand out in my memory. The first was Enoch Powell, speaking in a Pro-Life debate for almost an hour with no notes; his eloquence, breadth of subject matter, intellect and delivery skill were outstanding. I knew from a tip-off from the Speaker that I would be called next. As I waited to follow him the thought went constantly through my mind, now follow that! I did but not to his high standard. I had by then spoken regularly in the House and would never reach his standards but I have since realized that very few others could. The next great speech was Geoffrey Howe's resignation speech that was the turning-point in the Thatcher premiership; it convinced the party that there had to be change and that we had to have a new leader. It has been billed as a speech that changed history and I believe it did. It was well thought out, balanced and presented with the skill of a statesman. Geoffrey had the reputation of a rather dull speaker but on this occasion he set the political world alight.

We had all known for some time that the Cabinet was in disarray. Mrs Thatcher had fallen out with Nigel Lawson over the economy and she had clearly had a disagreement with Geoffrey Howe on the European currency issue; so much so that she re-shuffled him from the position of Foreign Secretary to the Leader of the House and deputy prime minister, much to his disgust and more importantly his wife's disgust. Obviously he could stand it no longer and he resigned on 31 October, making his famous speech the following week. As I sat there listening to him I also had a moment of change. I had, and still acknowledge that I had, ridden to Westminster on Margaret Thatcher's coat tails. I had received a good 'handbagging' in our heated debates when I voted against some of her policies but I had continued to support her personally. Geoffrey's speech was telling and he did influence my thinking. Even though I could not agree with his views on Europe, I did recognize the need for change.

Using cricketing parlance similar to that used by Mrs Thatcher at a recent Lord Mayor's banquet commenting that she was 'still at the crease and prepared to hit the bowling all round the ground', Geoffrey's response was that he believed that working with Mrs Thatcher was 'like sending your opening batsman in only to find that their bat has been broken – by the captain!'

I became convinced that we had to have change at the top. I had known that Michael Heseltine was keen to get back into government and he had worked hard for the party in the past two years building support. I had been working with him on several issues and respected his ability, believing that he could lead the party and could take us to another great election victory.

I believe Geoffrey's speech convinced Michael that the time was 'now' to challenge Mrs Thatcher for the leadership. He did just that and we headed into a leadership election that split the party. I returned from Westminster with the idea of the necessary change in my head but with a need to sound out Batley and Spen's opinion. A weekend of taking soundings convinced me that there was a positive majority among Conservative supporters in the constituency who were looking for a change of leader and a change of style. In my discussions I had said I believed that 'unless the party changes its leader the country will change the government.' After this weekend of consultation I declared that I would 'back Heseltine'.

I found voting for Michael Heseltine to be an 'agonizing responsibility', helping to decide the fate of a prime minister and leader of the party. Whatever decision I made I knew some people would be unhappy and so it proved; some people never forgave me for voting against Mrs Thatcher. I see from my scrapbook I said at the time Mrs Thatcher made us proud to be British and will go down in history for making Britain 'great again'. This remains true today but I had to vote for change for the sake of the party and the country. It goes to show the power of a well-timed, well-researched speech, even for someone who was never a great orator! Geoffrey certainly did it that day!

To meet the Heseltine challenge Mrs Thatcher had put together a campaign team made up of her 'yes men'. They were confident, in fact far too confident, that they could see off Michael Heseltine. They made a serious mistake. True, Margaret Thatcher won with a vote of 204 with 152 for Michael Heseltine. This fell short of the party's rules for a first ballot win and there would have to be a second ballot. When the result was announced Margaret was in Paris at a European meeting and was advised that she could easily win on the second ballot. She actually announced in Paris that she would stand to fight on.

As I went to vote I was convinced that there had to be change at the top. We were in political trouble and positive change had to occur to overcome Mrs Thatcher's intransigence against listening and the inability of her surrounding team to communicate. I knew I had to vote for Michael Heseltine and change; that I did and I was sorry to do so.

The following day, having decided to fight on, Mrs Thatcher met her Cabinet in turn and found that she did not have their support as they told her one by one that she could not win a second ballot. In other words they removed their support. By the end of the day on 21 November 1990 she had decided to resign.

First question to the Prime Minister, John Major, by the author with the former PM taking her seat on the back benches for the first time since her resignation, November 1990.

On the morning of 22 November 1990 Margaret told the Cabinet she was resigning and made a formal announcement in an unforgettable speech in the House of Commons in the afternoon. This was clearly the end of the Thatcher era; a truly sorry day. Someone once said: 'Political careers are great but they almost always end in tears.' The Thatcher years did indeed end in tears, with a tribute of 'We will not see the like of her again.'

However, a leadership contest was still in place and had a new urgency. Within hours the nominations for the second ballot closed with two additional candidates being added as they no longer needed to maintain their loyalty to Mrs Thatcher: namely John Major and Douglas Hurd, both of whom had made a rapid rise through the ministerial jungle during the later Thatcher years.

The ballot for the leadership was scheduled for 27 November, less than a week away, and I was left in a dilemma as to who I should now support.

I had supported Michael for change as I approved of his businesslike approach to issues and his wide experience. He was also someone you could talk to and be sure he was listening, even if he did not always agree. On the other hand John had been much closer to the newer members as he was not a minister in the earlier Thatcher government. He was pleasant and friendly and he seemed to be one of our team but he had risen through the hierarchy very rapidly. Was it too rapid? Douglas I did not know so well. He always seemed to be a proper statesman destined to be prime minister but did he have the necessary experience and drive to get the party out of its present troubles? In an era of television politics, which of these three equally suitable candidates could unite the party and lead us to win a forthcoming election?

Each candidate had offered to meet on a one-to-one basis with any member for a private discussion to help their decision-making progress. I therefore decided that I would take up this offer and meet each candidate in turn on the same day. I did just that. I interviewed three candidates for the job of Prime Minister! What a unique experience! I concluded then and still believe that they all could have done the job well. I decided against Douglas because I did not know him well enough. I wanted to vote for John because I liked him personally the most but I was not sure about his very rapid rise and lack of experience at the top. Could he lead us out of this political hole? Michael Heseltine had supported me often in Batley and Spen, he spoke good business sense and he had plenty of experience across Whitehall so seemed to be the best bet. After the 'interviews' I decided to vote for him.

On 27 November we elected a new leader and new Prime Minister, John Major. He had attracted 185 votes, Michael Heseltine 131 and Douglas Hurd 56. This result left John Major two votes short of a first ballot victory under the complex party rules. The contest had been friendly and continued to be so when John's rivals conceded and withdrew, thus leaving John Major as Prime Minister with the difficult task of following the world-recognized 'Iron Lady' and taking the party to a future success from an unlikely starting-point.

My conversation with Mrs Thatcher at John Major's first Prime Minister's Question Time
From the very first days of John's Premiership I seemed to get into some sort of publicity often without trying, which continued until 1997. On Thursday 29 November 1990, only two days after we had elected John as

Leader, I decided I would go into the Chamber at 2.30pm prior to Prime Minister's Questions at 3.00pm to take part in Treasury Questions, which were likely to be of interest to Yorkshire Industry. This allowed me to prepare myself to put a question to the Prime Minister I had drawn in the ballot.

As the Prime Minister's Question Time was John Major's first since his election there was a speculation on how he would fair against Neil Kinnock and even greater consideration of whether and when Margaret Thatcher would return to the Commons after her resignation. The press wondered whether she would have a 'Heath style' sulk and not appear or whether she would take the positive Thatcher approach. I sat down in my usual seat by the gangway on the fourth row from the front with my regular colleagues David Atkinson and Sir Michael Shaw (Lord Shaw) to await a call from the Speaker to join the debate. Suddenly, our Whip, Timothy Kirkhope, arrived by my seat and said: 'The Rt Hon Member for Finchley is coming any minute to listen to Prime Minister's Questions and give her support to the new Prime Minister. We are not sure where she wants to sit, it may be on the Privy Councillors Bench on the third row or it could be where you sit, Elizabeth.' At that very moment in marched Margaret Thatcher, the tears of resignation gone and replaced by the positive Thatcher attack. She arrived quickly by the side of the fourth row saying: 'Elizabeth do you mind if I join you on this row as it was from here that I made my Maiden Speech years ago.' I quickly replied in the habitual manner: 'No problem, Prime Minister. I'll move along and push these fellows up. Like you I am attracted to this seat as I also made my Maiden Speech from here.'

This exchange of greetings was hardly complete when I was called by the Speaker to join the debate. I suddenly realized that vast numbers of people would be watching television to see Margaret's return to the backbenchers and here she was sat next to me as I put my question. It is true that most British newspapers the next day had a photograph of me speaking with a listening Margaret Thatcher, some even on the front page!

John Major had opened the batting for Prime Minster's Questions and was holding his own with Neil Kinnock during the usual battle. During which I had a conversation with Margaret who was back to her competitive best. She had placed her famous handbag and her specs on the bench and as Question Time ended she picked up her handbag heading for the tea room with Michael Grylls, thanking me as she left but forgetting the specs.

Suddenly, with Cecil Franks (Barrow), I noticed the specs and rushed towards the tea room to hand them back to her. Out in the Members Lobby, before I got to the tea room, I was besieged by the press, who had been watching the television and wanted to know what we had been talking about. I was somewhat taken aback by their collective demands and decided I would not tell them anything, which made some of the Lobby Correspondents rather cross.

Having handed the specs back I headed for my office and made some hand-written notes on the conversation that I wished to remember. These notes, that I have now unearthed, revealed that having discussed our Maiden Speeches Mrs Thatcher commented that the seat gave a very different view of the Chamber, the people and especially the Public Gallery, something she had forgotten. She then observed: 'You can't hear very well from here'. I agreed – it was often difficult.

She then said: 'it will be interesting to see if Neil Kinnock appears as vacuous from this bench as he does from the Despatch Box'. I replied, 'You will soon see!'

An Opposition member then asked John Major if he was his 'own man' to which he replied that he was! Mrs Thatcher added rather loudly: 'He most certainly is!' As she got up to go she added: 'John has had a good Question Time.' I certainly admired Margaret's fortitude and the way she handled her removal from the front-bench of world politics to the backbench of the foot soldiers of British politics – a brave woman!

In the evening I relented and did BBC radio and TV interviews but still would not discuss the conversation and only do so now, more than twenty years later, as I confirm my admiration for the lady, if not all her policies.

My View

There will always be some unhappiness at the way Margaret Thatcher lost the leadership of the Conservative Party and the role of Prime Minister. The 350 people involved in the voting process may always feel some embarrassment about the way it was done and why. Clearly the party was in serious trouble and the leader was not taking enough notice of the party's concerns because she was too isolated from day-to-day issues by the group of people working for her. The party and the country had lost confidence and wanted change. It was a high-risk strategy to change leader but it had to happen. Now, in retrospect, it is much easier to justify that change but at the time we were not sure we had done the right thing.

Chapter 16

Characters in the Commons
II

In any consideration of the great characters in the House you must include the Speakers because to achieve this important position you have to be elected by your fellow members. To be elected you have to be recognized; you must, therefore, have to have character. For this reason anyone elected to the Speaker's chair must be exceptional; something I realized soon after I entered the House. In what is now a period of thirty years I have known or worked with the following five Speakers.

George Thomas 1976–83
I cheat slightly here because George Thomas had resigned in 1983 just before I arrived at Westminster and had been elected to the Lords as Viscount Tonypandy; therefore you may well ask why I include him in my list of outstanding characters. The answer is simple: the Commons includes a few grumpy men, it includes some charming men, but none who were as charming as George Thomas and nobody else had such a beautiful voice that many of us remember from early-morning radio.

I met him somewhat by chance soon after I arrived at Westminster when I was asked to serve on a Lords/Commons committee chaired by Baroness Faithful on children's issues. The new Viscount Tonypandy joined the committee. At the first meeting I sat next to George and we became good working friends. He was keen to know my background and recognized that although we had differing political views, we had similar family experiences. George Thomas was a coal miner's son from Tonypandy who had fought his way to university in Southampton before becoming a schoolteacher in the East End of London and later in South Wales. With a sound Christian family background he had a determination to get into politics. This he did, entering the House as a Christian Socialist

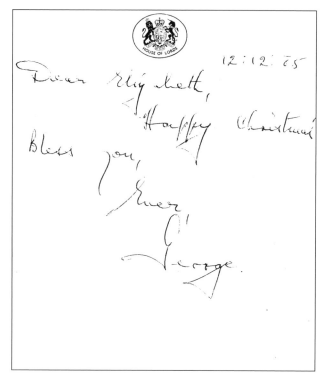

12:12:75

Dear Elizabeth,

Happy Christmas

Bless you,

George

A Christmas greeting, 1985 from George Thomas, former Speaker [Lord Tonypandy].

for Cardiff. He then moved rapidly from the back benches and into the Cabinet as Secretary of State for Wales and was elected Speaker in 1976. In the late 1970s the House was a turbulent place with the minority Labour government held in place by the Lib-Lab pact. The firm but charming Mr Speaker led the House with a style and control not previously recognized. In retirement he was full of fun and charm and I got to know him well on the Children's Committee.

Whenever I met him in Central Lobby or the tea room I got a great hug and kisses on both cheeks. Indeed, one day in Central Lobby we had just met in this manner as one of the rather left-wing members for South Wales went past, making the comment: 'Put her down, George! Don't you know she is one of those dreadful Tories?' When he wrote his book in 1985 he gave me a special copy in which he had already written: 'Elizabeth, God bless you, George Thomas 12 December 1985.' For many years we exchanged Christmas cards. I was moved to tears when he died in 1997 after I had lost my seat and I managed to attend the very suitable memorial service at Westminster Abbey. A charming man who I will always remember.

Bernard Weatherill 1983–92

Bernard [always referred to as Jack] Weatherill who was elected Speaker in 1983 had a tough act to follow in replacing George Thomas but again he proved to be the right man at the right time.

When I entered the Commons in June 1983 one of the first tasks after we had all been sworn in was to elect a new Speaker. At that point I had little knowledge who would be best suited to the job but the word on the street was that Bernard should be ideal and that the 'new boys and girls' should support him. I did just that, after having a look at his impressive record.

Bernard had the advantage of not only being an experienced politician; he was a businessman and had seen military service. He had a lifelong connection with tailoring, having been an apprentice in the family firm of Bernard Weatherill Limited of Savile Row, London. Later he became a director and chairman, resuming day-to-day involvement with the business when he retired from the Commons in 1992.

Bernard always had a distinctive trademark in his jacket pocket: his tailor's thimble, as a reminder of his time in the trade and as a sign of his humble background. His military service was equally full of achievement as he had enlisted at the beginning of the Second World War. He quickly reached the rank of captain, followed by an attachment to the Indian army, becoming a fluent Urdu speaker and a vegetarian.

With this experience he turned his attention to politics and was elected in 1964 as the Conservative Member of Parliament for Croydon North East. He rapidly became a party whip and deputy chief whip and vice chairman of Her Majesty's Household; the holder of this later post having the job of hand-writing a daily report to Her Majesty the Queen on the activities and opinions being expressed in the House of Commons.

Interestingly, Bernard Weatherill played an important role in the eventual defeat of the Labour government in 1979 involving my predecessor Dr Alfred Broughton, the much-respected member for Batley and Morley. As the hour for the crucial vote of confidence came near, the Labour deputy chief whip, Walter Harrison, MP for Wakefield, approached Bernard to discuss the gentlemen's agreement that should a member be unable to vote due to serious ill health, an MP from the other party would abstain to compensate. Alfred Broughton was seriously ill and the government looked like losing without his vote. Bernard pointed out that this so-called agreement was not designed to save a government and that he could not find a Conservative who would be prepared to

The Speaker, Bernard Weatherill, receiving Scouts and Guides, 1987 [on the left of the picture is my trusted secretary Lorna Humphreys].

abstain. However, after a moment's reflection he offered to abstain himself to honour the agreement, knowing that such an abstention would be the end of his career. Walter, without too much thought, turned down the offer and the Labour government subsequently lost the vote and the election that followed. Bernard Weatherill and Walter Harrison have to be admired for the courage in their decision-making, confirming to the surprise of many that politicians can be honourable. Because of this incident and my role in Batley, I got to know Bernard well as he liked to recall the story.

The role of Mr Speaker is very difficult to fulfil; the House has to be controlled, business has to proceed and political balance and fairness has to be achieved. When Bernard Weatherill took the chair I was greatly impressed by how he soon recognized the many new members by name, so that he could call them to speak. He presided over the House with firmness, allied with wit and humour. Throughout his time as Speaker he protected the rights of backbenchers and opposition members. He rightly insisted that government policy matters should be announced in the House of Commons before they were made public on the BBC *Today* programme or elsewhere.

Since the introduction of television cameras to the House and the regular broadcast of proceedings, the role of Speaker has become much more in the public eye, particularly involving Prime Minister's Question Time. Sir Bernard during his nine-year tenure became the first Speaker of the television age, a role he fulfilled with ease. He often declared that he was the only man who could walk around London in his tights and his Court dress without being arrested; he would always chuckle at the thought!

In truth the Speaker can be a frustration to a back-bench member, particularly if they have an issue they wish to bring to the notice of the government, the press or their constituents. If the Speaker fails to call them to speak for days or sometimes weeks it is really frustrating. To overcome this problem, the backbencher has to be noticed to be able to be called. I found being small among so many tall men a distinct disadvantage and this had to be overcome by wearing something brightly coloured. Thankfully, this tactic worked as Bernard gave me a fair share of speaking time.

The role of the Speaker is arduous and therefore time-limiting. By 1992 Bernard Weatherill had achieved his objective and decided nine years was long enough. He resigned with an appointment to the House of Lords and returned to his tailoring profession, regrettably for a short time as he died in 2007.

In my view Bernard, or Jack as he was usually known, was a gentleman who could deal equally well with Prime Ministers and backbenchers like myself with ease and grace; a truly difficult task.

Betty Boothroyd 1992–2000

Following my re-election to Westminster in 1992 and with the resignation of Bernard Weatherill, a new Speaker had to be elected. Under unwritten Parliamentary convention the Speaker has usually been elected from the ranks of the two major parties in turn. As we moved towards the election it seemed likely that someone from the Labour Party would succeed, with the popular Betty Boothroyd as a front-runner. However, there were several talented Conservatives who could have handled the challenge, including Sir George Young and my good friend and colleague Sir Giles Shaw, MP for Pudsey. I was therefore somewhat in a dilemma as to who should get my vote. Regrettably the Conservatives could not agree on just one candidate to put forward and it was soon obvious that a Conservative could not hope to win.

As Betty Boothroyd had been an extremely good Deputy Speaker dealing with the House in all its toughest moments I decided that she would get my vote regardless of party allegiance and time proved that I was right.

Betty is a true Yorkshire lass, born and educated in Dewsbury, West Yorkshire, next door to Batley and Spen. She had attended Dewsbury College of Commerce and Art with which I had regular contact. Betty, who originally worked as secretary and political assistant to various Labour politicians, had struggled to get herself elected and after five attempts was successful at West Bromwich in a 1973 by-election. From here her political career took off and she became an assistant government whip, a Member of the European Parliament between 1975 and 1977, and a member of the Labour Party National Executive from 1981 to 1987. Her potential as a fair and no-nonsense Speaker was noted on all sides of the House when she took the role of Deputy Speaker in 1987.

I always found Betty Boothroyd to be approachable and she remained so in the office of Speaker. She handled the House with a distinctive and friendly style that should not be underrated as she dealt firmly and speedily with troublemakers. Her approachable style was highlighted by a little story recalled by my husband. In the mid-1980s I was a delegate to the annual session of the Commonwealth Parliamentary Association in Kuala Lumpur and Betty was leader of the delegation. One day between seminars Betty declared that she wanted some time off to visit the local market but no one seemed to want to go with her because it was so very hot. Seeing the problem my husband Brian, who had travelled out to join me and to travel around Malaysia at the end of the conference, offered to go with Betty. They disappeared into town and spent two hours haggling for bargains in the local Chinese market. Brian was, as a mean Yorkshire man claims to be, good at bargaining and negotiating but he did admit that he was outgunned by our future Speaker who seemed to be able to charm the locals into some really good deals!

After her retirement as Speaker and her elevation to the House of Lords she has kept actively involved in political affairs including supporting the Association of Former Members of Parliament. Betty Boothroyd is to be greatly admired, having fulfilled a successful career at the highest possible level but never forgotten her humble Yorkshire roots.

Michael Martin 2000–09

Michael Martin arrived in Westminster well before my day and left after I had gone, having been elected for Glasgow Springburn in 1979 and remaining until 2009 as Member for Glasgow North East. I include him in my consideration of Speakers on the basis that he was one of my former colleagues, albeit on the other side of the House. Regardless of the eventual controversy surrounding him, he achieved much, becoming Speaker from a very humble background. He has to be admired for his efforts in moving from a sheet-metal apprenticeship through union and Labour Party membership to the House of Commons and the Speaker's Chair.

In my day Michael was a character of the tea room, always prepared to get involved in sensible and cheerful conversation on the issues of the day with members from all sides of the House. It was from this activity that he gained support from many members to elevate him to Speaker in 2000. Interestingly, on his election as Speaker he was the first Roman Catholic to serve in the role since the Reformation. During his Speakership he took active steps to harness the experience of former MPs and greatly encouraged the formation of the Association of Former Members of Parliament and became its first patron.

In my role with the Association I found him very helpful and determined to see the establishment of a worthwhile organization to provide a conduit between present and former members. MPs currently have a poor reputation but many former members have great experience gained in the House and elsewhere that is invaluable to the nation. Many Commonwealth and European governments have recognized this fact and give active support to former member organizations. Michael Martin helped us drive this project and we thank him for his efforts to establish a viable and vibrant association.

Regrettably for him and his family, his term of office was filled with controversy. In his early days in the Chair he seemed to have some hesitancy and he was also accused of allowing political bias. If we look back in history this has been an accusation levelled at many Speakers and is rarely proved. This was followed by a period of intense media attack on the control of the expenses of Members of Parliament, a responsibility of the Speaker. Therefore the media then attacked him on expenses. The turmoil was all compounded by the arrest of the government minister, Damian Green, by the police within the House of Commons, something that could not traditionally have happened if the Speaker had been in full control. With diminishing public and Parliamentary confidence in his role, Michael decided to resign.

I do recognize that Michael Martin resigned in controversial circumstances but he did achieve the Speaker's role on merit and he was a man you could do business with.

John Bercow 2009 to date

John Bercow, Conservative MP for Buckingham, was somewhat controversially elected Speaker following the resignation of Michael Martin. He appeared to be heavily supported by the Labour Party with interestingly little Conservative support; an intriguing start to a new Speaker's career. He made a torrid start in his role by attempting to change the style of dress and approach. He has equally had difficulties with publicity of the political and other activities of his family.

He is taking a new approach to the role; a new style with a new character and only time will tell whether the House of Commons is happy with this modern more liberal environment. However, he has been helpful in allowing the Association of Former Members to have a yearly reception in his state rooms; obviously an event for which all members pay!

The Speaker welcomes Scouts and Guides

Soon after I had arrived at Westminster I decided I needed to join the Parliamentary Scout Association so that I was able to invite a Scout from the constituency to have tea with the Speaker Bernard Weatherill. This I did each year until 1997. Originally Guides were not invited but as my secretary Lorna was a District Commissioner in the Guides in Bedfordshire, we persuaded the 'powers that be' in Westminster that Guides should be included.

The young people thoroughly enjoyed their tea, especially as the Speaker always invited special guests with interests in 'youth' to join us. One year I had invited a Scout from Batley who was a Huddersfield Town FC supporter and together we got in conversation with former Prime Minister Harold Wilson who was a guest. On hearing that my Scout supported Huddersfield, Harold took out his wallet and found a very old photograph of the Huddersfield team that had been successful in the 1930s. I was soon left out of the conversation as the elder statesman and a Batley Scout discussed the merits of the 1930s and 1980s teams.

Chapter 17

The 'Yorkshire Mafia'

Yorkshire has played a very important part in my life and obviously provided an even more important aspect of my political career. However, it was not just the county but the people from Yorkshire who influenced my approach and thinking. Clearly my constituents were key but so were my fellow Yorkshire MPs, almost regardless of party. In writing this book I wish to acknowledge their help and guidance over the years and say a big 'thank you'.

From my early days at Westminster I realized that members of whatever party from Yorkshire punched far above their weight in representing the county and that party differences could be put on one side while the interests of Yorkshire were defended.

When I arrived I was instantly given the job of secretary to the Yorkshire Conservative Members Group whose chairman at the time was Sir Michael Shaw, MP for Scarborough (now Lord Shaw of Northstead). Michael was one of my constituents as he maintained his family home in Spenborough; consequently he always kept an eye on my activities. Within the group as vice chairman we had Marcus Fox (later Sir Marcus) from Shipley; one of the liveliest members in the House with huge energy, ability and influence, later chairman of the Conservative Back Bench 1922 committee. Someone who really did punch above his weight was Giles Shaw (later Sir Giles) from Pudsey. While rather short in stature, he was a giant in the political world with big but measured comments and wisdom. Being a former 'After Eights' marketing director for Rowntrees Chocolate he knew his market, political and otherwise. I do believe he was the best Speaker the House never had.

The great character of the Conservative 'Yorkshire Mafia' was my whip and former butcher Donald Thompson (later Sir Donald) from Calder Valley, who gave me my one-stop first-day tour of the Palace of Westminster that took all of twenty minutes!

Donald was good on advice with a positive summary of the issues, as I recall during the 1987 general election when I was unhappy about the Poll Tax and how it would affect families in my constituency. Having abstained in the votes, I was faced with a Party Leaflet that I could not support. I discussed this with Donald on several occasions until he eventually got so fed up with me that he said: 'Elizabeth, just try for once to stop fighting the Party! Do you want to win this f...... election?' From that day on, Donald's response became my family's electioneering motto!

More importantly he was the man to know at Westminster on Thursday evenings because he always organized a taxi from the House to King's Cross immediately after the last vote to catch the Leeds train. 'If you were there you could have a lift but you could not share the cost, so you must buy him a gin and tonic on the train!'

At some point in time Donald had been a minister in the Thatcher government and told wonderful stories of his experiences that always ended with the comment: 'Then she (Mrs Thatcher) fired me.' I don't think he ever knew why!

For all his bluff approach he was well thought of across the House, taking interests in diverse areas such as war memorials and dogs (specifically Crufts).

Donald always had a fund of funny, respectable stories in a little book he carried around that emphasized the sort of pressure an MP has to endure as part of the job, namely the unscheduled speech.

Like many middle-aged men these days, Donald had to have a heart by-pass operation and often told the story of his experience. He had undergone the operation, had been in the usual intensive care unit and then been moved to a four-bed high-dependency ward where he slowly came round. Having realized where he was but still feeling groggy, he was suddenly addressed by the fellow in the next bed who said in a strong Yorkshire voice: 'Tha' nurse tells me you're Donald Thompson Member of Parliament, is that right?' Donald, still feeling less than 100 per cent, somewhat reluctantly nodded in agreement, hoping the fellow would shut up and leave him alone. To Donald's astonishment the fellow said: 'Now Donald, you're my Member of Parliament, it's now 9.30 and we've had no toast yet for breakfast, what are you going to do about it? As you're my Member of Parliament I want some action!' As Donald's response was reported to be somewhat negative he probably lost a vote but who could blame him?

Over the years the Yorkshire Mafia had a changing team: Sir John

Osborn, then Irvine Patnick from Sheffield and John Watson from Skipton.

Then the newly-elected William Hague arrived and at that point I was still secretary of the Yorkshire group. Someone said: 'Elizabeth, give this fellow something useful to do or else he will be bored!' So I did: I made sure he became the secretary of the Yorkshire Conservative Members.

The Yorkshire Mafia was not all Conservative, of course. We could all work together if necessary, regardless of party; especially organizing taxis from and to King's Cross! Michael Meadowcroft, Liberal Leeds, with whom I had worked in the voluntary sector, could be relied upon to get involved. The man from whom Michael had won his seat, Joe Dean, Labour was a lifelong defender of Yorkshire interests and he continued to do this from his deserved seat in the Lords. While a committed Labour man, he always had an eye on what I was saying and doing and was very supportive.

The Labour members for Doncaster and Barnsley from the mining areas certainly had their own mafia including Kevin Barron (Rother Valley), Michael Clapham (Barnsley) and Joe Ashton (Bassetlaw). David Hinchcliffe (Wakefield) was a great supporter of anything to do with Yorkshire and was a very friendly member of the opposition. Equally those great attackers of Conservative policies, Bob Cryer (Bradford) and Austin Mitchell (Grimsby), were always supportive of 'God's own county' as were Derek Enright (Hemsworth), the former Home Secretary Merlyn Rees and Barry Shearman (Huddersfield). I am not sure whether Alice Mahon (Halifax) or Helen Jackson (Sheffield) would subscribe to Yorkshire Mafia membership but I always found them very friendly and helpful, despite our political differences. One of the Yorkshire men I truly admire is Denis Healey as a politician who has seen the bad times and the good times throughout a wonderful career. It made my evening when in 1993 he was honoured as Yorkshire Man of the Year when I became Yorkshire Woman of the Year.

While party issues have to be fought long and hard, when the county needs support it gets it regardless of politics.

My View

I am biased, of course, but convinced that the Yorkshire contingent in the House from 1983–97 punched above their weight from all sides of the Commons. Thank you all, including those I have neglected to mention by name.

The Major Years

* * *

Chapter 18

Consolidating Thatcher
(1990–92)

Within hours of becoming prime minister John Major set about the daunting task of following Mrs Thatcher. His first move was to recall Michael Heseltine to the Cabinet as Secretary of State for the Environment, with the task of reforming the hated Poll Tax and putting something more acceptable in place. It was important that this issue should be tackled and quickly because the country was unhappy and an election was due by 1992. Certainly without rapid reform a Tory win seemed impossible.

I believe we were subconsciously in election mode almost from day one of the Major era. John had a problem in that he had not been elected by the country but by some 340 of his colleagues and of them only 185 had actually voted for him. He needed a mandate in his own right and many people expected him to rush to the country for such an endorsement.

Sensibly John and his team attacked the issues of the day as they were matters causing the party arguments and the country much concern. The Poll Tax was his first big issue to be addressed. It could have been made to work if it had been handled better and introduced over a period but this option was long gone. Nicholas Ridley got it wrong by going for a one-year implementation period and left local authorities to raise their taxes higher than was necessary. It was now all too late for the Poll Tax and it had to be replaced. Michael Heseltine was given a free hand to do just that and propose a new property-based tax to be called Council Tax and that is the direction in which we headed, albeit with not too much confidence. We originally set out to reform local taxation with the collection across a wider base but along the way we got it all wrong. My reason for never supporting the legislation was its mode of introduction: it should have been phased in over a number of years across a wider base. The property-based council tax was the best alternative to the old rates system that Michael could put together in the limited time available. However, a retrospective view now shows that it is little better than the old rates because to make it work efficiently it needs updating every few years.

Successive governments have, since its introduction, failed in the main to carry out this updating as it becomes particularly sensitive so they 'chicken out' on this potentially vote-losing process. Michael Heseltine's council tax thankfully got the Conservative Party out of a political hole but it did not solve the real issue of local tax collection, a matter that has still to be resolved.

The big change I recall being discussed as soon as John took over was a different style of Cabinet meeting that encouraged teamwork and conversation. Someone even said they were fun compared with the aggression of the Thatcher meetings. Despite this new style it was clearly recognized that John was in charge and led the decision-making process.

Issues soon arose to test the efficiency of working in this manner. Michael Heseltine clearly found he could work with John Major as they had a similar outlook and Michael adopted a system of pre-discussing issues with John before their official Cabinet consideration. Equally there was a good degree of harmony between the Prime Minister and Party Chairman Chris Patten that became more important as the election approached.

The economy

As 1991 opened, the economy was still in difficulties with high unemployment and it fell into recession with high borrowing. The course had already been set by the Thatcher administration and then became lost in the issues around the Gulf War.

However, in March 1991 new Chancellor Norman Lamont's first budget found a way of providing £140 towards each person's Poll Tax bill. This in the short term eased the pain of this ridiculous tax but it was as usual a 'give with one hand and take away with the other' situation when he changed VAT levels in later years.

At the same time John agreed to some special help to be given to the homeless and for cold weather payments.

By March 1992 the Gulf War had been won and we were in positive election mode with Norman Lamont unveiling his budget with a new 20p in the pound income tax band for the first £2,000 of taxable income but also with a huge £28 billion borrowing requirement.

International affairs

'Events, dear boy' as Harold Macmillan was reported to have said about things that influence government, certainly affected John Major. John, who had been Foreign Secretary somewhat reluctantly in the Thatcher government, moved rapidly when he was elected to become better acquainted with the international scene by the visit to Westminster of President Bush. It proved a sound strategy as he inherited the Gulf problem brought about by the Iraqi invasion of Kuwait in August 1990. Mrs Thatcher at her last Cabinet meeting approved the deployment of additional troops to the area.

In true British style John grabbed control of the issue, working through the United Nations hoping to avoid war if Saddam Hussein withdrew from Kuwait. My scrapbook is rather thin on Gulf matters as it did not on a daily basis concern my first objective, the constituency. I do, however, recall tea-room discussion about how helpful and supportive Neil Kinnock and Paddy Ashdown were to John as he made the decision that it had to be war.

The outbreak of the Gulf War in January 1991 brought John Major from obscurity to the world stage as he worked with the Americans following Saddam Hussein's invasion of Kuwait. The combined mass of British and American troops soon got Hussein out of Kuwait and then they marched through Iraq, stopping before reaching Baghdad. This they did to allow Hussein and the Iraqis to carry out reform of structure and government. In retrospect this was a mistake but John and his team were not to know that. The Gulf War brought John to the international scene with issues in Russia and regularly dealing with President George Bush Senior in the USA.

To my surprise in August 1991 President Gorbachev who I had met in London was toppled by a revolt involving Boris Yeltsin, only to be reinstated within days. Gorbachev tried to hold Russia together but failed, with the Soviet Republic becoming independent and Boris Yeltsin taking over as leader in Russia; all very confusing at the time.

As a bystander to the main action in these events but being sufficiently near to hear informed comment, I have always admired John Major's handling of the Gulf War. The way he picked up the challenge has, in my view, been under-recognized.

As I had at an earlier date visited South Africa and been in discussion with the then Botha government I was invited to meet State President F.W. de Klerk when he visited London in 1991. He clearly had a different

10 DOWNING STREET
LONDON SW1A 2AA

THE PRIME MINISTER

29 January 1991

Dear Elizabeth,

Thank you for your letter of 23 January expressing the support
of the Yorkshire Area Conservative Trade Unionists for the
Government's handling of the Gulf crisis.

It is extremely helpful to know that I have the support of so
many people at this difficult time, and I am most grateful to
you for taking the trouble to write.

Yours Ever,
John

Mrs Elizabeth J Peacock JP MP

outlook on the future of South Africa to the hardline Botha position. I did
not at this time realize how different and how quickly things were to
change in South Africa following the release from prison of Nelson
Mandela and the founding of the Rainbow Nation.

Europe

Following Margaret Thatcher's anti-federalist speech in Bruges, Europe
became an emotive issue, splitting the Conservative Party. Mrs Thatcher

had clashed with Ted Heath on the issue, each accusing the other of telling lies. John Major was soon attacked by certain sections of the party because he was seen to be too friendly with his European colleagues. The party was badly split on Europe with the Thatcherite anti-federalist anti-single-currency supporters with whom I had sympathy on one side and the Europhiles on the other; a difficult problem that became very clear as John entered Downing Street.

This matter dominated Westminster and John for the remainder of his premiership, with the EC continuing to discuss ever-closer political and economic union and the single currency. I recall a Commons debate before the crucial Maastricht meeting in November that was dominated by Mrs Thatcher who called for a referendum and warned, as she put it, 'of the conveyor belt to federalism', thus placing John in an even more difficult position. He rejected the idea of a referendum, went to Maastricht to negotiate and came away with success, the Europeans agreeing to a treaty allowing Britain to opt out of the single currency and to go ahead without Britain on the Social Chapter. With this John kept the two wings of the party happy, at least until after the 1992 general election.

As already indicated, I have always been in favour of a European Common Market but strongly against a federal structure involving a single currency and interference in the internal affairs of the UK. I understood John's problems within the party and I was doubtful about the Maastricht approach but voted in favour. In retrospect John was right, thankfully, and he kept us out of the single currency and Social Chapter. This treaty kept the party together when it could have permanently split but that was not to last.

Citizen's Charter

Politicians are always looking for fresh ideas, some sort of change, and John Major was no different. He needed a new approach to the British way of life and to put his own stamp on government. As a response he introduced the concept of the 'Citizen's Charter'; the idea of which was to make administration accountable and citizen-friendly and was to include setting maximum waiting times for surgical operations, providing refunds for rail passengers when their trains were late, and fixing appointments for meter-reading.

The concept never took off: it had little impact on people's lives; it was too esoteric and could not be measured. As I write today, the current Cameron administration is having a similar problem trying to get over the concept of the 'Big Society'. We should keep trying in this respect but the British are an independent lot and do not really want politicians attempting to interfere in their daily lives.

John had done a great job of pulling the party together after Mrs Thatcher's resignation. He had sorted out an alternative to the hated poll tax and kept the party reasonably together on Europe. He consolidated the best of the Thatcher regime and corrected some of the mistakes by his balanced action.

1922 Committee

The reader will recall that I had gained my seat on the Executive of the 1992 Committee in 1987 shortly after the election, a rather surprising back-bench victory. As I had demonstrated my independent views, I suspect I had gained votes from a rather secretive right-wing subgroup co-ordinated by my good friend and fellow Yorkshire member John Townend (Bridlington) and including Sir George Gardiner MP for Reigate and a columnist for several national newspapers. Over a period I found their political positioning too rigid and this began to constrain my commonsense Conservatism. This became apparent in 1990 when I had some very open disagreement with Margaret Thatcher, telling her the truth on several matters, and got me into trouble with the secretive '92 Group when the party became unhappy with Mrs Thatcher over the poll tax. I was accused by George Gardiner and the dreaded Alan Clark of speaking against her in a '92 meeting. It is true I did point out that the backbenchers and the country were unhappy with the situation and that to win again there had to be changes and that we must give the PM the facts. When recording the discussion at this meeting Alan Clark (Plymouth Sutton) said: 'None was quite as awful as Elizabeth Peacock, who spoke squarely and fairly against Margaret. Why bother? She won't be here in the next Parliament anyway.'

Suddenly the details of discussion and debate in the 1922 Committee started appearing in the press, obviously leaked by someone but by whom? George Gardiner and Lord Colnbrook tried to blame me and we had a good row, with the chairman trying to divide 'the fighting dogs'. Months later I got clear evidence that George was doing the leaking himself to give his newspaper articles more bite.

In passing I mentioned this to Angela Rumbold who was by then Minister for Prisons in the Home Office with Kenneth Baker as Home Secretary. Her response was as follows:

Elizabeth, it's about time you moved on from the 1922; we need you on the ministerial ladder for an eventual government job. I am supposed to have appointed a Parliamentary Private Secretary (PPS) to work with me on my responsibilities. You must do the job. I will ask for Kenneth's permission to appoint you.

I agreed on the spot as it was time I moved on. Kenneth Baker approved and so I became PPS (unpaid) in the Home Office looking after parliamentary matters for Angela. Each morning I attended the Home Secretary's business prayer meeting to pick up my tasks for the day that I integrated with my own activities. By this route I became thoroughly involved in the Home Office and the Prison Department, soon noting the tensions between politicians and civil servants. It became obvious that without a strong Home Secretary the civil servants would totally control and implement their own policies; a problem I understand still applies today. Having resigned from the 1922 Committee, I remained as PPS in the Home Office until the election in 1992 when Angela did not continue in John Major's government.

Towards an election with a rejuvenated opposition

John Major considered calling an election in 1991 but following discussions with Chris Patten he abandoned the idea. Having dealt with the budget, John decided in March 1992 that he had to go to the country and get his own mandate to govern. The polls had throughout John's sixteen months in Downing Street been very volatile with the Conservatives losing seats at by-elections in the Ribble Valley and Monmouth.

A Labour lead of some 10 per cent in early 1991, reversed to a Tory lead later in the year and soon reversed back to Labour, highlights the volatility. Labour and Neil Kinnock were at this time struggling to tame militants especially in Liverpool, so the game was on for an interesting election with Labour clear favourites.

Having survived the massive Tory majorities in the last two Thatcher-dominated parliaments, the opposition parties were beginning to fight back by 1991/92. The Labour Party was, I recall, particularly active locally, following and commenting on my activities. Neil Kinnock was making a good job of leading and gave John Major plenty of trouble at 'Questions to the Prime Minister', on a few occasions having a better day than John.

In John Smith, Labour had a Shadow Chancellor of real ability and stature who I rather admired. Of equal importance, they were developing a team with a good mix of experience and youth. Clearly the Labour Party had the potential to be difficult to beat when this election was called.

My View

The importance of John Major's contribution to Britain and the Conservative Party in the time between the resignation of Mrs Thatcher in 1990 and his re-election with his own mandate in 1992 has been seriously underplayed and under-recognized. He sorted out the local taxation debacle that Mrs Thatcher had allowed to develop; he handled the Gulf War with skill; he began to get some sense into the European dilemma; he stabilized the economic situation; and, most importantly, he did all of this well enough to satisfy the British people who gave him another term in office despite a rejuvenated opposition.

Regardless of difficulties in later times, his initial consolidation of the Thatcher years was outstanding.

Chapter 19

Soapbox Election
(1992)

When John Major called the general election in March 1992 there was a view among the pundits that he could not possibly win. He was a 'grey man' carrying the legacy of the problems of the Thatcher era. I took a different view. I thought that the British public was beginning to realize that he was different from Mrs Thatcher and he was making a sincere effort to change direction and correct some of the troublesome issues like Poll Tax and the Maastricht negotiations on Europe. As for myself I could never, with my small majority, be confident of winning in Batley and Spen. I had to lead my campaign team with the motivation that we were going to win but always went to the count with an A or B, win or lose, speech in my head, if not in my pocket. However, if you think you can win and work for it, then often you can. The opinion polls said the Conservatives could not win; Labour were too far ahead. Local polls indicated that I could not win; I was destined to lose my seat. However, this had been said in 1983 and 1987 and we won on both occasions.

There were some members of the Conservative Party who were saying it would be better if John did not win. This would allow Labour one five-year parliament with the Conservatives then coming back with a different leader; all very pessimistic and a very difficult environment for an election campaign. For once I was reasonably confident that we could do well in Batley and Spen as we had done a lot of work locally and I seemed to have good support from people and areas not usually supportive of the Conservative cause. I appeared to have a reasonable personal vote but was it big enough to overcome the poll predictions?

The election announcement had been expected for a few weeks so everyone was ready to 'go' once it was given. John allowed his Chancellor Norman Lamont to launch his 'Budget for Recovery' which introduced a

Michael Heseltine visiting Batley to assess the need for City Challenge funding.

PLEASE
VOTE

ELIZABETH
PEACOCK

Election literature, 1992.

CITY CHALLENGE
Batley needs
Elizabeth Peacock
at Westminster and
Michael Heseltine
at Environment for
a Brighter Future

Vote
PEACOCK
for PARLIAMENT
...please

new 20p tax band that effectively reduced tax for the lower-paid. The Labour Party voted against this proposal as it was linked with an increase in government borrowing; a tactical Labour error in the recession that was gripping the country and it contrasted with Labour predictions of the need for high taxes.

The Conservative campaign was launched around the slogan 'Don't let Labour ruin it' that led to 'You can't trust Labour'. Labour's obvious attack on thirteen years of Tory government was 'Time for a change'.

As the campaign got into gear Labour did not increase their position in the polls as would have been expected. Their threat of increased taxes brought the thought of a hung parliament into press speculation. This stimulated John Major to say that he would not do deals with the Liberal Democrats in order to stay in power, nor would he get into discussion on devolution for Scotland.

It became a fairly negative campaign with Labour leaving the Conservatives to lose the election with equally negative tactics: 'Don't elect Labour; they will ruin everything.' Labour were vulnerable on tax matters but the Chancellor's measures had not helped the Conservative cause. Still all to play for in Batley and Spen and elsewhere!

Michael Heseltine, a leading figure in the campaign, played the tax issue with John Major and Douglas Hurd, questioning Neil Kinnock's experience and authority for the role of prime minister.

The Labour manifesto 'It's time to get Britain working again' was short and sharp, threatening to take public control of the National Grid and the water companies plus support for greater commitment to Europe and surprisingly the retention of a nuclear deterrent.

The Tory manifesto 'The best future for Britain' went for franchising British Rail services to the private sector and investment in inner cities, something that eventually helped in Batley with City Challenge money. The government remained vulnerable to poor economic and trade figures and unemployment levels being too high. An argument, referred to as the 'War of Jennifer's Ear' (regarding a controversial delayed medical procedure with reference to the actual eighteenth-century War of Jenkins' Ear), contrasted treatment in the NHS and private sectors, completely dominating the media for days and in the end benefiting nobody.

As the campaign drew to a close there was concern in Conservative circles that their campaign was going nowhere, despite the fact that Mrs Thatcher had joined a party rally, thereby acknowledging her successor. John Major's response to this level of concern was to fight back in an

'SOAP BOX COUP'
JOHN MAJOR PM, ELECTION VICTORY......APRIL 9th 1992

effective and simplistic style that intrigued the media and awakened the public: he went around holding public meetings from a traditional soapbox, taking on hecklers if necessary. This unusual mode of electioneering with the aid of television cameras brought the people to him and they liked him; he might have appeared to be a bit grey but he was likeable and someone they could trust.

In contrast Labour, still in front in the opinion polls, made the mistake of underestimating the new Major style and overestimated the strength of their opinion poll position. They, together with Neil Kinnock, staged a large and well-televised rally in Sheffield; the triumphant nature of which alienated voters who suddenly changed sides. Despite all the campaigning, Labour did not appear to have achieved the 8 per cent swing needed to form a government on their own and a hung parliament seemed likely by election day.

The pundits put their money on Labour to win and handsomely but John Major countered this with his novel soapbox approach to electioneering. It may have been a throwback to an earlier era but it worked and the public liked his style.

On the morning of 12 April as the results were announced it was not Neil Kinnock heading to Downing Street but John Major to remain in residence. The British people liked the Major approach and disliked the Kinnock brashness that had come across as triumphal at the Sheffield rally.

In a funny way I have always had some sympathy for Neil Kinnock; a pleasant fellow who I thought talked too much with his long-winded responses but he had tried for many years to reform the Labour Party and remove its militancy. However, he never got the electoral thanks that went eventually to Tony Blair; such is the luck of the political jungle!

John may not have won the campaign but he won the election with his approach of 'trust me'. The people did.

What of the election locally?

We had our usual small but strong team of planners and canvassers, led of course by Doug Brewer and my election agent Mary Bentley, the association secretary. Additionally my London secretary Lorna Humphreys took holiday from Westminster, transferred her operation to Cleckheaton and became a major member of the team. Indeed Lorna, who sadly died far too young, had by handling my postbag come to know more about the area than many local people and her knowledge was invaluable to me.

Thankfully the fund-raising team had done a sound job and we had enough cash to mount a full campaign. My opponents fought a good clean fight with Labour represented by Eunice Durkin who had a sound union background; the Liberal Democrats by Gordon Beever; and the stalwart of many elections Clive Lord for the Greens. It was pleasant for the first time to have a woman as the major opponent through which was raised a better balance of domestic matters.

We did all the usual but tiring election things: house-to-house canvassing, visits to businesses and meeting the public in the town, in the supermarket or wherever they were. This has to be done if you want to win but it gives you a false picture of the likely result; more people say they will support you than ever do! Many people just dislike saying 'No'.

My motivational phrase 'We only need one more vote than the others to win' adequately sums up the situation.

Once again, despite my unusual approach to Conservative politics and my ability to react on issues that I considered not in the interest of Batley and Spen, we had a good spread of government visitors to give support. I suppose that with my involvement with the Executive of the 1922 Committee I was, after ten years, considered to be a serious if ill-disciplined player. We attracted the former party chairman Cecil Parkinson, European Commissioner Leon Brittan, Giles Shaw and Chancellor of the Exchequer Norman Lamont who was especially helpful as we got direct reaction to the Labour tax proposals.

Along came election day . . . then the count. I thought we might win but I could never be sure so as usual I had two speeches available. When we saw the boxes being emptied we realized we could win, albeit by the usual close margin, and so it turned out. I had beaten Eunice by 1,408 which was a slightly increased majority and I was now for the third time the Member of Parliament for Batley and Spen. I was delighted, as the local newspaper headline said. I had won and increased my majority by forty-six! This was particularly pleasing because the national opinion polls had predicted that Batley and Spen, being the thirteenth key marginal in the country, was one of the constituencies Labour had to win to form a government. From my results and others that had come in it looked as though John Major would win enough seats to form the next government. So the result was finalized with a majority of twenty-one but without Party Chairman Chris Patten, who had lost in Bath.

Yes, we had won locally and we had plenty of fun on the way. Politics is a serious business but you have to enjoy being involved.

Why did we win again locally? I have never been really sure. When one of the Yorkshire political pundits was asked why Batley and Spen remained Conservative, he replied: 'That was the Peacock factor!'

My View
As I write some twenty years on, why do I believe we won locally in 1992? I think I summarized it in an interview with the *Telegraph and Argus*:

Asked after the count what Mrs Peacock thought had swung it for the Tories, she said: 'I have worked hard to put Batley and Spen on the map and we did have many people saying "I'm not happy with what the Conservatives are doing but as you have been a hard-working representative for us I will vote for you."'

As for the national scene, Labour should have won but people did not trust their tax policy and they were in the end not sure about Neil Kinnock as prime minister. Neil, as I came to know, is a pleasant man but if I had to choose between Neil Kinnock and John Major as prime minister I would have to choose John and that is what Britain did on 9 April 1992.

General election 9 April 1992

Batley and Spen

Elizabeth Peacock	Conservative	27,629
Eunice Durkin	Labour	26,221
Gordon Beever	Liberal Democrat	6,380
Clive Lord	Green	628
Conservative majority		1,408

National Result	Seats
Conservative	336
Labour	271
Liberal Democrat	20
Others	24
	651
Conservative majority	21

Chapter 20

The Difficulties of Government (1992–97)

Yes, we had won the election nationally: John Major with an unexpected majority of twenty-one and I had been returned for a third term, my majority slightly increased. I went back to Westminster with enthusiasm; my foot on the bottom of the ministerial ladder as a PPS under a leader of measured style. Little did I realize the problems that John Major, his government and the Conservative Party were going to run into in the coming five years.

As I review this five-year parliament and affairs of the period it is easier to emphasize the problems we got into than highlight the successes. The commentators in the media castigated the Prime Minister and the party to the eventual satisfaction of the public and the delight of the opposition. However, as I write now some twenty years on I see things somewhat differently. Despite the problems, and they were many, the Major government fulfilled all its 1992 election manifesto promises and it got all its proposed legislation in place. Through the hand-to-hand fighting of daily politics, objectives were achieved. For this reason I believe that John Major's seven years as Prime Minister are important in consolidating the Thatcher revolution into history. John's government, for all its faults, dotted the 'i's and crossed the 't's of many of the Thatcher initiatives. Throughout all his challenges, John, dubbed unfairly the 'grey man' of British politics, did not lose sight of his objectives and at the same time created a strengthening in the British economy that benefited the Blair regime of the 1990s. He deserves better treatment than he usually gets and I will come back to this theme later.

I arrived back at Westminster with high spirits and a hope that I could contribute to the government. I was to be initially disappointed because

Angela Rumbold lost her ministerial job in the reshaped government after the election, so I also lost my PPS role in the Home Office that was personal to the minister and unpaid.

Europe and European issues were to be the recurring theme throughout the five years of this parliament and almost every issue caused me some problem. As I have explained elsewhere I have been in favour of being a member of the EU as a trading group with certain understandings to provide an open market; nothing more, with Europe having no input in any other British matters or legislation. Because of this constraint my support throughout the five years had to be measured against this yardstick.

Soon after we returned to Westminster the Maastricht Treaty raised its head again. It had made progress in the previous parliament confirming our membership but following John Major's endeavours, excusing us from the single currency and the Social Chapter. Denmark had rejected the treaty in a referendum putting the proposal on hold. This made my Euro-sceptic colleagues demand a re-think that began a five-year Conservative battle on European policies.

This indecisive position on European policy encouraged a sudden run on the sterling exchange rate that was constrained due to its membership of the Exchange Rate Mechanism (ERM) which John Major and others had encouraged Margaret Thatcher reluctantly to join in 1990. Following huge speculation on Wednesday 16 September, control of the pound exchange rate was lost. In an attempt to regain control the Treasury was forced to pump billions into the market and the bank rate was pushed to unknown heights of 15 per cent and above. By evening, with the exchange rate still out of control Chancellor Norman Lamont had to take Britain out of the ERM, hence the name 'Black Wednesday'!

I have, however, never subscribed to this title. The British media blamed John Major and Norman Lamont for this humiliation and the Conservative Party never led the opinion polls again in the coming five years. In my view, exit from the ERM was a blessing for Britain.

Mrs Thatcher was right: we should never have been involved in the first place. Once outside the mechanism we had full control of our currency and interest rates which led eventually to the vibrant economy that Chancellor Ken Clarke handed over to the Labour Party in 1997.

Perhaps the title should really be 'White Wednesday'.

The press hounded John Major to sack Norman Lamont for this so-called debacle. He clearly did not want to do so but eventually had to appoint Ken Clarke in his place, thus gaining an unjustified reputation for weak management. I know and respect both these talented men, so recognize John's dilemma.

Back as a PPS

I had been a little disappointed when I lost my PPS role but thought no more about the matter until one day a little while after the election my car phone rang as I was leaving Batley. The caller, to my surprise, was Minister for the Disabled Nick Scott (later Sir Nicholas), who came straight to the point:

> Elizabeth, I'm looking for a PPS to help me with my role in the Department of Health and Social Security. I hear you did a good job in the Home Office with Angela and I would like you to be my PPS.

I replied by saying I was delighted and interested and as I was just driving to my home I would ring back in an hour.

I liked the idea of working with Nick as he was a pleasant and dedicated man with an interesting area of work. So within the hour I rang back: 'Yes, I'd be happy to do the job on the understanding that the demands of my constituency have to come first.' Nick was happy with this arrangement so I was back with a junior appointment in government that with luck should have headed me up the 'greasy pole' of politics.

As we shall see later, because of my independent nature it did not last long but I did enjoy the challenge while it lasted!

Chapter 21

Positive Government

The five years from 1992 to '97 have been billed as a period of turbulence for the Conservative Party, moving from the large majorities of the Thatcher period to the rebirth of the Labour Party and the inevitability of a Labour government. It is true they were turbulent but I believe in retrospect that they were immensely important for the Conservative Party to confirm and consolidate the advances that had been achieved by Margaret Thatcher. Misguidedly, some senior Conservatives at the 1992 election had said we would be well served, for the longer term, if we lost the election and were out of office for a whole parliament.

I have always believed that this was nonsense. I am of the opinion that despite the problems that arose during these years, the benefits of the Thatcher era would not have been so well-recognized had John Major not consolidated them. He was the right man at the right time and as the years go by this becomes more apparent. I am convinced the Major years were important to Britain and that the Major premiership was a much more important period than is generally accepted.

Maybe Neil Kinnock gave the election away with his Sheffield performance but John also won the election from his soapbox. His 21-seat majority would normally have been very workable but because of the Conservative inability to agree a common line on Europe, it remained fragile throughout the parliament. Consequently John had a constant struggle to hold his government and party together.

As I have already reported, the parliament started well with the bill implementing the Maastricht European Treaty getting a solid majority in the Commons, although some twenty-two Tory MPs voted against. However, when the Danes voted against, the re-think began and further progress on the bill had to be delayed.

As we have noted, the greatest problem for the government was the economy and the ERM. Norman Lamont, the Chancellor of the Exchequer, had failed to get the German government to reduce their interest rates which would have solved the issue. Speculative trading of sterling carried on, so to curb this activity interest rates were increased twice during the day but to no avail. As we already know, by evening Norman Lamont announced that Britain was withdrawing from the European Exchange Rate Mechanism.

True, the Cabinet was shaken and John had a tough time at Prime Minister's Questions with John Smith, the leader of the opposition, on the issue. The matter played heavily at the Conservative Party conference in October and John Major was criticized for not sacking Norman Lamont for his part in the affair. Shortly, among all this turmoil, to my great annoyance and dismay Michael Heseltine suddenly announced the almost immediate closure of thirty-one pits with the loss of thousands of jobs in the mining industry. The timing was terrible and caused a great row that I helped to ferment; so much so that the government was forced to step back and review its plans before proceeding.

Such was the disarray in government that the revived Maastricht Bill only just survived by three votes when it returned to the Commons in November 1993. John Major and Foreign Secretary Douglas Hurd helped the Danes find a solution for a new referendum. The government got the bill into law by July 1993 but then lost a crucial vote on the Social Chapter. This triggered a vote of no confidence that it managed to defeat.

All in all this period of total disarray in government and party was later, with a series of scandals, to cause the downfall of the government under a tide of public demand for change. After his defeat in the 1992 election Neil Kinnock had resigned to be replaced by the respected right-wing John Smith. To the horror of all sides of the House, John suffered a heart attack soon after his appointment and died. In electing a replacement the Labour Party moved to a new generation by choosing the charismatic Tony Blair as their new leader and leader of the opposition; a choice I soon recognized as befitting the television age.

Tony grabbed the role with vigour; surprising the Labour conference with a controversial proposal to scrap Clause Four of the Labour Party constitution referring to nationalization of British industry. Tony Blair considered that the removal of the demand for common ownership represented a major shift in thinking for the modern Labour Party and had to be achieved.

It was a difficult time to be at Westminster with the pressure to get the legislation through the House and the media constantly looking for comment and more stories. I began to find it trying.

John Major was now beset with problems from all sides: the economy, Europe, a new Labour leader and a spiral of scandals from within his party.

National Heritage Secretary David Mellor had to resign because of his involvement with an actress, as did Northern Ireland minister Michael Mates because of his support for the businessman Asil Nadir who had fled to North Cyprus.

Several MPs were alleged to have taken money from Mohamed Al-Fayed for raising matters in Parliament, dubbed 'cash for questions'. This caused continuing press comment and challenge to the MPs involved and to the party concerning the conduct of MPs in general; so much so that in October 1994 a committee on Standards of Conduct in Public Life was established to investigate the matter. The 'cash for questions' affair was to raise its head again in 1996 with a libel case brought against the *Guardian* by Neil Hamilton MP. This all happened when John Major launched his 'back to basics' campaign to provide old-fashioned standards of behaviour in British life. I always thought it was a pleasant idea but did not describe a modern Britain.

Throughout this period the Conservatives lost several by-elections and in 1994 also took a heavy defeat in the European elections.

Once again in 1994 Europe caused major disruption for the party when the government turned the second reading of a European budget bill into a confidence vote. My colleagues rebelled and had the Party Whip removed; I, for once, was well-behaved! In revenge the rebels then voted with Labour on the imposition of VAT on domestic fuel. John Major had by then had enough of the party rebellions and decided that rather than resign as prime minister he would resign as party leader and seek re-election with the party's support. This he did, to great surprise making a statement in the rose garden at 10 Downing Street. He was challenged, not from the troublesome backbenchers, but by John Redwood from within the Cabinet. John's resignation caused plenty of media noise, though the result was never in doubt with an easy win for John Major with 218 votes to John Redwood with 89 votes. This was sufficient to confirm John Major's leadership, allowing Michael Heseltine to take the position of deputy prime minister to provide some extra thinking. However, this dramatic action did not stop disruption as several leading figures 'crossed the floor' to join Labour (Alan Howarth) and the Liberal Democrats (Emma Nicholson and Peter Thurnham).

Matters European continued to plague the party into 1997 with the imposition of a ban on the export of British beef due to foot-and-mouth disease and pressure to ensure that the single currency was not accepted. A firm stance was taken by government, even with a pro-Europe Chancellor of the Exchequer like Kenneth Clarke.

164

Chapter 22

Pit Closures and Privatization

Restructuring coal mining

My big disagreement with the Major government arose in October 1992 on industrial policy and the re-structuring of the British coal industry. Suddenly without any notice Michael Heseltine announced the closure of thirty-one pits and the subsequent loss of around 30,000 coal-mining jobs. I took serious exception to the way this issue was handled. My problem was that there had been no meaningful investigation and discussion into the long-term energy needs for Britain and what part coal was to play in competition with oil, gas and other sources. I accepted that many of the pits in question were losing money and could not compete with imported coal and that a closure programme was therefore necessary. My issue was with the manner and speed of implementation, so I opposed government plans, making friends in the mining industry and enemies in the Conservative Party. I indicated my unhappiness with the proposals to my whips, stating that unless they were reviewed and the timescale of implementation was significantly modified I could not support the plan and would vote against.

My dilemma was that ministerial responsibility was with Michael Heseltine who had made the initial announcement of the proposal. Michael had been a good supporter of my work in Batley and Spen having visited on several occasions and was instrumental in progressing Batley City Challenge funding. He had also been my choice of leader in the election when Mrs Thatcher resigned so I wrote to him explaining my position.

This I did jointly with Winston Churchill, pointing out that in our view the government, together with Michael Heseltine and Minister for Coal Tim Eggar, had got the process wrong and they should think again. The press were soon on the issue and all hell broke loose in the media, particularly when Roy Lynk, leader of the Union of Democratic Mine

Workers, declared he would go on hunger strike down in the workings of the Silverhill Colliery near Nottingham.

Winston and I decided that we should visit Silverhill to support Roy, which we did. Winston had already rung Brian Redhead on the *Today* programme before he set off for Silverhill and told him of our plans, therefore when we arrived at Silverhill we were met not only by the regional manager of British Coal but a mass of media people who had heard the *Today* broadcast.

Understandably the regional manager refused our request to go underground but he did take us to the canteen where a great number of miners were meeting to consider the government's proposals. When we joined them there we got a tremendous reception with TV cameras exposing the problem at national and international level. Arrangements had been made for us to speak to Roy via the pit-surface-to-coal-face telephone system and we were able to assure him and everyone else present of our support.

We then gave press interviews and photographs were taken for many newspapers and radio stations building on the story. The big question was: 'Why are you as Tory MPs supporting the miners?' This was something many people just could not understand.

The answer was simple:

Our government has not adequately considered British energy policy, especially the place of coal in the future mix. It must do so before we have a major re-structure of British coal-mining. We are not against re-structuring but it must be done in a considered and controlled manner.

On a personal level I did understand the position of the miners and the 1974 Heath government and the traumas of the industry after Arthur Scargill's defeat by the Thatcher government in 1984. During that time I had worked with the then Coal Minister, David Hunt, and had arranged for working miners' wives to attend a meeting in the House of Commons to inform the government of the very difficult circumstances that they were having to live with because their husbands wished to go to work. Their views, comments and photographs were taken directly to the prime minister by me and the coal minister. I did have great sympathy for those continuing to work during the strike.

Clearly Batley and Spen did not have any mines left but several local

16 NOV 1993

1O DOWNING STREET
LONDON SW1A 2AA

THE PRIME MINISTER

15 November 1993

Dear Elizabeth,

Thank you for your letter of 26 October. I am sorry that you felt it necessary to vote against the Government on 27 October but I appreciate your courtesy in forewarning me.

I know we share a common aim in wanting to see a viable industry continue in this country. I consider that the structure of privatisation announced recently will provide that future.

I am pleased that British Coal are close to finalising details on leasing Clipstone pit to R. J. Budge. British Coal are still considering bids for other pits.

It is also good news that Ellington pit has been able to take advantage of the Government's offer of extra subsidy, both for their sales to British Alcan and for exports. We will continue to examine any other applications for subsidy sympathetically.

Yours Ever,
John

Mrs. Elizabeth Peacock, J.P., M.P.

George Gale cartoons on the pit closure debate.

companies did supply equipment to the industry and needed to keep their manufacturing programmes running.

The TV and press coverage from Silverhill turned the whole issue into a national protest with me and a few other Conservative MPs as the leading protestors. Our attack on our own government came just as some poor economic figures were being published on production output and unemployment that turned the debate into an economic argument, thus widening the problem for Michael Heseltine and his team.

Archbishop of York Dr John Habgood called the proposed pit closures economic madness. Cardinal Basil Hume, the Archbishop of Westminster, wrote to Michael Heseltine saying he was 'distressed at the social and human costs of these drastic closures'.

The Labour Party demanded a statement and an emergency debate in the House or they would use their opposition day in the coming week to run such a debate.

Suddenly I seemed to become the unofficial spokesman for the Tory protestors, even though we had a Churchill on the team; maybe because I was the only woman or maybe because I gave them the story 'straight from the shoulder'. Wherever I went I was invaded by the media and on several occasions we had two or three TV or radio crews in our drive at home. I just could not escape. Almost every day I had a telephone conversation with Michael Heseltine to see if we could find an answer and stem the rebellion that looked as though it could overturn the government.

An emergency debate was held with the opposition pressing the need for a re-think but avoiding support for a possible miners' strike. I spoke in the debate, saying:

"I am totally opposed to the wholesale closure of British coal mines, particularly in Yorkshire, until we have an agreed policy including coal together with oil, gas and so-called sustainable sources. Without this policy, pit closures on this scale could be strategically dangerous for our economic future. It's fine to say 'We've got cheap imported coal at the moment' but remember if we do close a mine it cannot be reopened! In five years coal prices will have gone up and we will then be held to ransom by those countries on which we have become dependent for our coal supplies."

A series of debates was held in the House on the issue. As the story unfolded and the government began to see some sense, I got some good support and an equal amount of abuse, even from the Labour Party who I was likely to support. Having made a detailed speech setting out my position, I was surprised to be attacked by Ron Davies, Labour MP for Caerphilly, who accused me of being undecided and that my claim to be an independent-minded Yorkshire woman was no good if I was not strong-willed and that he knew I would abstain. I was angry as I had no plan to abstain and tried to intervene in his speech but he would not give way. I appealed to the Speaker Betty Boothroyd but she could not help. To my further surprise (as I was being a nuisance to the government), Michael Heseltine and David Hunt (then Secretary of State for Wales) took Ron Davies to task for his rude behaviour; David Hunt saying: 'That was a disgraceful and discourteous speech. In the debate Mrs Peacock and Mr Churchill expressed concern about important issues, yet the Hon. Gentleman chose in an arrogant way not to give way and give them the opportunity to intervene.'

Michael and David were gentlemen, even though we disagreed!

Many other Tory MPs spoke on the lines of an economic problem. John Townend (Bridlington) called for further interest rate cuts; the former Trade and Industry Secretary Nicholas Ridley (later Lord Ridley) joined the argument from the Lords by warning of a 1930s-style slump. John Carlisle (Luton), who was unhappy that Norman Lamont was still in place as Chancellor despite the ERM debacle, used the coal argument to call for his resignation. All very confusing but following widespread public protests and our threatened revolt Michael Heseltine backed down temporarily and ordered a review. This kept the argument going for several weeks with me almost drowning in press interest. During this review and consultation period I visited Grimethorpe colliery to meet local people and miners' union representatives. Following this I went underground to the coal face at Maltby, in each case receiving a rousing reception for my support. I was receiving messages of support from around Britain and in particular from Yorkshire, including the then Bishop of Wakefield Nigel McCulloch and his chaplain for the coalfields the Rev. Ian Gaskell.

I took both of the latter to a meeting with the head of British Coal to discuss the implementation of the plan. On the way to the meeting we very nearly needed a new Bishop of Wakefield because as we rushed across the road the bishop was very nearly run down by the traffic; a fact he remembers to this day.

Michael Heseltine, having accepted that the issue had been badly handled, put the matter before the Commons Trade and Industry Select

The author visiting Maltby Colliery during the threat of pit closures.

Committee. To lessen the furore he provided lengthy consultations, especially with the protesting Tories. I took part in this consultation process, discussing the issue directly with Michael Heseltine. When he wanted to speak to me the phone would ring and a very important-sounding voice would say: 'Number 10 here, Mr Heseltine wants to speak to Elizabeth.' This worked well through my office but not so at home if my husband answered the phone as he had grown tired of the performance. When the voice said 'Number 10 here' he would reply 'Number 10 where?' and then await the reaction at the other end that was often frosty!

One day my office reported that a Mr Scargill had been on the phone saying he would like to meet me and would I go to his headquarters in Yorkshire for a meeting? We replied 'Happy to meet' but it would have to be at my office in 1 Parliament Street. This meant with our House security we would not have a media scrum, ensuring that there would be no publicity. So the very next day Arthur Scargill arrived in my office for a discussion on mine closures and the future. He opened the discussion by saying he was not entirely happy discussing the topic with a Conservative Member of Parliament but believed he had no viable option if the closures were to be stopped or slowed down. Arthur was a perfect gentleman and we had a sensible discussion over a cup of coffee. I emphasized that I was not against re-structuring the industry that would require some closures but I was totally opposed to the way the government was proceeding. Obviously he could not agree to re-structuring but thanked me for my efforts on behalf of his members.

At long last after weeks of consultation the government decided to proceed as planned, starting with another debate in the House and a vote. The speculation in the days leading up to the debate and vote was that it would be a close-run thing for the government. However, I knew that some of the early Tory protestors now considered that the government had reviewed energy policy and the proposals in sufficient depth for them to abstain or even vote with the government. I was not convinced that our energy policy had been studied in sufficient depth and the demand for coal quantified. I therefore announced my continued intention of voting against the government.

To my horror early on the day of the debate and vote my House of Commons secretary, Lorna, rang to say that Alastair Campbell in his column in the *Daily Mirror* that morning was saying that I had changed sides and would vote with the government. He then suggested all miners and their supporters should ring my office telephone to express their disgust and proceeded to provide my House of Commons internal office telephone number. So many angry and in some cases obscene calls came in; so much so that the Sergeant-at-Arms closed down the switchboard completely for a short period to relieve the pressure.

As my husband Brian was in London I discussed with him what action should be taken to ensure the truth was told long before the vote was taken. I felt, at that time, unable to deal with Alastair Campbell and needed to concentrate on my speech for this important debate. In response Brian organized a press release reconfirming my intention to vote against the government, adding that we intended to instruct solicitors to sue the *Daily Mirror* and Campbell. This went to all radio and TV stations within the hour. He then rang the *Daily Mirror* and Campbell to confirm our action.

After some difficulty he did get through to Alastair Campbell and after an exchange of some basic Yorkshire language Campbell agreed he had got the story completely wrong and that the *Mirror* would change the story in their later edition, taking out my telephone number, and they would apologize in print later. To be fair they did apologize somewhat belatedly but well after the event.

Throughout the whole of this drawn-out affair I had remained PPS to Nicholas Scott, Minister for the Disabled, and continued working on his behalf. The convention was that when a member of the government team votes or threatens to vote against government, they should resign their position. As a PPS is a very small cog in the government wheel I told Nick Scott, subject to his agreement, that I did not intend to resign before the vote as I had not yet committed the crime! He was very understanding and as I knew he would not sack me I carried on working with him.

During the debate the issues were aired again and I repeated my position. However, the protestors reduced in number so the government won the vote with a majority of thirteen; six Tory rebels voted with the opposition, with five other Conservatives abstaining. My colleagues who held their resolve to the bitter end and voted against the government were Richard Alexander (Newark), Dr Michael Clark (Rochford), Richard Shepherd (Aldridge Brownhills), Nicholas Winterton (Macclesfield) and Ann Winterton (Congleton).

The five abstaining were David Nicholson (Taunton), Toby Jessel (Twickenham), Peter Fry (Wellingborough), Sir Richard Body (Holland with Boston) and Sir Patrick McNair-Wilson (New Forest). These colleagues were not convinced that the government had gone far enough with their concessions but would not vote against. Eight Ulster Unionists (who would normally vote with the government) also abstained and were the subject of much ridicule from Labour MPs.

I had voted with the Labour Party before but some of my fellow rebels found it a 'different experience'. My greatest disappointment during the debate and subsequent vote was when Winston Churchill announced that the government had now done enough to satisfy his concerns and that he would vote with the government. My reaction was 'Turncoat!' as I was disappointed for the miners. However, I had been warned that Winston might change his mind as he had used this sort of tactic before. Eventually I got over my disappointment and as he was my office neighbour we remained friends until his untimely death.

As the result of the vote was announced I headed across the lobby to meet the press as I had agreed earlier. On the way out of the Chamber I was met by the Conservative duty whip Nicholas Baker (Dorset) who was obviously waiting for me, saying simply: 'Elizabeth, you're sacked forthwith as a PPS.' My reply was 'I was about to resign!' and on I went to meet the press. The very first press question was: 'Elizabeth, when are you going to resign as a PPS?' My reply was: 'I don't need to, I have just been sacked!'

The BBC who had been covering the vote on TV flashed up my photograph at the end of the 10 o'clock news with the subtitle: 'Rebel Yorkshire Tory MP sacked for supporting miners.' This caused comment for days in the media and in my postbag.

Some people in the Conservative Party were not happy with the way I had supported the miners and some have never forgiven me for the part I played. In my view governments have to learn that they must prepare their ground and take their supporters and the people with them as they formulate policy and action. The government did not do this when announcing pit closures, so I opposed their action and would do so again in similar circumstances. I certainly understood the party view the next day when I met Virginia Bottomley in the Members' Lobby and she told me in a very loud voice what a disgrace to the Conservative Party I was. Unfortunately for her, she did so in the hearing of the badge messengers and some Labour MPs who reacted by saying she had gone too far. Similarly I believe it was my efforts to force the government to review energy policy and my support for the miners that upset the late Alan Clark and encouraged him to make two disparaging remarks about me in his

'Diaries', which then reached the newspapers. I reacted by saying I did not think much of him either, that he was a terrible snob and philanderer who lived on his family's financial success. Maybe he was an old-fashioned Tory but never a modern Conservative!

Some years later I did get the opportunity to get a little revenge for his diary comments when Alan Clark who had given up his Plymouth seat suddenly wished to return to the House as Member for Kensington and Chelsea, replacing my old boss Sir Nicholas Scott who had died. When Alan was unexpectedly selected as the Conservative candidate I was asked by a Yorkshire newspaper to comment and I did so in the following manner under the headline: 'How could the Party pick this reprobate?' I said I thought it unbelievable that anyone would choose this self-confessed philanderer, reprobate and adulterer. I said he was an unpleasant and arrogant man who was extremely rude about the North and people in trade, which was surprising as he was not a true aristocrat, his family having made their money in the cotton trade. His comments about Michael Heseltine having to 'buy his own furniture' were the last word in arrogance.

The media and communication response
The weeks between the original announcements of the pit closures and the final vote were, and remain, a blur of activity among government ministers, colleagues and the media. The media interest was stimulated by the involvement of 'a Churchill' and by my decision with Winston to go to Silverhill Colliery at the very start, following the government announcements. The British media, particularly radio and TV, wanted constant comment and by the day of the final vote I had also appeared on TV and radio for several countries around the world including Russia, the USA and Canada, often at odd hours of the day or night!

As I began to write this chapter I remember the huge response that I received on my initial decision to oppose the government plans and an even greater response when I really did vote against the government and got sacked on the spot from my PPS job.

My office received thousands of letters and messages; so many that we just did not have the capacity to acknowledge or reply. We received letters of support for my stance from all parts of the United Kingdom and some from around the world. We had obviously attracted great interest. At the time I did read all the letters but there were so many and I was in such a whirlwind of TV and radio interviews explaining the basis of our opposition to the government and our disappointment with the outcome that there was not time to absorb all the comments.

As they arrived and I had read them, my dear secretary Lorna filed them in date order to be eventually brought from London to Yorkshire in a substantial packing-case. As writing began I decided I must look through the collection but once again I discovered that the task was almost impossible, so what I have done is take a sample of the letters and cards on which I will now make some comment. However, before doing so I must apologize if you wrote to me and I have not noted your interest: sorry, but the archive is just too large!

The first point I noted was the number of women who wrote, probably a majority. Letters came from business unions, local authorities, doctors and the clergy in addition to the individual. Indeed, I received letters of support from Yorkshire with some sound backing from Scotland, Wales and the Isle of Man.

As would be expected, there was great support from the unions as they had a deep interest in the outcome of the debate. This included the NUM, the National Association of Colliery Overmen, Deputies and Shotfirers, and local authority communication and health unions.

What I had not expected was the support of two petitions, one national and one from Sussex, certainly a non-mining area.

The clergy provided wide-ranging support from many denominations, from vicars and bishops including the Right Reverend David Konstant (Leeds) and my good friend Nigel McCulloch (Wakefield), who was most helpful throughout the whole period together with his chaplain the Rev. Ian Gaskell. What did particularly please me was a note from one of my former North Yorkshire county council colleagues, Gerald Turton, as my stance was not too popular in some Conservative circles.

In my recent review of the correspondence I did also note letters from Ireland and Scotland including one from the 'Friends of the Gordon Highlanders'!

Leaders of local authorities took time to write, also the Mayor of Barnsley and others from Kirklees and Mansfield. Of great value to me was a hand-written note from Dr David Skidmore, the former Conservative candidate for Stockport and one of the heroes who had helped the injured after the Brighton hotel bombing.

However, the outstanding point that I think I appreciated in 1992 and certainly do now was the great number of non-Conservatives, especially Labour supporters, who wrote with their congratulations and thanks for my efforts. I feel I should now quote from their letters and I give examples below:

"Dear Mrs Peacock
We wish to express our admiration for the way you have supported the miners at the risk of your own political career. We are very sorry that you lost your post at the Ministry for the Disabled but we are sure you have gained many friends and admirers, not only in the mining community but throughout the whole country."

"We are Labour supporters who wish there were more people in all political parties as honourable as you. We hope your determination will help to encourage the government to formulate a more sensible energy programme in the future."

"We wrote to you prior to the 'pit closure' debate on Wednesday last and would like you to know that we are filled with admiration for you and the support you gave to the miners and mining communities. You showed great courage, unlike many of your colleagues."

"While we are Labour Party members, we appreciate what you are doing for the mining communities."

"I am not a Conservative supporter in any way but your stand this week has restored my faith in the British parliamentary system where individuals, who are prepared to be counted, can accurately represent their constituents in spite of pressure from the party whips. Thank you for your sacrifice; it won't be forgotten."

"As lifelong Labour voters we are writing to thank you for your principled stand in the House of Commons yesterday."

"We have admired your independence of spirit since long before the general election, and your constituents are fortunate indeed to have you as their MP."

"I never imagined I would ever be writing a letter of support to a Conservative MP. I am an ex-miner, still unemployed after four years but I am still concerned about mines, miners and their communities.

I have to say that you have earned my respect and admiration for your courage in standing by your principles in the face of what must have been terrific pressure."

It was gratifying to see that my commonsense endeavour was having some influence.

"Dear Mrs Peacock
You're a wonderful lady! Keep up the good work. What a pity your fellow colleagues haven't got your good Yorkshire common sense.

Thank you for all your efforts on behalf of the coal industry and the miners.

It has cheered me enormously to know that common sense and logic can prevail over party politics and I am only sorry that some of your colleagues dropped out at the end."

I was forever grateful for the notes of encouragement I received from the establishment including my fellow MPs Glenda Jackson and Helen Jackson and those two men of letters, Sir Philip Goodhart and Woodrow Wyatt. Not only did I receive letters and cards, I got poems describing the affair such as this from Carlton Hardy:

BLACK DEATH
I hear the marching feet of men,
And hear the women cry.
I hear the politicians say,
That all the pits must die.

There is no future for the coal
That lies beneath our earth.
Other methods, other fuels,
Are given greater worth.

The government sees no profit
In supporting coal communities,
So casts them on the slag heap,
As in the threadbare 'Thirties,

When blue-scarred men
With hardened lungs were told:
'No work for you', 'till wartime
Made their labour weigh as gold.

Once Britain's wealth was built
With British coal and British sweat,
And miners' lives, and Aberfan.
How easily they forget!

Again there's the marching feet of men,
And grief as women cry,
When affluent politicians say,
That all the pits must die.
CARLTON HARDY
(October, 1992)
Reproduced by the kind permission of Mr Carlton Hardy.

Probably some of the most interesting are the short notes that go straight to the point, some of which are just scraps of paper:-

"CONGRATULATIONS MADAM, SACKED BUT NOT SILENCED"

"Dear Mrs Peacock
You have got more balls than any of those other nodding dogs!
Good girl.
I love you for it."

"YOU LOST YOUR JOB BUT KEPT YOUR WORD, GOOD FOR YOU AND THANKS. YORKIE"

"Dear Mrs Peacock
Walk Tall!
    God bless you and keep showing 'em and let them know what Yorkshire folk are made of."

My View

Looking at the issues now some twenty years on with a clearer eye and less emotion I can say the following.

Yes, the British coal-mining industry had to be rationalized and re-structured; even Arthur Scargill knew that but would not say so. Many of the pits were inefficient and losing huge amounts of tax-payers' money. The cost of taking coal from these inefficient British deep mines was considerably greater than purchasing international open-cast coal and therefore re-structuring had to happen. The question was when and how.

The government's timing in the autumn of 1992 was probably correct but Michael Heseltine and Coal Minister Tim Eggar got the 'how' part wrong. They should have had the energy review first and then announced the rationalization programme. Michael is a big-picture businessman who clearly said to Tim Eggar: 'Get the industry re-structured and privatized now.' Eggar did not put in the detailed review work required and just pushed on regardless. His personal style upset the coal industry, the politicians and others who reacted with vigour.

The proposal could and should have been handled better but the government got its way in the end. Ten mines were closed and the remains of the industry privatized.

Privatization

You would have thought that having been fired from my albeit small government job I would have had enough of coal and coal mines but I was determined to remain involved with the industry and try to bring some stability to the trade.

The government had clearly decided that it would close the planned pits that were not economic and that it would put the more commercial pits up for tender. This tender would include pits in Scotland, Wales and England that would be of interest to local operational companies. The main player was likely to be Richard Budge and his colleagues. During the pit closure argument I had been regularly to meetings with the NCB at senior level including their sales director Malcolm Edwards. Shortly after the debate Malcolm invited me to lunch, during which he said he would like to get involved in pit operations and in the tender process. He then said he was considering setting up a company and raising funds from the stock market and banks. It transpired that his plan was to buy the shell of the former Cornish tin-mining company Geevor Mining and to change the name to Coal Investments. In doing this he must build a board to manage the company. He then suggested that I might join as a non-executive director, concentrating on government and trade union matters. This would be done in such a way that it would not conflict with my constituency and parliamentary duties, and as it looked like a new challenge I said yes; a fresh 'coal challenge' for me.

Shortly afterwards Malcolm left the NCB and Coal Investments Plc was brought into being by bankers, solicitors and accountants. The Geevor company with its stock exchange listing was purchased with international bankers' support. This City activity was an eye-opener to me and gave me a new insight into industry and in the long term helped my parliamentary/industry understanding.

To get the ball rolling Coal Investments shares were sold and began trading on the stock exchange, and I was now a director of a public company; or as my mother-in-law often indicated in a friendly manner, 'a pushy Yorkshire lass'.

To help launch the project I decided that I must invest and put my money where my mouth was and support the industry. My husband agreed that he would also invest. The Peacocks were taking a risk again!

We got Coal Investments going just in time as government minister Tim Eggar published the privatization document, having already decided which pits must close. In a great rush we tendered for mainly English pits, clearly in competition with Richard Budge, with others tendering for those in Wales and Scotland.

We waited for some weeks and then lost. Budge was better funded and got the pits with land and property that he wanted. This was disappointing. However, it did not kill us off but left us having to license the best of the government-closed pits and those that Budge did not want. In the meantime Malcolm Edwards had got our sales and marketing going from day one by signing power-station contracts using imported coal with options to transfer to a UK supplier at a later date. So to cover these contracts we arranged to license pits from the government that had the good geological potential and sound surface facilities we needed for a quality product. We then progressively opened pits at Hem Heath, Silverdale in Staffordshire, Markham Main, Coventry, and Cwmgilli in South Wales for anthracite.

Things looked very promising: we had contracts, we had coal and we were creating jobs but we needed more funding so off we went to the bankers and the stock exchange. This secondary fund-raising exercise was successful, with the Peacocks joining in again!

As usual I wanted to get thoroughly involved in the business as far as my other duties would allow, and made a tour of each pit as it was reopened. I thoroughly enjoyed these visits, being allowed to ride on the

With Denis Healey receiving the awards of Yorkshire Man and Yorkshire Woman of the Year, 1993. [Ross Parry Agency]

Receiving the Yorkshire Woman of Achievement Award, 1993.

coal conveyors from the coal face. This was exciting as I had to lay flat on my stomach on the conveyors that were conveniently slowed for our comfort but still sufficiently fast to be exciting, all the while keeping one's head down to miss the overhead beams.

I soon learnt about Joy mining machinery, roadway cutters and long wall production with the necessary roof-bolting and mine safety issues. I spent a full morning at the coal face at Silverdale, Stoke-on-Trent with my husband when we were allowed to drive the Joy cutter. I do not think I have ever been so hot, deaf or dirty before or since.

I therefore learnt at first hand some of the challenges facing the coal miner.

Then things began to go wrong. The bulk price of coal (open-cast) dropped and seriously undercut our deep-mined product. In the meantime Richard Budge had got his pitch and sales going better, power stations began to move their contracts around and we lost sales volume. After a few months it became somewhat obvious that we and Budge had opened too much production capacity in a falling coal price market. To add to our problems we ran into geological problems at our pits that did reduce availability for a time and also put up our production costs.

We began to lose money but hoped that the world price would change. However, after twelve months these problems began to cause us to lose serious money. We tried all we could to stop these losses but they began to mount and our bankers, particularly our international bankers, took fright and UBS removed their financial support, causing Coal Investments to go into administration with an eventual loss of £millions.

A sad day for the miners we had re-employed, an unfortunate day for the bankers and a terrible day for those who had privately invested, including the Peacocks.

My View

Coal Investments had had a good team. No one knew the coal industry and its markets better than Malcolm Edwards, and Brian Nicholls from Australia was the best mine director we could have found. In truth we opened too much capacity and were too ambitious with five operational collieries. Our financial and management resources were just too thinly spread. We should have concentrated on one or two pits at most, with tighter financial control. Maybe we should have been more ruthless and stripped out the early coal, 'asset-stripping' as it was called, which Richard Budge was good at and Malcolm Edwards opposed.

In retrospect our management structure was wrong: Malcolm had too

much to do; too many responsibilities as chairman, chief executive and top salesman. In my view the roles of chairman and chief executive should not have been combined and we should have had a non-executive chairman.

In summary it was an interesting but expensive experience with a particularly sad end for those employed by Coal Investments and a more disappointing end for the investors. However, the simple truth is that coal was losing the fight for its place in the energy mix and deep-mined coal cannot compete with open-cast.

This time I lost money, not just votes. Obviously I was not happy but still have an interest in what remains of the industry as patron of the National Coal Mining Museum for England near my home in Wakefield. This gives me the opportunity to keep in touch with those who remain in the industry and help when I can.

Memories and awards

We had lost the argument and the vote and the pits would close but I have the memories provided by the letters and messages I received during the fight. Yorkshire recognized what I had been trying to do and thanked me with the awards of Yorkshire Woman of Achievement and Yorkshire Woman of the Year 1993, the year in which Denis Healey was Yorkshire Man of the Year as mentioned before.

On a pleasing note, I was suddenly faced with the fact that I had been chosen as 'Campaigner of the Year' in the awards sponsored by the *Spectator* magazine and Highland Park whisky for my pit closure fight. I was approached by the *Spectator* to attend their annual lunch but refused as I was due to be in Batley at the time. Pressure was put on me to attend, which I eventually did and I now know why. I was honoured, gaining a case of special Highland Park whisky that my friends tested on my behalf! I found myself in good company as Speaker Betty Boothroyd was named 'Parliamentarian of the Year' and Michael Forsyth was the 'Member to watch'!

On a more frivolous note, I was delighted in December 1992 when Waddingtons of Leeds, the makers of Cluedo, decided to produce a special edition of the game. They used me in the Mrs Peacock role; all very frightening as Waddingtons had just attempted to kick off the board game the murderous Reverend Green, replacing him with a trendy business character. All rather confusing as I had rarely played the game.

I was honoured then and remain so today. Thanks again to everyone concerned for the messages and awards.

Chapter 23

Pushing on – Difficulties Continue

I have already outlined the main factors that beset the Major government of 1992–97 and had an influence on my political future. I now analyze them in more depth and look at them in the context of subsequent events, thus allowing a better assessment of the Major government.

Boundary changes

Of particular concern was the regular ten-year review of constituencies and their size in terms of number of electors. There was quite obviously a problem in Yorkshire, especially in West Yorkshire. Batley and Spen had many more electors than other local constituencies, while Normanton had too few. Consequently the Boundary Commission tabled a proposal to change constituency boundaries in West Yorkshire, around Wakefield, reducing the number of electors in Batley and Spen from around 77,000 towards the national average of 65,000. The proposal was that they would remove electors in Heckmondwike to a re-shaped Dewsbury and Wakefield.

I had always considered that Heckmondwike was crucial to my electoral success. I had many friends in the town and some good supporters. In a good year for Conservatives we could elect Conservative councillors but would revert to Labour in a poor year. Heckmondwike seemed to be an important way to my continued success at the next election scheduled for 1997; we therefore objected to the planned change.

As there were other objections across West Yorkshire the whole plan went to a public enquiry and consultation that allowed discussion on counter-proposals. The Labour Party was well-organized with a team of lawyers putting forward variations across West Yorkshire. By contrast, the Conservative Party could not agree among themselves so did not find any

186

lawyers or counter-proposals for discussion. I had been so much trouble to the party that they were not prepared to support me. However, we had a good young supporter, Chris Saul, who being a barrister was also very keen on developing a political career for himself. This was sadly something that was not to be because he died from cancer as a very young man. Chris, on hearing that the Conservative Party did not have legal support, offered his services to attend the enquiry and put forward a Batley and Spen counter-proposal that we had produced. This he did, proposing that Heckmondwike should remain in Batley and Spen and that the Leeds Road area of Batley adjacent to Dewsbury should be moved into the Dewsbury constituency. This plan had the approval of many people in that area as they already considered that they lived in Dewsbury and as I write this, a proposal for further boundary changes in 2015 is suggesting just that action.

Despite his efforts, Chris did not succeed and would take no fee other than a case of wine from the Peacocks. When finalized the boundary changes went ahead almost as originally proposed and as Labour wished, which I knew placed a big question mark over my ability to retain my seat, regardless of the political scene in 1997. All rather depressing, because if West Yorkshire Conservatives could have agreed an overall plan, we might have had a different outcome that could have saved some Conservatives from the 1997 tidal wave that was to come!

My View

Did the boundary changes really influence the eventual result in 1997? In truth the answer must be 'No'. The Conservatives were never going to be re-elected in 1997. Britain was looking for change: Tony Blair and New Labour were ready and willing. We had assessed that I had a possible personal vote of around 2,000 that had got me re-elected in 1987 and 1992.

In 1997 I lost by much more than 2,000. However, in a less dramatic election the outcome could have been very different.

Sunday trading

The reader may recall that in an earlier attempt to legalize Sunday trading I had voted against the proposal. In December 1992 a new Sunday trading bill was introduced with better safeguards. I commented at the time that: 'Everyone agrees that the existing law is unsatisfactory.' For once, this long-standing issue seemed to have a commonsense proposal that looked workable. When the matter came to a vote, I changed direction and voted for Sunday trading, as the Keep Sunday Special campaign and others had been consulted on these new proposals that included government provisions protecting shop workers from being obliged to work on Sundays. At the time I realized not everyone would be satisfied or pleased that I had changed direction but change was needed with the necessary controls and safeguards in place. When the vote was taken the government won and Sunday trading as we now know it came into being.

My View

I have never been entirely happy with shopping on Sundays. It is not a religious position but it never seems right and I still avoid shopping on what I call a 'rest day'. For this reason I voted against the original legislation as it was not workable.

However, looking back John Major's government was right to persist with new legislation that I then supported. A few simple changes to the rules have changed the British way of life forever. John should be congratulated.

City Challenge

There is one initiative for which the people of Batley can thank the Conservative government and that is the City Challenge monies that we managed to attract to the town under the government Urban Regeneration policy that was pushed hard by Michael Heseltine. Michael, with whom I had crossed swords on pit closures and on the possible privatization of Royal Mail and who I had supported for party leader in 1990, was remarkably sympathetic to putting regeneration funds into the town, including the question of housing and its refurbishment.

In early 1992 Kirklees Council was invited by Michael Heseltine to put forward a scheme and a bid for £7.5million each year for five years to tackle employment, housing, and social and environmental problems in the town.

After plenty of the usual government delay, the scheme was accepted with public backing and the funds were made available. Houses on council estates were refurbished and buildings cleaned for the first time since the days of the shoddy trade. The impressive buildings on Station Road, some of which were used as warehouses and others left unused, were cleaned and brought back into use for the first time in decades and this improved the overall appearance of the town.

My View

City Challenge money did help the refurbishment of Batley and we got a greater share of the available funding than we might have expected because the local team and Kirklees Council put forward a very sensible plan that impressed Michael Heseltine, particularly when he visited Batley to inspect the town.

However, I can still say a big 'thank you' to John Major and Michael.

Europe and party division

Europe and European problems and issues were a constant irritation to the government and the Conservative Party throughout the whole of the 1992–97 Parliament and I found it completely frustrating. The party could never find a cohesive policy around which we could all agree: we were totally split on the issues, not just into Europhiles and Euro-sceptics but also into groups between these two extremes.

John Major wanted to be in a central position in Europe; steering the ship but at the same time trying to get the best deals for Britain. This he can claim to have done successfully with the Maastricht Treaty but he was seen to be less successful elsewhere. As a long-term supporter of being in the EU for trading purposes only, I had regular problems with John's position. I was always happy to support trading matters but totally opposed to European interference in British issues. On reflection, John Major got his European strategy wrong with the then state of the Conservative Party. With many members remaining unhappy about the removal and replacement of Margaret Thatcher, he might have done better keeping out of the European mainstream and taking a much more robust independent line. This may have brought the party together but who can tell? It was a judgement call.

Bosnia was the one European challenge around which British political consensus could be achieved. Internationally there was a difference of opinion between the countries involved on how to stop the complex war between the Bosnian Serbs and Muslims that raised questions of arms embargoes and direct air strikes. John and his team steered a good course through this problem to the overall satisfaction of the House. The House, as you would expect, took time to consider these matters but to be honest it did not seem to be of great concern to Batley and Spen so received very little of my time and attention.

The ratification of the Maastricht Treaty in 1993 was the start of our problems as the Euro-sceptic members of the party were vehemently opposed to certain provisions considered to be federal. As the opposition,

The Rt. Hon. John Major
Prime Minister
10 Downing Street
London SW1A 2AA

EJP/mef
12th January 1995

I am concerned about the way Britain's policy towards Europe is portrayed and I know many more people are concerned about the way the European Union is planning to develop.

I believe there is a growing need to allow everyone in Britain the opportunity without party political influence, to express their wishes to the extent that we will allow the European Union to influence our lives. Hence the need for a Referendum. As a keen supporter of our manufacturing industries, I am convinced that if we are to remain prosperous we must be a member of the European Union. The great debate is what form the Union should take. My view is clear. It should be a <u>union of sovereign independent self governing trading nations</u>, maintaining their own heritage and traditions, but with a common defence and security policy ensured by common NATO style armed forces.

It positively must not be a United States of Europe controlled from Brussels with a common currency and the power to interfere with the lives of people from Finland to Portugal and from Ireland to Greece.

As yet we do not know what will be on the Agenda for the 1996 Inter Governmental Conference, however, if this included items which will establish the sort of European Union we will have well into the next Century, I believe the people of Britain must give their approval to the consequences when their implications are known. I am, therefore, of the view that depending upon the outcome of the 1996 Conference a referendum is essential to allow the country to clearly confirm the sort of Union they will be happy to be a member of in the 21st Century and to confirm how much power, if any, they are prepared to hand to a European Parliament and Government.

Of a more pressing nature, I believe there is a need to hammer out a cohesive party line on this exasperating issue. Undoubtedly a new and different approach is needed to bring us together. May I suggest that we hold a Special One-Day Private (no media) Parliamentary Party Conference in the Spring to include those who do not take the Whip, structured in such a way that brings together our divergent views into a strategy that allows us to go forward in Europe along an agreed route to agreed timings.

I believe this different approach could bear fruit within the Party.

ELIZABETH J PEACOCK

Letter to the Prime Minister expressing my reservations on European Policy.

who basically supported the treaty, decided tactically to vote against the government the Maastricht rebels defeated the government. This then required a vote of confidence the following day to clarify the issue. The government was badly damaged, as this set the scene for constant arguments within the Tory Party.

I was, as usual, in a dilemma on how to vote on the Maastricht Treaty. I did not want to support any further integration with Europe and I thought John Major was beginning to get too close to our European colleagues. However, he had done a good job in negotiating opt-outs for Britain that were beneficial. So on balance I decided to support the government, which I did. The difficulties with this issue were multiplied by John himself in an unguarded moment during an interview with ITN News when he thought the microphones were switched off. Responding to a question from the interviewer Michael Brunton as to why he did not sack the ministers in his government who were opposing his European policy, his reply was along the lines of ' … with a majority of 18 I don't need three more bastards out there!' Somebody leaked the tape to the *Daily Mirror*.

Various names (John Redwood, Peter Lilley and Michael Portillo) were linked with this comment, causing even greater and continuing problems for the party.

Throughout 1994 there were constant heated arguments regarding Europe: about who we should support as president of the European Commission; about qualified majority voting; and a ban on British beef due to 'mad cow' disease. Our Euro-sceptics became so wound up that Tony Marlow MP demanded John's resignation.

The main issue for the remainder of the parliament was whether Britain should join the planned European single currency. Again we were split: Chancellor Ken Clarke and other senior members within government were in favour but a considerable number of members at Westminster and within the party were opposed. I was firmly in the latter camp and would not have supported any move to join the single currency.

The issue remained a thorn in the flesh of the party until the 1997 election when the people of Britain recognized that we had no confirmed policy and this was one of the reasons we lost so heavily. John in my opinion should have taken a more Euro-sceptic stance when some of our openly Euro-sceptic colleagues Tony Marlow, Bill Cash and others allowed their understandable opposition to get out of hand. Even by the next general election in 2001 we still did not have a cohesive policy.

10 DOWNING STREET
LONDON SW1A 2AA

THE PRIME MINISTER

1st February 1995

Dear Elizabeth,

Thank you very much for your letter of 12th January.

I share your concern about the way our policy on Europe is sometimes portrayed. I have said on a number of occasions that it is ridiculous to think in terms of extremes: either one agrees that everything that comes out of Europe is right or dismisses out of hand. I do not stand at either extreme. I believe that Britain must be in Europe, protecting her interests and arguing for the kind of Europe we want: a free trading, prosperous community of nation states.

I made clear the Government's position on the outcome of the Intergovernmental Conference at the beginning of the year. You are right that no one knows what will be on the Conference agenda. I doubt that there will be any proposal for major constitutional change but, should one arise, I would oppose it. If, for some reason which I cannot fathom, such a proposal was passed without our agreement, I would keep the option of a referendum open.

With regard to your idea of a one day seminar on Europe, I am always willing to listen to the views of all those in the Party. I am sure you are aware that Policy Groups are being formed at the moment to gather and discuss policies across the Board, and that will obviously include Europe. I do hope you will take part.

Thank you again for your letter,

Yours Ever,

John

The Prime Ministers reply to my letter.

My View

By 1995 I was convinced that Europe was going to ruin John's government and that he was not sufficiently positive about the issue. He had handled the Maastricht Treaty well but then failed to recognize that Britain does not want European interference in British matters. Consequently we had an exchange of correspondence that I believe illustrates the point that we were a split party and John had got his positioning wrong.

In truth the European question remains unresolved some eighteen years on!

Leadership election

In addition to the problem of European policy, John Major was confronted with a series of scandals that were given the title 'Tory sleaze' that at the time portrayed us as a 'party out of control'. From the distance now of twenty-plus years, they seem less important. By June 1995 John Major had had enough of constant attack from the media and the equally constant attack and threat of a leadership election from the parliamentary/ Conservative Party that never came. He grabbed the initiative and resigned as party leader while remaining prime minister until the consequent leadership election was completed.

I have included a copy of the press statement that John gave in the garden of 10 Downing Street explaining his frustration and disappointment with the party so that the reader may be familiar with John's thinking at the time.

John stood for election again and was challenged by John Redwood who had resigned as Secretary of State for Wales. John Major's win just gave him the confidence to carry on.

When I first heard, from a London taxi driver, that John had resigned, I was shocked and thought we would all be out of work in the next few weeks as both the taxi driver and I had misread what John Major had done.

My View

It takes great strength of character to put your way of life on the line as John did and I greatly admire his strength of resolve to get the party together. It helped within the party for a limited time but did it help the Conservative cause with the people of Britain? Not really. As we were later to learn in the 1997 election, the people, ably assisted by the press, had decided to punish us.

PRESS STATEMENT

I have been deeply involved in politics since I was sixteen. I see public service as a duty. If you can serve, you should do so.

I have now been Prime Minister for nearly five years. In that time, we have achieved a great deal. But for the past three years I have been opposed by a minority. During those years, there have been repeated threats of a leadership election. In each year they turned out to be phoney threats. Now the same thing is happening again in 1995. It is in no one's interests that this continues until November. It undermines the Government and damages the Conservative Party. I am not prepared to see the Party I care for laid out on the rack like this any longer.

To remove this uncertainty, I have this afternoon tendered my resignation as Leader of the Conservative Party to Sir Marcus Fox, the Chairman of the 1922 Committee, and requested him to set the machinery in motion for the election of a successor. I have confirmed to Sir Marcus that I shall be a candidate in that election. If I win, I shall continue as Prime Minister and lead the Party into and through the next General Election. Should I be defeated, which I do not expect, I shall resign as Prime Minister and offer my successor my full support.

The Conservative Party must make its choice. Every leader is leader only with the support of his Party. That is true of me too. That is why I am no longer prepared to tolerate the present situation. In short, it is time to put up or shut up.

Statement made by Prime Minister the Rt. Hon. John Major in The garden at Downing Street. Thursday 22nd. June. 1995.

Conservative misdemeanours

Our cause was eventually completely drowned under a torrent of so-called 'Tory sleaze'; the effects of which were felt throughout the party and the public. To make matters worse, John Major had homed in on a theme and topic of 'Back to Basics' at the 1993 Conservative Party conference with the emphasis on moral and family values and standards. Members of the Party let him down across the board.

The scandals came thick and fast to the delight of the media, the shame of the Party and the disapproval of the nation. David Mellor, a Cabinet Minister, was having an extramarital affair and a series of other members were connected to scandals, including Alan Clark, my old sparring partner, a flamboyant minister who admitted affairs with the wife of a South African judge and his two daughters, then involved in an 'arms to Iraq' embargo.

This was followed by the high-profile 'Cash for Questions' affair involving in some way Graham Riddick, David Tredinnick, Tim Smith and Neil Hamilton with the financier Mohamed Al-Fayed. Furthermore, Defence Minister Jonathan Aitken was accused by the *Guardian* and ITV's *World in Action* of doing secret deals with Saudi Arabia. He took them to court but when winning he was subsequently shown to have committed perjury and eventually served a prison sentence.

This torrent of Conservative misdemeanours drowned the Major government and helped to turn the British public against the Party.

My View

It is now, in retrospect, much easier to put this whole issue of 'Tory sleaze' into context. At the time it was a big issue in the Westminster village and in the press with plenty of editorial comment. This all added to the Conservative problems elsewhere. If we now look at some of these misdemeanours they are no worse nor better than some of the scandalous matters subsequently suffered by the later Blair and Brown administrations with much less public and media disapproval. 'Sleaze' certainly damaged the Tory Party at the time but some of the matters would now be looked at in a different light.

Constituency concerns (1992–97)

As I have made comment on and reviewed each of the three parliaments I spent at Westminster I have noted that people and in particular the local press showed an interest mainly in constituency issues, often with very little concern for central government activities. I have found that many of the so-called important national issues received no local reporting. In some cases I stirred up national issues myself making comment; this I sometimes did deliberately because I needed constituency opinion. For instance, when I demanded that the signs on the M1 motorway near Wakefield should be changed to include Batley, we got acres of press space. We did eventually get the signs changed but it took years. Even taking local Scouts and Guides to tea with the Speaker got more space than the serious politics of the day!

Tory 'rare bird' whose wings they can't clip

In the early 1990s we were looking at our railway system and how it should be structured in the private sector. What would a franchised system look like? Would it be commercially viable?

At about the same time there was a great debate on school standards and in particular testing and measuring of standards and performance that caused plenty of local comment. This remains today, as ever, a question for teachers, parents and Ministers of Education.

The local debate and airing of these issues at meetings, in my surgeries, on the street and in the supermarket was helpful in my decision-making process.

This certainly included Sunday trading and the proposed legislation to remove historical barriers. I was unhappy with the initial 'free-for-all' legislation and voted against, causing the government to have a re-think. This brought forward more balanced legislation. I got a very mixed local reaction to my original vote against and my local press helped my decision-making after the re-think when I voted in favour of Sunday trading.

The second topic that excited great local interest in the media and again assisted my thinking was the question of post offices and the privatization of Royal Mail. At this time there was a major campaign to close post offices and sub post offices that in many cases became emotive and gave me plenty of discussion and campaigning on behalf of users. The other discussion point was a plan put forward by Michael Heseltine to privatize Royal Mail. With some of my fellow MPs I considered his proposal, the conclusion being that we did not like his ideas. My local press once again assisted the opinion-forming process, often with startling headlines such

Cartoon following protests on a possible M1/M62 link road.

Breaking the ground for the Drighlington by-pass with colleagues Merlyn Rees and Bob Cryer.

as: 'Coal rebel fights Heseltine again on post offices.' Enough of us argued with Michael to convince him he could not get it through the House and he abandoned the idea. In retrospect we were wrong: Royal Mail should have been privatized years ago.

True, I did sometimes cause some of the local press comment myself; for example, by urging council-house tenants to get on and purchase their houses. I also got thoroughly involved in the House once again attempting to reintroduce the death penalty for certain offenders.

The question of VAT on domestic fuel and newspapers got a local airing and received some publicity but surprisingly never became a big topic. One issue that did get attention with campaigning was a proposal for a new link road from the M1 near Wakefield to the M62 west of Cleckheaton, cutting through Ann Taylor's Dewsbury constituency and through Batley and Spen. This became a long-running campaign for us all as neither we nor the local media liked the idea.

The big personal and press issue was the Boundary Commission's proposal to re-draw our constituency boundaries by moving the electors in Heckmondwike from Batley and Spen to Dewsbury. I did not like this idea as it looked terminal for my small majority, virtually handing this seat to Labour. Locally the media had gained a red tinge but played the proposal down the middle when they discovered that the Peacock family was prepared to have a barrister argue against the proposition in court when the Conservative Party could not achieve a common front.

All the way through the scrapbooks covering my fourteen years in office, three topics appear in some guise: law and order; industry, particularly wool textiles; and Pro-Life/abortion matters that are dealt with elsewhere.

Chapter 24

The Irish Threat

Margaret Thatcher, John Major, and me in a small way
The threat of Irish terrorism had a significant part to play through the Thatcher and Major premierships, both at a personal and national level. At the personal level this threat must have had an influence, not just on the workload but also on their own lifestyles. This is an aspect that I became fully acquainted with through my own limited experience of a terrorist threat.

I will not go into details of all the acts of terrorism inflicted on the British people during this period but there are certain incidents that should be noted and commented upon. Throughout these years tremendous political efforts were being made to find a solution to this long-standing issue.

A terrorist outrage perpetrated before she became leader had a significant impact on Margaret Thatcher. That was the death of her great friend and supporter Airey Neave in 1979, caused by a car bomb. Airey Neave was a man of action with an impressive following and a high profile as a war hero who had escaped from Colditz where he had suffered greatly in the Second World War. After the war he became a barrister in the same Chambers as Margaret Thatcher and was one of her neighbours in Westminster Gardens. He was elected MP for Abingdon being briefly a junior minister in the Heath government but resigned due to poor health. As an alternative he became Chairman of the Select Committee on Science and Technology. Thus as a neighbour and barrister with a positive interest in science, he and Margaret became firm friends.

Airey was her manager in Margaret's campaign to become party leader and when she was successful he became head of her private office and subsequently Shadow Secretary of State for Northern Ireland. This would presumably have led to a ministerial position in the future government, clearly making him a target for Irish terrorists.

On 30 March 1979 his car was blown up by a bomb that exploded as he drove up the ramp from the House of Commons car park. The bomb had been planted in his car by the Irish National Liberation Army, a breakaway unit from the IRA. The bomb, detonated by a mercury-level switch, wrecked the car and blew both his legs off. Airey Neave died in hospital shortly after arriving there. Margaret Thatcher was very seriously upset by Airey's death. As she paid tribute to his memory, little did she know that regrettably she was to lose other friends during her premiership to terrorist acts by the IRA or its splinter organizations. These organizations became a constant threat throughout her years in office and to John Major and other Prime Ministers.

Clearly Margaret Thatcher became a target for terrorism from an early date, being attacked in October 1984 during the Conservative Party Conference by the planting of a bomb by the Provisional IRA at the Grand Hotel, Brighton. This act had the objective of assassinating the Prime Minister and members of the Cabinet who were using the hotel for the conference and it very nearly succeeded.

During September Patrick Magee, a member of the Provisional IRA staying at the hotel, planted a long-delay time bomb in one of the best bedrooms, likely to be used by a senior Conservative. At 2.54 am on 12 October 1984 the bomb exploded, badly damaging the bathroom of Margaret Thatcher's suite where she was busy writing her conference speech. By some miracle she and her husband Denis escaped injury, though they were badly shocked. They were eventually escorted from the building and spent the rest of the night in Sussex Police Headquarters in Lewes where Margaret decided the conference must go on, despite the injuries and loss of life.

Five people had been killed and thirty-four taken to hospital with injuries, some very serious. Those killed were Roberta Wakeham, wife of the Parliamentary Treasury Secretary John Wakeham; Sir Anthony Berry MP; Eric Taylor; Lady Jeanne Shattock; and Lady Muriel Maclean in whose room the bomb exploded (her husband Sir Donald Maclean, though badly injured, did recover). Among those seriously injured was Margaret Tebbit, wife of Norman Tebbit, then President of the Board of Trade, who was disabled for life. Many of those who were injured including the Tebbits had to be cut from the wrecked building by the fire brigade. This took many hours during which time many received medical assistance from the eminent surgeon Dr David Skidmore who volunteered to go into the building to help. I had become one of David's friends when he was the

Conservative candidate for Stockport while I was training to be a Conservative agent. I had great admiration for David anyway but more so when he volunteered for the dangerous task of providing medical help in an unstable building with the possibility of a further bomb.

Like the rest of the world I was shocked by the atrocity, particularly as I had been in the Grand Hotel the previous day until 7.00pm. I had left at this time to go to Australia and New Zealand with the House of Commons Employment Select Committee together with Gerry Neale MP.

The Thatcher determination not to be derailed by anyone or any incident came to the surface following the bombing. She insisted that the conference open on time the following day despite the lives that had been lost and the disruption caused, and it did.

The Thatcher message was positive: 'We will not be driven off course by anyone.' Clearly the Brighton bomb had an influence on the lives of all the people involved, including John Wakeham for the loss of his wife and Norman Tebbit for the lifelong disability of his. It had a significant part to play in the lives of many others, especially those who were injured. Walter Clegg MP for Wyre, a good Northern colleague of mine in the House, was badly injured by the blast and I do not believe he ever fully recovered. He was still a great character but for the last ten years of his life he seemed never to be the old 'Wally' that we knew.

In truth the Irish question or 'the Troubles' was a problem throughout the Thatcher era with regular acts of violence in Northern Ireland and across Britain. Attempts were made to devolve power of government to Northern Ireland to involve all shades of opinion in the community. This was progressed by Anglo-Irish agreements with the government in Dublin to provide balance. Limited progress was made and such progress that was achieved was impeded by the hunger strikes of political prisoners led by Bobby Sands.

Clearly at that time the various parties were not ready to talk and move towards a solution. The Thatcher government put in plenty of effort but got little in return, other than more acts of violence on the British mainland. These included a bomb in Harrods, a blast at the Royal Marines School of Music that killed ten bandsmen, and a device at the Carlton Club in St James that injured four people, one being Sir Donald Kaberry, our colleague from Yorkshire. Like Walter Clegg, Donald was badly shaken and never seemed as lively and punchy as he had been before the incident. These violent acts included the assassination of another of Margaret's friends and supporters: Ian Gow MP for Eastbourne who had held various ministerial positions in Thatcher governments. He was killed by a car bomb outside his home.

Real progress towards a solution was never achieved in the Thatcher era despite plenty of effort as no one seemed ready to talk.

John Major and the 'Irish Problem'

When he became Prime Minister, John Major had little experience of Northern Ireland and its issues. He had rarely travelled to or visited Northern Ireland and the portfolios he had held to date did not bring him into contact with the detail of the issues involved. This was to change in his premiership and it became his most regular domestic visiting destination. He realized at the outset that something different had to be tried. Too many initiatives had failed in the past: the Whitelaw talks (1972), Ted Heath's Sunningdale deal (1973), John Prior's Assembly (1982), and Margaret Thatcher's Anglo-Irish Agreement (1985).

When John took over the reins in 1990 he left Peter Brooke in place as Northern Ireland Secretary as Peter was putting all his efforts into finding a solution. With great skill he brought together the Ulster Unionists, the DUP, the SDLP and the Alliance party with the Irish government to search for a solution using a three-stranded approach to establish a Main Assembly. By the time of the 1992 election, Peter Brooke was in need of a rest so John appointed the very competent Paddy (Patrick) Mayhew to the post. Using his strong personality and commanding presence, Paddy picked up the three-stranded approach introduced initially by Peter. With the aid of his wife Jean he made their official home, Hillsborough Castle, a place of welcome to the parties involved. Paddy was a great supporter of my activities in Yorkshire, visiting us on several occasions. Each time upon reaching Wakefield we had to stop to collect meat pies from Hoffmans. Being a very good lawyer he was keen to see others succeed and gave good advice to our eldest son Jonathan, then a junior barrister.

As I cover this topic, I have come to the conclusion that while Tony Blair has quite rightly been given the plaudits for solving the Northern Ireland issue, the background was laid out for him by Paddy Mayhew and John Major. Paddy has not been given the thanks he is due for the sterling work he did in trying circumstances. From his own autobiography we learn that the British government and the IRA had found some dialogue to progress grounds for negotiation after John became Prime Minister. However, this did not prevent Irish terrorists from attempting to kill John and his Cabinet with a rocket attack on Downing Street in February 1991.

On the day in question the full Cabinet meeting had been delayed to allow a meeting on Kuwait to take place, chaired by John and with a good number of Cabinet members present. Suddenly there was a tremendous explosion in the garden outside the Cabinet room window. The windows buckled and everyone took cover, some under the table. It soon became clear that the IRA had launched three mortars from a stolen van parked in Whitehall near the Ministry of Defence. Luckily nobody was hurt. Once again Irish terrorists had attacked at the heart of British government with the objective of killing the Prime Minister of the day, his Cabinet and their officials. I remember the noise to this day as I worked in my office some 300 yards away. I cannot imagine what it was like in Downing Street.

Like Margaret Thatcher after the Brighton bomb, John resolved that as nobody was hurt and regardless of any damage the Cabinet would meet at 11.00am as planned, thus preventing the IRA claiming a propaganda victory. For the remainder of his premiership making progress in Northern Ireland became a priority. John's Downing Street Declaration issued jointly with Albert Reynolds, Prime Minister of the Republic of Ireland, looked as though it would make progress. However, Sinn Fein on behalf of the Republicans asked for clarification of the terms. Regrettably it was opposed by Ian Paisley and made no great progress. Suddenly there was a chink of light when the Provisional IRA announced a temporary cessation of hostilities for three days at Easter of 1994 that was followed in August by a formal 'cessation of military operations'. This led to demands for a permanent 'peace process' aided by an intervention from US President Bill Clinton on a visit to Belfast.

The grounds for the eventual 'peace settlement' achieved by Tony Blair were laid down by the 'International Body on Arms Decommissioning' (the Mitchell Report) set up by John Major. This laid down the rules for decommissioning and talks to agree an effective election process involving all parties concerned. Again the Unionists could not agree and terrorism continued in Northern Ireland and elsewhere. The Major government continued to search for a solution, which Tony Blair went on to achieve using Paddy Mayhew's sterling work.

My interest
How did I get involved with the Irish terrorist threat? Undoubtedly due to my outspoken approach and straight talking.

I suppose I had three brushes with Irish terrorism, if I count the fact that I was in the Grand Hotel in Brighton on the evening prior to the bomb exploding during the night. Many others had the same experience I know but it brings home the fact that it is impossible to know when this sort of attack is likely to occur. Having had this passing experience it remains with you for years, particularly when you knew the people involved in the incident as I did.

My first brush with Irish terrorism occurred in July 1989 when a constituent of mine, a soldier serving in Germany, was assassinated by the IRA for no known reason. He was off duty and with his family began to get into his car when it blew up. He was killed instantly but luckily his family escaped with injuries and lived. He was a member of the well-known Smith family from Cleckheaton who were my constituents.

I was interviewed by the press, making very positive statements about the need to have the death penalty available for murder and in particular for acts of terrorism. I now remember my exact words. I said that I thought the IRA were evil bastards to inflict such terrible tragedy on one family and I hoped they could be caught and that they should then be hanged forthwith!

This issue continued for some time as his family decided they wished to return from Germany to West Yorkshire, so I got involved in helping to arrange the move. For some reason that I never knew, Special Branch indicated that his wife and children could be in danger of further attack; consequently they had to return to a secret address in Yorkshire. Again vigorously I attacked this need in the press, which then caused Special Branch to warn me that I had annoyed the IRA and should take security precautions myself at home and they would monitor my surgery meeting-places. This entailed additional security lights around my home, some barbed wire on fencing and large drive gates, together with mirrors on sticks to inspect the underside of our car for bombs! As a family we got into a security routine but it all seemed futile and unnecessary. All I was doing was looking after the interests of my constituents. Maybe there was a link with this affair and my further brush with the IRA. I will never know.

Some years later in 1996 we were still suffering from the threat of Irish terrorism with attempts being made to bring Sinn Fein, the political wing of the IRA, into the political scene to find a solution. Sinn Fein members had been elected to the House of Commons as MPs for Irish constituencies since the 1920s but as a matter of principle abstained from taking their seats. Despite this, they or their colleagues were regularly invited into the House by interested Members of Parliament for discussions. On one

Question to the Prime Minister on Irish Issues, 1996.

occasion in 1996 Ken Livingstone, then a Member of Parliament, invited three Sinn Fein members into the House but for some reason left them to wander around the House alone. In a period full of terrorist attacks or threats this was considered a serious breach of security, being picked up by the *Independent* newspaper in the following day's edition with a front-page headline: 'IRA Army Council Members in House of Commons.'

On this particular day, I had Question No 1 to the Prime Minister. Question No 1 is, by tradition, expected to be topical and of wide interest to the country. That morning I reviewed the newspapers for the question and concluded that the IRA Army Council at Westminster was the best option so I went into the Chamber armed with a copy of the *Independent*. When the Speaker called, I waved the *Independent* and asked John Major the question. The exchange was as recorded by Hansard:

> **Mrs Peacock:** Is my right hon. Friend aware of the report in today's issue of the *Independent* which states that, yesterday, three members

of the IRA's Army Council were brought to the House of Commons by Labour Members? Is he aware that one of them was allowed to wander around for twenty minutes unaccompanied? Will he please instigate an immediate investigation?

The Prime Minister: I understand that my right hon. Friend the Leader of the House has written to Madam Speaker about the incident. My understanding is that those representatives of Sinn Fein were invited to the House to meet a number of hon. Members, that no prior notification about the meeting was given and that the representatives were, from time to time, left unattended. I do not know what the outcome of the inquiry will be, but I think that it is stunning naivety on the part of any hon. Member not to realise the connection between Sinn Fein and the IRA.

This all seems rather simple today in retrospect but it excited the press at this time when Irish terrorist issues were raised. As I came out of the Chamber I was grabbed by the press for further comment; would I give an interview and take part in a programme for BBC London? This I agreed to do and made similar comments about the IRA Army Council being in the House of Commons.

By tradition I had no problem making these sorts of statements in the House as I was legally covered by parliamentary privilege. However, this did not cover me outside the House and certainly not on BBC radio. I do not now recall my exact words on radio but they linked the individuals in the House of Commons with the IRA Army Council as the *Independent* newspaper had claimed. Even though no names were mentioned by me I clearly caused them some concerns as about two weeks later I received a letter from an East London firm of solicitors acting for Sinn Fein, claiming that my words on radio had libelled their clients as IRA Army Council Members and demanding damages. The BBC received a similar letter, as did the *Independent* for their original publication.

As my sons and daughters-in-law are all lawyers I asked for advice and as often happens with lawyers I got a variety of opinions, albeit with the theme: 'You need a proper libel lawyer, this could be a problem.' Luckily one of my colleagues in the House looked at the details, advising that I allow the BBC to handle the issue and inform Special Branch of the facts, which I did. However, during the two to three weeks it took to consider the matter and respond I had a frightening experience one evening.

I was using my husband's Mercedes to go to a school prize-giving event in Heckmondwike and returned home on a dark and rainy night at about 10.00pm. I stopped the car outside our large gates that were then locked with a padlock and chain. As I was unlocking the gate, a car shot out of the farm lane some 30 yards from my gate with its headlights on full beam. As it passed there was a loud 'popping' noise and the rear window of the car totally disintegrated onto the back seat. The offending car disappeared through the village at very high speed. I eventually got the gate open and drove the damaged car into the drive just as my husband was opening the front door and I shouted that I had been shot at.

He instantly rang the police who responded very quickly by closing local roads south of Wakefield. The police came at once to inspect the car, decided it had to be taken away for forensic analysis and arranged for it to be collected on a trailer. The next morning George Lane in Notton was closed for some time to allow the police to do a detailed finger search on the road. After some days of analysis but with nobody stopped and no sign of a bullet in the car or on the road, the view was that someone had decided to frighten me on the libel challenge and had deliberately shot at my car window with a high-velocity air rifle. Was it a Sinn Fein/IRA sympathizer? We will never know but it certainly was a very frightening experience at the time, particularly in view of the events of the 1980s.

Months later the BBC and the *Independent* settled the libel damages and claims with a payment including the claim on me. The details of the settlement were confidential and remain so today.

I was once again advised to step up my security which was almost impossible and eventually unnecessary.

My View
Both Prime Ministers Margaret Thatcher and John Major and other Prime Ministers before and since were faced with a dual challenge from Irish terrorism: they had the pressure of personal safety and the responsibility of trying to find a solution to the threat with its many-sided aspects. They are all to be admired for their courage and endeavour.

In my more limited case I became involved because I took high-profile stances and used the sort of language that described my outrage and that of my constituents, regardless of the fact that it irritated terrorist organizations. I would not change my stance!

Chapter 25

Characters in the Commons
III

There are several groups of people within the Palace of Westminster that provide the backbone of the institution. Of course the permanent staff; the police, catering teams and the officers run the organization but other groups provide the atmosphere. The media men and women record and tell the story; the lawyers provide the expertise; and the party whips attempt to keep the troops in order, voting in the right lobby!

Media men
MPs welcome a good news story or hate the publicity if it is bad news.

As would be expected, there are always plenty of media men and women around Westminster but there are some who stand out from the crowd. During my years in the House I was involved with many of these very professional people and I built up an understanding and working relationship with them and the way they work to report the activities of the government, the House and Members of Parliament.

Westminster is often referred to as the 'Westminster village' because of the close working environment of all those involved. There was always a danger that some issues seemed of great importance within 'the village' but were of little or no interest to the British public. This is where the experience of the media boys and girls comes into play, as they can usually analyze the topic and decide whether the story will run and be worth reporting. In their terms, will the story 'have legs'?

When making a selection of media people to highlight I have too much choice, not only from among those with whom I worked but also from the ranks of the many with whom I never worked but who are, or were, true House of Commons characters in their own right.

Almost all MPs can write a decent report or contribution to their local paper. If they have difficulty when they are first elected, they soon learn. However, among their ranks are the real professionals who can describe the issues of the day with well-chosen prose and infinite detail. This is a skill honed by many while in the House and that blossoms when they move on, often to better and greater things. Many of these talented people qualify as exceptional characters around the House and I am happy to pay homage to the power of their pens.

Two of my former colleagues from the 1983 Thatcher brigade displayed journalistic potential during their political adventure in the Commons and have since gone on to make a name for themselves in the media. They have, however, built on their experiences as members to provide informed views and opinions on the Westminster scene. These are Matthew Parris and Michael Brown.

They were 'characters in the Commons' in the sense that they were honing their contacts and experience to become future able communicators. As Winston Churchill Senior and Junior found, journalism is a useful activity to combine with a political career and this they both did with great skill.

Sir Bernard Ingham

As I am homing in on the importance of my Yorkshire roots, I have to start by cheating slightly, beginning my comments with a Yorkshire man who was never in the Commons but played a significant part in the media as press secretary to Margaret Thatcher. I refer, of course, to Sir Bernard Ingham. Bernard is a typical down-to-earth Yorkshire man with exactly the sort of experience and background to stand no nonsense. He is well-organized, well-read and an interesting person to know but is still quite capable of smoothly putting idiots in their place. A Yorkshire grammar school education followed by an apprenticeship in the Yorkshire media, the *Hebden Bridge Times*, the *Yorkshire Evening Post* and *Yorkshire Post*, should set up any young man for life in the world of journalism and it did just that for Bernard. A period of sophistication with the *Guardian* and a spell with the Labour Party and union movement provided the balance to advise any politician, let alone the Prime Minister. I cannot remember when I first met Bernard but it must have been in my early days when he had taken up the role of Chief Press Officer to Margaret Thatcher. At that time I must have been a 'new girl' on the large political scene but we understood each other from day one. He was a straightforward Yorkshire man with a job to do for the Prime Minister and I was a Yorkshire woman with an independent streak who would knock the bowling around if I thought it necessary for Yorkshire and Batley and Spen.

Over the years, Bernard has obviously migrated from the left wing of the union world to the right wing of the independent-thinking tendency. I have moved without losing my roots from a poor family background to a world not of privilege but of entrepreneurial right-wing politics driven by common sense. The tall bushy-eyebrowed Yorkshire man with a commonsense approach to politics has to be my media idol. I can fully understand why the positive Margaret Thatcher could work with Bernard and how he could give her sound advice on the whole gambit of British life. He just has to be included in my characters in the Commons, where he had influence but never served as a member.

For ease of reference, the remainder of this section of 'characters' appears in alphabetical order:

Michael Brown

Michael Brown was first elected in 1979 for the marginal seat of Brigg and Scunthorpe and was re-elected in 1983 for the new Brigg and Cleethorpes seat. On entering Parliament he had quickly established his ability to communicate. However, with a marginal Northern seat similar to Batley and Spen I always assumed he was looking over his shoulder as to where he would go next. Like Matthew Parris, he has harnessed his writing skills to beat out a career as a leading political journalist and pundit as the parliamentary correspondent for the *Independent*.

Michael studied law at York University and Middle Temple and got into politics as a researcher for MPs Michael Marshall and Nicholas Winterton. Once in the House he made progress as a PPS in Trade and Industry, the Foreign and Commonwealth Office and in Northern Ireland, and then achieved the doubtful role of assistant government whip. Like many others he lost his position in 1997, needed something to do and found life difficult as good opportunities for former MPs are rare. Michael is bright and knows the political scene and can get along with people across the political spectrum.

For some years now he has held the position of political sketch writer for the *Independent* and regularly appears as a political pundit on BBC and Sky News programmes. I have always admired Michael Brown's style – probably due to his, to coin a phrase, independent approach to issues, not being wedded to the Conservative path – an independent mind that I can understand. Like Matthew Parris, he has not hidden his homosexuality;

tsomething that I may not understand but I do recognize his openness and bravery in making this public.

His articles in the *Independent* are always worth a read!

Nick Budgen

I include Nick under the media banner but he could equally qualify as a lawyer as he was a well-respected barrister (and farmer) MP for Wolverhampton South West. As a political sideline he wrote a column for various newspapers and became a character around the House because he could never decide the topic or get down to writing until an hour before his deadline. When I had an office along the Embankment in Norman Shaw North it took too long to get to the lobby for votes so in the evenings I worked in the library where Nick stationed himself for writing. Regularly he would bounce ideas off me for his column but was never satisfied with my answers and often became frustrated, saying: 'Elizabeth, how could you have produced two brilliant barrister sons like yours?' My initial answer was: 'Their father brings the brains and I bring the good looks!'

However, on the second or third (albeit friendly) attack, I too became frustrated and replied: 'Nick, how can someone as bright as you write such bloody awful rubbish in your columns?'

We had boxed a draw!

Conal Gregory

I would add Conal Gregory to my list of former colleagues (York 1983) who were characters in the House and who have built on this experience to hammer out a media career. Conal has taken a slightly different approach, building on his business and financial interest to write an interesting column for the *Yorkshire Post* on Saturdays. During his time at Westminster, Conal was always full of life and activity.

Roy Hattersley

I could not compile this limited sketch of media characters in the Commons without commenting on a fellow Yorkshire native who has achieved more in the political area than I shall ever aspire to and who should be noted as a linchpin in the socialist movement covering the past fifty years. I refer to Roy (now Lord) Hattersley, noting that I am finding as time moves on, maybe his dog became just as famous as his master.

True, Roy and I do not know each other well. I know him as the guiding hand of the Labour Party in the Commons and a character to be noted.

He probably knew me as that upstart of a woman who luckily won the Labour seat of Batley and Spen and who kept on winning (until 1997).

Roy, having been Secretary of State for Prices and Consumer Protection, Shadow Chancellor, Home Secretary and deputy leader of the Labour Party, knows his way around the Westminster village and can translate the issues of the day for a wide audience as an experienced author and journalist. Like many ambitious young men, with a Sheffield Grammar School and Hull University education Roy had a determination to become an MP, and this he achieved for Birmingham (Sparkbrook) in 1964.

Roy has long been recognized as being on the right of the party which probably explains why Labour were slow to use his talent. Also he entered the House in a period of Tory domination but being in opposition this gave him the time and incentive to develop a journalistic skill and career prior to his important roles in the Labour Party including that of deputy leader.

By his skills of authorship his somewhat wayward dog Buster who killed a goose in a Royal Park and then through Roy's pen claimed self-defence became as well-known as his master. As a leading politician Roy was in my day a character in the Commons, albeit somewhat 'peckish' and less of a Rottweiler than the late Buster. He continues as a character around the 'village' from the Lords.

Chris Moncrieff

My next media character in the Commons also fails to qualify as a member of the House but he has been in and around the Westminster scene for so many years that he appears more important than many of the statues of the long-forgotten politicians littered about the building. He was around in my fourteen years and many more before and since, having seen off seven Prime Ministers during his tenure: Chris Moncrieff, long-time Political Editor of the Press Association and then a freelance journalist with a bar named after him in the House of Commons. It has been said that he has been involved with the House so long that he should be recorded within the accounts of the Palace as 'an asset with no depreciation'. Chris, who I always found helpful to a Yorkshire lass while unfortunately being born in Derbyshire, spent some of his early life in Yorkshire learning his trade as a reporter in the better end of the county, Harrogate. Stories about Chris and his activities in his heavy drinking days to his teetotal stance of the last thirty years are well told in the House. However, he is a real professional with an ability to tell the story as it is: no flannel, just straightforward reporting!

I got this message loud and clear when I worked with him on various issues. If I had been a nuisance to government by rebelling in a vote he was good at getting to the core of my objection to the government proposals. I am happy to note that my friends agree with me on the importance of Chris Moncrieff in the House of Commons. Nick Winterton (Sir Nicholas) said: 'To me, the best journalist in this place is the oldest: Chris Moncrieff. You tell him something and he reports it; he is the straightest man you could ever come across.' I agree with my friend; if I wanted to tell a story, the most reliable way was to tell it to Chris. This reliability was recognized at the highest level by Mrs Thatcher who made him a CBE.

Once Enoch Powell agreed to be interviewed by Chris and while Chris was awaiting Enoch's arrival he put his socks in the local launderette and then had to interview the great man minus his socks as he had forgotten to collect them. I should have recognized Chris as maybe the character of the Commons, not only for his journalistic professionalism but also for his appearance. His trousers were always at least two sizes too wide and too long. It was said that his wife bought his trousers and other clothes from a charity shop and could never remember his size. It must be true.

Matthew Parris

Matthew is South African-born with a colonial background of Zimbabwe, Cyprus, Swaziland and Jamaica, supplemented by a Cambridge law degree (another lawyer!), followed by a spell with the Foreign and Commonwealth Office. He then decided he wanted to become an MP and did so for West Derbyshire (1979), beating future ministers Peter Lilley and Michael Howard for the nomination, when presently employed as Mrs Thatcher's correspondence secretary. He was soon recognized as someone with communication talent.

I found he was a good man to know as he was at the hub of the party communication process and his information could be relied upon. His political connections and his talent were recognized outside the House when he resigned his seat to become presenter of the ITV current affairs programme *Weekend World* and joined *The Times*.

During his career as an MP Matthew had supported gay rights and openly confirmed his homosexuality in a late-night Commons debate and in his newspaper columns.

It is probably true to say that with his knowledge and understanding of the political machine and his ability to communicate, he came to have influence through his columns in *The Times* and *Spectator*. In his position as parliamentary sketch writer for *The Times* he had some influence on MPs with his observant, funny and even caustic, critical comments about members' appearance, garb and behaviour.

On occasions I suffered from his pen, albeit in good faith. On one occasion he 'took the rise' out of the hat I wore for the State Opening of Parliament, describing it with humour. His successful move away from Westminster confirms that for someone with talent and character, there is a life after politics!

Woodrow Wyatt

There is a recognized tendency for certain people to move across the political spectrum during their careers, normally from left to right. This appears to have been true of Sir Bernard Ingham who was a Labour Party member and now holds right-wing views, and Matthew Parris who moved as a student from Liberal to Tory. Similarly Woodrow Wyatt moved from the left as a Labour Member of Parliament for Birmingham Acton (1945) and a junior minister in the 1951 Attlee government to an admirer of Margaret Thatcher and a supporter of many of her policies.

It was later when I got to know him well and admired his style. As well as being an experienced politician, author, journalist and broadcaster he certainly had lots of style. He was considered by many as a man of firm convictions and by others as a maverick not suited to permanently keeping to the party line. Maybe it was this independent tendency that I found stimulating. In or out of Parliament, Woodrow was an accomplished journalist whose column in the *News of the World* regularly supported the Thatcher line, attracting attention and attack from the left. By the mid 1980s he had become something of a 'fixer' with the unions, brokering negotiations with the electricians' union and assisting with the Murdoch News International move to Wapping.

During the miners' strike and the mine closure dispute he yet again got involved in an advisory role as he was trusted by both sides of the argument. It was in this area that I got involved with him, holding several meetings with mining interests and in particular working with miners' wives.

Woodrow summarized his maverick career with his posthumously publicized indiscreet and candid diaries that are worth reading, even though my former colleague, the equally prolific historian and writer Robert Rhodes James MP for Cambridge advised 'caution in believing the diaries in modern times'. Although I only worked with Woodrow for a very short time, he was indeed a great character.

Lawyers

My survey of characters in the Commons would not be complete if I did not make some comment on the smart men of politics: the lawyers.

Someone once said to me there are too many lawyers in politics, there are too many lawyers in the House of Commons; avoid them, they are just too smart. This I have never achieved; I have found them to be the really clever chaps who are often helpful. I have some personal difficulty in ignoring lawyers, having two sons who are both QCs, one daughter-in-law who is a solicitor and another who is a barrister. Consequently I have never attempted to avoid the lawyers in the House; nor would I wish to as some were real characters!

I start with my late friend and sparring partner, the notorious and outrageous Nicholas Fairbairn:

Nicholas 'Nicky' Fairbairn (Sir Nicholas)

The tea room in the House of Commons has always been a place for socializing and the exchange of ideas and views. It comes into its own in the afternoons after the major debates have got under way in the Chamber. It is a more suitable place for a woman to visit than the bars, which can get a bit tough at times. In my years in the House I found it a good place to visit from time to time, particularly if I needed a view from a member of an opposing party.

The tea room always has its 'habitees' and among these were to be found many interesting people including the notorious and colourful character Nicky Fairbairn; colourful both in turn of phrase and appearance, usually wearing dramatic highland trews designed by himself. Nicky, the Member for Perth and Kinross, was at home in the tea room or smoking room being well known as an advocate, wit and raconteur. Having made his name as a successful Scottish defence lawyer in noteworthy trials and Solicitor General for Scotland before he came to Westminster, his skills of speaking and storytelling were well known and admired.

For years he was considered the 'enfant terrible' of the Scottish bar, being a conspicuous champion of permissiveness in Edinburgh and getting himself into a series of scrapes and 'adventures'. Thus he brought his reputation to Westminster, becoming a recognized raconteur of 'blue' stories. He initially tried to shock me but being broadminded I overcame the problem. I soon discovered that if he saw me approaching, the story became suddenly 'bluer' to see if he could embarrass me. It took some time before he realized he could not win; I just ignored the story until he finished and then opened a sensible conversation. It took him months to get the message!

I did, however, have some fun at his expense. One weekend I went to Gleneagles in Scotland to speak at the annual dinner of the National Bed Federation and having changed for dinner went into the cocktail bar where guests were to have a pre-dinner drink. As I arrived in the room there was great shout from the bar that I recognized as coming from the notorious Nicky Fairbairn: 'What are you doing in my bloody constituency?' When I told him I was speaking he then asked (with special whisky-driven adjectives): 'What are you doing addressing a meeting in my patch? Don't you know that no MP visits my constituency without my knowledge and no woman can speak at a meeting in my patch before I have bedded her?!!' Well, of course, this loud outburst brought the conversation in the large room to a complete halt. Luckily I had the wit to reply instantly: 'Well Nicky, I am speaking in ten minutes; we'd better do the "bed" bit now as there are plenty of beds around, but can you perform in time in your state of intoxication?'

This, of course, brought the house down and caused much merriment for days in the bedding industry. Having then introduced the notorious local MP to the delegates, I got a free drink from Nicky which was rare. After making my speech I had the need for the 'Ladies' and followed what I thought was a skirt through a door, only to find I had followed a kilt and was in the gents' loo! Oh dear.

Sir Nicholas died in 1995, far too young for a man with his combined abilities for serious endeavour and flamboyance.

I now move from the outrageous to the equally talented but more stable Ivan Lawrence (Sir Ivan):

Ivan Lawrence (Sir)

Ivan made an impact in the House of Commons, not just as an MP for Burton-on-Trent but for his ability to understand the needs of the law and his great ability to speak at length on an issue of little substance. His ability was transferred to his storytelling! Ivan was particularly helpful as a guiding hand when I was first elected and I thank him for his support.

Speaking to him recently, when discussing his latest book on his experience in law and politics he said: 'I now understand the maxim "You need to watch who you tread on as you move up the greasy pole of a career, because you are likely to meet them again on the way down."' He gives a good example of this. When Michael Howard was Leader of the Conservative Party Ivan went to see him each week, as a friend, to put him in touch with back-bench opinion. I quote: 'On the way in I always ignored the teaboy/scribbler in the outer office. Now when the teaboy/scribbler comes into the room he totally ignores me – he is Prime Minister Cameron – serves me right!'

Two lawyers come to mind for the important parts they played in the Thatcher government and who should be recognized for the manner in which they worked as part of the team:

Peter Rees (late Lord Rees)

Peter had made his name and reputation as a leading tax barrister before he came into the House. Once established, he took on the role of Chief Secretary to the Treasury as the financial brains in the Thatcher treasury team. He qualifies as a 'character' in my view because he, like many lawyers, was a true gentleman. I knew him well as our eldest son, Jonathan, shared a room in Chambers with Peter as a newly-qualified barrister.

Sir Patrick Mayhew

Like many skilled lawyers Paddy Mayhew, as he was usually known, could pick up issues and challenges without hesitation; this he demonstrated with the herculean role of Northern Ireland Secretary. This he undertook when we were faced by the ongoing threat of Irish terrorism, not only in Northern Ireland but also on the mainland. Paddy, ably assisted by his wife, made a real impact on the Irish question, getting to grips with the various and often competing terrorist organizations. As stated before, I think it can be said that he laid down the foundations for the decisions and compromise that were eventually progressed with success by the Major and Blair governments. True, he was not the one who made the eventual breakthrough but he made it possible and so he deserves recognition for this work. Among all this pressure he was always a colleague who would give support. He visited Batley and Spen on several occasions and always had to stop in Wakefield to buy Hoffman's meat pies!

On a personal basis he helped and took an interest in the development of our two barrister sons, wanting detailed reports on their progress.

Kenneth Clarke

I don't really need to include Ken Clarke in my lot of 'characters' because most of the nation recognizes him as a leading political figure of the era; a tenure he has extended long after my days at Westminster. Like his lawyer friends, he has demonstrated a talent for picking up a political brief across the whole spectrum of government and turning it into a success, taking with him along the way the Great British public. This ability is unique as he can make unpopular decisions acceptable to the nation as people like his style and trust him.

I have never worked with Ken, who I understand can be frustrating when he does not get round to reading the papers. However, we have one thing in common: a liking for traditional jazz. During our long day and night sessions a little party would sometimes escape from the House of Commons to Ronnie Scott's club to listen to jazz for an hour or so. Ken was always at the forefront and received a great reception at the club, not only from Ronnie himself but the musicians and members too.

Ken is a man of true political skill who I am sure would (and should) have been leader of the Conservative Party (and Prime Minister) if not for his deeply-held but misguided views on the position of Britain in Europe. I forgive him for this defect as he must be Britain's leading jazz guru!

Michael Howard

Michael is one of my contemporaries who were elected in 1983. He always appeared, in a pleasant way, somewhat different to the rest of us. He was a leading lawyer who had developed a successful career, now wanted a change and had picked up the challenge of politics. We soon recognized that Michael would not be on the back bench for very long as he was destined to take a role in government. He had the talent and skills with the appropriate style to lead the party (as he eventually did). From time to time someone new arrives at Westminster and it is very clear that they are going to lead. Michael, who was always friendly and approachable, was that person and it was not too long before he was given his first post in government, just as several of us had predicted. His progress was then onwards and upwards but he remained supportive of those from his initial circle of friends.

In my case he visited Batley and Spen on several occasions. I distinctly remember when he visited to speak at one of our Patrons' dinners when he was Home Secretary. As it was a late-finishing dinner, he agreed to stay at our home in Notton, near Wakefield. I had always known about the security surrounding a Home Secretary but I did not appreciate the detail. On the day before his arrival our home was thoroughly searched by the bomb-squad beagles and our garage was turned, using summerhouse furniture, into a command post for the four policemen who were to guard him during the night on a rota, two on duty and two in the garage.

On arrival Michael introduced himself to the policemen who were from the local team. During his visit he spotted my husband's Lotus Elan which interested him as he had at an earlier date owned a similar vehicle. Hence four policemen, the Home Secretary and husband Brian discussed the attributes of the Lotus that had been specially prepared for racing; all much more interesting on a Friday night at approaching midnight than boring politics! As we all eventually went off to bed I said naively to one of the policemen: 'I think I need to put the burglar alarm on.' He looked at me and laughed, saying: 'Mrs Peacock, I don't think so, with four policemen guarding all night.' I did feel rather silly!

Michael's final visit to Batley and Spen in my day was during the 1997 election when he came to support me and my son Jonathan who was busy campaigning as Conservative candidate for Wakefield. The three of us had a photograph taken under the Parliament Street sign near Wakefield Westgate Station; all rather unhelpful in the end as we both lost.

Tony Beaumont-Dark (Sir Anthony)
Tony Beaumont-Dark, Member of Parliament for Birmingham Selly Oak from 1979 to 1992, was truly one of the great characters in the House, something I soon recognized when I arrived in 1983.

Tony was not a lawyer but a stockbroker and I just had to include him somewhere! He had the great skill of providing an instant quote or comment on any subject before the House, in the media or in everyday conversation. Sometimes they were unprintable but always witty and to the point. The media loved him and chased him for the quote of the day. I got to know him because he took me to task on some line I had taken in the House and we had a good verbal sparring match. From then on we became friends; so much so that when we met around the House I would be greeted with a kiss on both cheeks and 'How are you today, darling?' which to his satisfaction made heads turn. He would then test the latest chat-up line or his quote of the day on me and often get a 'raspberry'.

Initially I found this embarrassing but I soon got used to the routine, except on one important day.

On the day in question my husband Brian's parents, Jessie and David

Peacock, came to visit me and have lunch. They never seemed to be sure why I wanted to be an MP. Certainly in my early years I do not think Brian's mother really approved; probably on the basis that wives should be at home looking after the family, although our two boys were by then at university!

As we headed along the bottom corridor towards the Terrace Restaurant for lunch, who should we meet but Tony Beaumont-Dark who went into the daily routine, kiss on cheeks and 'Hello, darling' etc. Then he suddenly realized I had visitors and was embarrassed, particularly when I introduced my husband's parents. Any embarrassment soon disappeared and he launched into a statement saying that I was one of the most popular members in the House who would fight my corner on issues taking an independent line when necessary, something that suited his philosophy. This sorted the matter out, especially when I pointed out the various notables having lunch that day, thus dismissing Tony into the distance.

My visitors enjoyed lunch so much that as we passed the House of Commons shop they suggested that they would like to buy me a present to commemorate their visit. I chose a House of Commons coffee set which I treasure to this day as it reminds me both of Brian's parents and of Tony.

Luckily the quick-thinking Tony Beaumont-Dark, having initially headed me into trouble, saved the day with some fast talking.

It was a great shame that he lost his seat in 1992. Without him, the House was a duller place!

Whips
The Rottweilers of Westminster; the prison guard of politics
Members of Parliament have a love/hate relationship with the whips, regardless of party, normally more hate than love. In any political structure that relies on a party system there needs to be someone who attempts to ensure that members are informed of the party's policy and to ensure that the member will turn up to support that policy when it comes to a vote in Parliament.

To ensure that this objective is achieved, a party appoints some senior members to ensure communication, to enforce discipline and get the best vote result. The difficulty for members is the enforcement of discipline that can cause all sorts of personal and domestic inconvenience due to the need to be at Westminster to vote through legislation on the party's programme. This is where the hate part soon bites and where the whips are recognized as the camp guards holding the prisoners in the camp to vote.

During my days at Westminster I had continuing fights with my whips about what I could or could not do, particularly when I wished to support events in Batley and Spen during the week. Soon after my election, I ran into the problem of my County Council seat. My County Council colleagues did not want me to resign and my Westminster whips would not give me time for North Yorkshire issues, so we soon had a fight! On many occasions I voted in Westminster at 10.00pm, travelled north on a sleeper train to be in Northallerton by 10.00am and had to be back in Westminster again by 10.00pm to vote the next evening. This was just crazy when we had a majority of 144 but the Westminster whips showed no sympathy.

I had regular fights with my whips, particularly when I rebelled against party policy as I did on various occasions. The job of the whip was to 'read the riot act' and put on the thumbscrews to ensure I did not rebel again. In the end they gave me up as a bad job as I knew the words of the Riot Act by heart, the thumbscrews did not work and by the end of my period at Westminster the whips just left me alone.

While we had regular fights, they were in the main 'good chaps' who had a job to do and I was just ongoing trouble. The senior whips were all going on to greater things or had already done ministerial jobs, so they knew their politics and drove the party along.

Donald Thompson

When I was first elected the Conservative Whip team was formidable! My Yorkshire whip was my good friend Donald Thompson who features elsewhere in my contribution so I will move on to others. The Chief Whip was John Wakeham, a victim of the Brighton bombing in which his wife Roberta sadly lost her life.

The whips' office was often a training ground for people going on to greater things. One of these was David Waddington, who followed John Wakeham as Chief Whip.

David Waddington (now Lord Waddington)

David went on to be Home Secretary and Governor General of Bermuda. He was in my view one of the real characters in the House. Recently as I was writing this contribution I met David at a reception in Downing Street and he said:

Elizabeth, you know the whips really did have trouble with you when you were in the House. Your rebelling made you a great nuisance and you took no notice of us when we tried to get you in line but I now recognize you were often right as you were fighting for your constituents, who did not agree with government policies. Your independent approach made your political career!

He also went on to say how he enjoyed coming to Batley and Spen to speak in my support. I recall one visit when he came to speak at a meeting on Immigration matters with my Asian friends in Taylor Street of Batley. David was at the time a Minister in the Home Office requiring Special Branch cover but as it was a weekend political event could not use his official car, so turned up in a rather battered Ford Escort that would not start due to a flat battery!

We held the meeting at Taylor Street and this was going well until a group of youths began to get excited outside the hall and eventually began to throw things around at the police who had been summoned by David's Special Branch men. Things got so unruly that the police demanded we abandon the meeting which we eventually did and smuggled David out to his car. The problem was the thing would then not start and had to be pushed! To this day I can see the scene of a group of my helpers, policemen and Special Branch pushing David's car along the road with the Minister leaning out of the window giving instructions. At long last the engine fired and away he went, waving.

Usually the Chief Whip was civilized, probably because he had to negotiate business with his opposite number in other parties and had to get the business through the House.

Another incident reminds me of David Waddington. In 1986 my husband had a suspected brain haemorrhage and was rushed to hospital. I attended Parliament on a three-line whip and then asked to be excused to return home to check on Brian. I asked my whip David Lightbown to let me off for at least twenty-four hours so I could be in Yorkshire if needed at the hospital. He refused and was really nasty. I was very upset and decided to return to Yorkshire anyway, which did not please David Lightbown. However, I did first consult with Sir Michael Shaw, Chairman of the Yorkshire Conservatives, who gave me his blessing to go. So I put my foot down and said: 'I'm going. My husband is more important than your 10.00pm vote!'

When I did return to Westminster I was met by David Lightbown, shouting that I had missed votes. In these circumstances I usually give as good as I get but on this occasion I was tired, had not eaten properly all day and was worried about my husband so I burst into tears but this made him worse so I just walked off. As I walked away, around the corner, who by chance should I meet but Chief Whip David Waddington who spotted that I was upset and wanted to know the reason. I told him the tale and he walked on, passing no real comment.

I voted that night as promised at 10.00pm and went back to my flat to find a bunch of roses by the front door with a note of apology from David Waddington saying: 'We are not all that bad.' I did not know for a long time that David Waddington had ordered and sent the flowers but David Lightbown had to pay! David Lightbown was a big man and a bit of a bully but sadly he was not with us much longer as he was taken ill and died, still a fairly young man; a sad story. David Waddington tells this story a little differently in his autobiography but the roses did arrive.

Irvine Patnick

Another whip who gave me difficulty was Irvine Patnick, a fellow Yorkshire Member of Parliament. He was a pleasant chap but a difficult whip who wanted to stick to the book. At this time I had some very bad dental treatment on my front teeth and had to have remedial work done in Yorkshire. You would have thought that with our good majority, I could have missed an occasional Thursday night vote, allowing me to get treatment in Yorkshire on Friday morning. For weeks this did not suit the whips so I had to vote at 10.00pm and catch the last train to Wakefield, arriving at 2.00am the next morning. No wonder I rebelled!

Tristan Garel-Jones (now Lord Tristan Garel-Jones)

From time to time a whip could be useful and helpful but not often! Tristan was one such whip and I have to thank him for his quick thinking in getting my private member's bill out of the House of Commons and into the Lords and onto the Statute Book. As we have already outlined, the Liberal Party opposed my bill so it had made little progress. The word on the street was that this opposition would continue so I was advised to get on with other business and on the Friday when my bill was listed for a further reading I was in Batley on constituency work. For some reason that morning the opposition to my bill did not arrive; the Liberals had either lost interest or forgotten. Quick as a flash Tristan, who was the Duty Whip, re-tabled my bill that then went straight through all stages in the Commons and into the Lords where it became law in April 1984, less than a year after I had been elected.

I continue to thank Tristan whenever I see him. This is always slightly tempered by the fact that on the night in May 1989 when I collapsed in the Commons, Tristan was the whip who immediately checked whether I had voted before I could be dispatched to hospital for a check-up!

Opposition Whips

If you knew the opposition whips, deals on voting could be done if you could find a 'Pair'. In my later years I had an unofficial 'pairing' arrangement with Helen Jackson (Sheffield). Between us we could sometimes get the two sets of whips to co-operate to allow us to be in Yorkshire late on Thursday evening rather than Friday lunchtime and it sometimes worked!

I will not say any more about opposition whips as I had enough trouble with my own. However, I will include an appreciation of the work ethics displayed by Walter Harrison (Wakefield):

Walter Harrison

Walter was the Labour Chief Whip for the Callaghan government and had the responsibility of keeping the party in power which he did with skill. When it came to the crucial vote in 1979, he with Bernard Weatherill had displayed true courage in the voting procedure when the respected Member for Batley Dr Alfred Broughton was ill and dying.

The Labour Party lost the vote and the government fell but Walter Harrison with Bernard Weatherill gained respect.

My View

I realize that most of these comments are Conservative-led but I still have the scars of fourteen years of battle! Opposition whips were sometimes more friendly.

I admire the media people, recognizing that I could not have handled the written word but have always enjoyed radio and television work where we have something in common.

I have often wished that I had been a lawyer. As a magistrate I have seen them working in court. I have seen their contribution to the House of Commons which is important to ensure that the correct sort of legislation is put in place.

Could I have been a whip? Not really!

Chapter 26

Issues and Pressures of the Period

In order to provide context, I have written some comments on the issues that have driven me during my political career and in most cases still do today some twenty years later. These topics are the ones that I regularly addressed, both in Westminster and in Batley and Spen.

My comments describe the background thinking that on occasions led me to rebel against my own government when I considered they had got it wrong.

Law and order

One theme that has been on my agenda throughout my political career is the need for a firm line on law and order that was confirmed by my time as PPS in the Home Office. Long before I wrote my first election address I was expressing my views, particularly in the discussion I had with constituency selection committees. I did not want anyone to misunderstand the strength of my conviction in this area; I made it clear that I was in favour of the reintroduction of the Death Penalty. During my years at Westminster we had several debates and votes on the issue without success. However, this failure has not changed my overall view. I remain in favour of the availability of the death penalty for acts of terrorism, for the murder of police officers and all premeditated murder. Furthermore, the sentence of life imprisonment for other murders should mean just that: life. I recognize that with the current political views we are not likely to get a majority for change. I have discovered, in the House and in debates elsewhere in which I have taken part such as the Durham University Union, that my proposition creates heated confrontation.

The questionnaire that I sometimes circulated in the constituency always showed that the House of Commons view is not the view of the general public. The public wishes to see a much firmer approach and I am certain that a referendum would support my position. The application of criminal sentencing and the level of the prison population are constantly debating topics for the press and a concern for the Home Secretary and Justice Minister. I have always subscribed to the view expressed so clearly by Michael Howard when Home Secretary that when the criminal population is in prison the level of crime falls; prison works!

The consistency of sentencing by Judges is, and always will be, an issue. I, like many others within the population, am looking for effective punishment, either in prison or on real community projects. I remember getting into big trouble in the press some years ago when I campaigned for the use of deterrent tough boot camps to punish and at the same time train young people who have committed crimes. I am still of the view, having sat in the past as a magistrate, that our fines system has its limitations and that positive deterrents are necessary.

I am convinced that law and order regimes have gone backwards due to the implementation of the Human Rights Act. The interference in British Justice by the European Court using this act has not helped. The widespread use of this act by defending lawyers in a spectrum of court cases has made our laws and Parliament less effective. There is a case for a human rights policy but it must be a British version and not European. If the public is to support law and order in our society, there has to be change. This change has to be a totally British system with no exterior interference from Brussels.

A British Bill of Rights could easily be written and administered by our courts system. Admittedly its application would be hotly debated but if we are to regain public confidence in the law, action is required now!

I took a look through my scrapbook that shows I took an equally positive view on the reintroduction of corporal punishment for certain offences. At one stage an interview I gave to the press was taken totally out of context and had me saying that corporate punishment, flogging, should be shown on television. I most certainly did not say that but clearly we do need a more dramatic and effective punishment regime.

Along these lines of discovering effective punishment I at one point got involved in a debate about the use of the stocks to humiliate hardened and regular petty criminals. Again this caused great merriment at my expense but I really did mean that we had and still have to be more innovative with punishment and rehabilitation. I recognize that it requires a brave government to progress innovation. In making this sort of remark then, and again now, I draw on my experience of working in the Home Office as PPS that confirmed my views.

I see from my scrapbook that my old colleague Matthew Parris had a good go at me in his political sketch in *The Times* on 24 March 1995. He starts his sketch with a wary glance at Prime Minister's Question Time between John Major and Tony Blair concerning the Royal Yacht *Britannia*, then launched into me on flogging and I quote:

"And I saw the same wary glance when Madam Speaker called Elizabeth Peacock (C. Batley & Spen) to question the Prime Minister. The Chamber erupted. This lady is going through one of her celebrity phases. Mrs Peacock displays her feathers rarely – but when she does: wow!

The last time we heard of Peacock was nearly three years ago, in 1992. She stunned her party by rebelling against the closure (that affected her constituency) of coal pits. It was brave. She was on every news bulletin and most television screens. Her photograph graced the front pages of newspapers. She was mobbed by journalists for about a fortnight.

Then the curtain fell. Peacock has no need for continuous publicity. A quick burst every few years will do.

Well, it's that time of the decade again. Last weekend, Elizabeth Peacock was on all our screens with a new plan for criminal justice. She suggested certain lawbreakers should be punished by a short time in the stocks.

Yesterday she did not elaborate. She simply told Mr Major that there was 'massive public support for the reintroduction of corporal punishment'. From behind him came growls of support from Tory backbenchers.

But it was not to them that the PM was listening. It seemed to me that he was cocking an ear across the floor, in case there should be an admonitory 'hear, hear,' from Tony Blair. Unable to promise Mrs Peacock the public stocks she desired, Major was alive to the danger of the next *Spectator* lecture but one: "Bircher" Blair says Labour will flog yobs."

Moral issues: Pro-Life and the Pope

As a woman with a Catholic upbringing I had always understood the moral issues and debate concerning abortion and the position taken by

Presentation to Pope John Paul II in the Vatican.

Introducing my Partial Birth Abortion Ten Minute Rule Bill, 1996.

various religious faiths. When I arrived at Westminster I recognized the great importance of Pro-Life issues, including abortion, on the political scene. With this in mind I was happy to support the aims and objectives of the Pro-Life movement and take part in their activities.

However, I always held a rather different approach to the matter that I should explain at the outset. I have taken, and still take, the view that women need abortion to be available in certain circumstances. The way abortion availability is applied needs to be controlled by legislation with firm but workable constraints.

The necessary constraints had initially been provided by David Steel's 1966 Termination of Pregnancy Bill and subsequent legislation. However, with continuing medical advances these constraints need to be regularly reviewed and where necessary challenged. Throughout my time at Westminster there were regular challenges to this controlling legislation; these being aimed at control of new and developing techniques, timing of terminations and the whole human reproductive area. This included the controversial use of human embryos in developing medical science. At an early date after the 1983 election I got involved in these issues and in the autumn of 1987 I co-sponsored David Alton's Abortion Amendment Bill proposing changes in the termination timing limits. This sort of challenge was mirrored by associated issues when in 1986 I urged the introduction of legislation to control test-tube babies, surrogate mothers and experimental pregnancies.

Such initiatives were continued throughout my fourteen years in the Commons. In 1987 David Alton introduced a further abortion-curbing bill during which I cited Christopher Nolan, the talented handicapped Irish writer, stating: 'Now they have threatened to abort babies like him; Britain is fast becoming the foetal dustbin of Europe.'

Abortion was not the only Pro-Life matter in the public debate.

The defining work in the sector was provided by Baroness Warnock in her very detailed report in the 1980s that highlighted the dilemmas in the whole area of human reproduction and embryo research. On reading my speeches and notes used in this period, I recall how emotional the issues were and how much effort was made to get legislative action. I see I even used a Latin legal principle in a speech to summarize the position: *res ipsa loquitur*, 'the thing speaks for itself'. Clearly, abortion was not the only Pro-Life ethical issue but it was of major concern then and remains so.

Embryo research is important to the advancement of medical science. In 1985 I supported Enoch Powell's Private Member's Bill in this area by

Receiving award on behalf of the Wool Industry from HRH The Duchess of Kent, 1993.

Presentation of the Queen's Award for Export to MELTOG by the Lord Lieutenant John Lyles with Donald Thompson, 1995.

agreeing that when a human egg is fertilized it has the capacity of becoming a person and that this sort of development can be seen after fourteen days. I therefore opposed scientific experiment on embryos after fourteen days that was the subject of Enoch's bill, which failed.

The ongoing debate on euthanasia and the 'right to die' created all sorts of ethical questions that were never resolved during my time at Westminster and have made little progress since. Continuing debate in Holland and a tolerant position in Switzerland accept the right to die and have led to several high-profile cases involving British citizens. More time is needed to find a balanced solution to these difficult issues.

In my view, the tide is moving slowly in the direction of greater tolerance. However, this should not, as I said in the 1980s, allow doctors to 'play God' and requires legislative control.

My work in the Pro-Life area brought me to Rome and the Vatican in December 1986 as a member of a delegation of MPs, from all parties and religions, tasked with presenting an illuminated address to His Holiness Pope John Paul II at a private audience at the Vatican.

The objective of the address to the Pope was to re-affirm the concern of members of the House of Commons and support for the Pope's stance on the sanctity of the human embryo and his opposition to the use of human embryos for research.

It was a very great honour to be invited to a private audience with the Pope, particularly as I was the only female MP in the delegation. A private audience with the Pope is a special honour for anyone but especially so for a woman brought up in the Catholic faith and educated at a convent school. I was proud to be a member of the delegation. I had an even greater honour as I was chosen to make a presentation to His Holiness of a leather-bound book on the Palace of Westminster.

We were a relatively small delegation of some forty people with families so we were ushered into a small audience room with a low stage at one end. Shortly after our arrival the Pope was carried into the room on a sedan-type chair from which he descended to a throne and made a speech of welcome in English. Sir Bernard Braine MP, our delegation leader, responded and presented our illuminated address and I followed with my presentation.

As the formal part ended the Pope jumped down from his throne, saying: 'Please shut the door, I will now meet you all' and proceeded to walk around the room, blessing the children present and shaking hands with everyone else. As he completed his tour of the room he announced in

Minister Angela Knight meeting Wool Industry Executives at Thomas Carr in Batley.

*The author speaking to an
audience of 800 at
Grosvenor House during
the Timber Trades
Industry International
Week, 1994.*

a loud voice: 'Now I'm in charge of the delegation photograph. Everyone onto the stage please, tallest at the back and leave room for me in the middle!' He then reorganized us until he was satisfied and allowed the photograph to be taken. Suddenly he rang a bell; the door opened and in came his sedan chair. He climbed aboard and left with a wave; a most human and friendly Pope, to be greatly admired. Indeed, to my surprise my husband, who has never been a great supporter of any church was so impressed that he became an admirer of Pope John Paul II. It was a wonderful experience for us all.

In 1996 I launched a nationwide campaign with a House of Commons Early Day Motion to outlaw what many critics believed was the most barbaric form of pregnancy termination: 'partial birth abortion'. Partial birth abortion had at that time become a political talking-point in America following President Clinton's decision to veto a ban on the procedure.

This controversial technique, developed in the US for use in late abortions, involves withdrawing the foetus through the birth canal until only the head remains which is then sucked out. This is to ensure that the child is born dead and no charge of murder can be levied. The extent of the use of this practice was at the time difficult to measure as it was not specified on abortion report forms.

Following the massive support for this EDM I eventually managed to get a Ten-Minute Rule Bill to expose the problem to an even wider audience. I got plenty of support from colleagues, from the media and from the public but we did not get any legislation to ban the practice. In truth an EDM and a ten-minute rule bill never would. This sort of legislation requires government support or a lucky Private Member's Bill.

It is difficult to get a Ten-Minute Rule Bill as there is always great demand. To achieve such a bill necessitated traditional British queuing outside the clerk's office throughout the night on chairs provided that were usually occupied as the bars closed around 1.00pm!

I did not fancy spending the night on a chair in a corridor full of men well topped-up with beer but I wanted a bill. So I bought the largest teddy bear we could find in the Toys R Us store, who instantly gained the name 'Sneezer Bear' as he went straight from the shop to a service at the Hanging Heaton Ebenezer Chapel in Batley. He was then smuggled into the Commons with a notice around his neck saying: 'I am Elizabeth Peacock's Assistant and I am queuing for a Ten-Minute Rule Bill.' I rejoined my bear at 5.30 the following morning to be confronted by several angry men who claimed I was cheating. I stood my ground and managed, to the great

Visiting a refugee camp in Azad Kashmir, 1994.

My favourite 'bear' who assisted me to obtain my Ten-Minute Rule Bill.

annoyance of some others, to get my bill. In the afternoon there were questions and points of order to the Speaker, complaining about my activities. The press picked up the story and the bear gave a series of radio and TV interviews. I got my bill so I was happy and the bear, who now sits on a sofa in my bedroom, endlessly tells the story of his exploits. Indeed, Gyles Brandreth former MP for the City of Chester, now the well-known raconteur, broadcaster, eccentric and fellow bear-lover, has been known to mention 'Mrs Peacock's bear'.

The media headlines were:

'MP's bid to stop "barbaric" abortions.'
'Peacock promotes new Bill.'

Mrs Peacock is one of a group of MPs to table a motion in Parliament calling on the government to take action to stop the availability of abortion on demand, and ensure people are better educated on the realities of abortion.

Pro-Life MPs say that many are unaware that the permission of two doctors is needed before an abortion can be carried out, and that the 1967 Abortion Act was never intended to allow abortion on demand as a woman's choice.

My View
I remain a supporter of the efforts of the Pro-Life movement to demand a continuing review of ethics and practice across the whole area of human reproduction, although I take an opposing view to the mainstream with the unusual position of approving controlled abortion and the death penalty for certain murders.

Communication, broadcasting and the BBC
I have something of a fascination with the spoken word; as my husband says, I 'talk too much and write too little'. Certainly, I like to talk and will avoid writing.

I claim this statement is untrue as I wrote a regular piece for our local newspapers on topics of the day at Westminster or in Yorkshire. It was always the job for Sunday evening and needed great discussion each week to confirm the subject. Some weeks I could encourage Brian to do a draft while I did some cooking with half an eye on the draft. This sometimes

Interview with Pakistan TV with Michael Colvin MP, 1994.

Dinner with the Prime Minister of Azad Kashmir.

worked but I usually needed the editor's red pen. We did produce some good articles that people seemed to like and these gave me a means of direct communication that an MP must have.

From my days as a charities administrator in York I have been involved with local radio and TV, having taken part in debate, discussions and local programmes. Since those days I have remained a dedicated supporter of local radio as a means of informing and bringing people together. I place so much importance on local radio that I believe it is the second most important objective in the BBC's responsibilities, after provision of the national radio and television news service that binds the United Kingdom together.

In my early days as a 'rookie' politician I was a bit naughty and did gain air time on two occasions at a Conservative conference. I spoke in the debate on the topic of the day, opposing the motion with some sharp headline-grabbing phrases. These indicated that I opposed the motion because the proposals were not going far enough! On each occasion I made the BBC 6 o'clock evening news programme, once as a headline. All a bit naughty because I cannot now remember the substance of the debate but it was a clear indication to me of the power of communication.

However, when I got to Westminster I had not taken part in a structured television programme other than giving short interviews during the election campaign and after the count when I was elected. This was soon corrected as I took part in an early evening news programme for Yorkshire TV with my new fellow MP Kevin Barron (Rother Valley), where we had to explain what action we intended to take in Parliament to resolve the miners' unofficial strike. We were both new to TV and both very nervous but we made a good programme with the help of the interviewer. Since then I have never stopped taking part in radio and television programmes and phone-ins at home and around the world. I made a major programme for Pakistan TV on refugees in Kashmir that got me banned from visiting India for a few years as the Indians did not like our reporting.

While I was being a nuisance at Westminster rebelling against government legislation, someone in the whips' office decided it would be a good idea if this troublesome woman could be found a job outside the House that would utilize her energies and get her out of the whips' hair! Consequently I was appointed as a government representative on the BBC General Advisory Council, chaired at that time by Marmaduke Hussey and on which I served for five years. Experience gained during these years on the council provided me with a detailed insight into the planning and management of radio and television with an emphasis on programme selection to meet the needs of the audience. In later years I had the opportunity to repeat the process as a member of the BBC Audience Council for England and chairman of the BBC Yorkshire Audience Council from 2006 to 2009.

After the Pakistan programme I with some help made my own TV programme on cycling safety for the BBC and the politics spot for Channel 4 after the evening news. I took part in *Any Questions?*, the political discussion radio show in Harrogate chaired at that time by John Timpson. The Labour Party was well-represented and I got into an argument with the audience rather than with my fellow panellists. I did not get invited again!

At one stage I did join a consortium of Yorkshire people including Austin Mitchell (Labour, Grimsby) and his wife Linda McDougall and others to bid for a licence for a private Yorkshire radio station; we did not succeed but it was fun trying. I was rather sorry we did not get the franchise because I would have enjoyed some first-hand experience of radio station management.

Some of the most interesting political television programme production came from recordings made throughout my election campaigns of 1987 and 1992. I agreed to be 'wired for sound': linked to a TV camera crew for several days to catch actual sounds and conversations at meetings, factory visits, canvassing house-to-house and meeting people on our 'walkabouts' in the streets and supermarkets. Being wired for sound has its challenges: I had to watch my language and I needed to turn off the sound when I went to the loo! I did forget on occasions, to the amusement of the crew! A further challenge was when the crew arrived at my home for breakfast to discuss the campaign plans for the day. I just had to 'put my face on' before we made the toast and allowed the camera to roll.

These programmes broadcast two or three weeks after the election were enlightening, especially as we won.

My View

As a consequence of this long-standing experience of broadcasting in Britain and elsewhere, when I look at the current position of the BBC and the onward development of the private sector and especially Sky, I am convinced that the BBC has to be restructured. The BBC should not be allowed to continue in its present format as it is almost unmanageable. It is too big, too complex and has too many non-core activities. The corporation needs to concentrate on broadcasting items of national importance: news and local interest. It currently has too many programmes, some of which would be more appropriate to the commercial sector. We need a streamlined BBC to compete with a vibrant BSkyB with a radical change in structure, remit and financing. The present BBC and the separate Trust is a nonsense, preventing proper management of the BBC and a failure by the BBC Trust to regulate.

Encouragement of industry

From the very first day I was selected as the candidate to fight the Batley and Spen seat in the spring of 1983, I knew that industry and jobs were going to be a major challenge.

It is not the role of politicians and government to be involved in businesses of any kind; politicians cannot run anything! The question is why? The answer is simple. Politicians and government, though they will deny it, are always looking to the next election. This leads to short-term, often irrational decision-making that is useless in business. It could be agreed that the nationalization policy of the 1945 Attlee government restructured sectors that had suffered in the Depression of the 1930s and during the Second World War. However, collectively-nationalized industries were never a business success due to the so-called government management.

Their return to the private sector by the Thatcher government has produced competition and dynamism to the country's benefit but even now a greater degree of competition is needed in some sectors, particularly energy and services.

From day one in 1983 to my last day in 1997 I spent a large part of my time in some way encouraging industry. Encouragement is the appropriate word: business will invest and respond, creating new jobs, if government provides an encouraging environment. The encouragement is not all about government grants, which do help, but more about minimizing bureaucracy, helping with planning issues, support for exports, in some cases control of unfair imports and a sensible tax policy when profits have been made.

I came to Batley and Spen in 1983 much better equipped and more knowledgeable of the local business scene than many people recognized as I had built and run a business in my early twenties in Keighley and my husband's family had business interests throughout the West Riding extending into East Lancashire and what is now Cumbria. I therefore knew of the business and industry challenges in and around Batley and Spen and

I had some knowledge of the people involved. Consequently I understood the difficulties experienced by local industry, especially the decline of the wool trade and its associated supply and engineering businesses.

My first impression of the state of local businesses when I became the Conservative candidate in 1983 was that if I was successful, I would have to concentrate my efforts on finding new business and creating new jobs for the area. My maiden speech in 1983 accepted this challenge. A review of my scrapbook covering my fourteen years confirms that I did just that, making jobs and business my major priority.

I concentrated on getting businesses to relocate to the area, encouraged urban regeneration to aid this process and involved myself in activities of the wool textile industry and campaigned for a national energy policy using, where possible, British coal.

As you would expect, I had some successes and some failures. I got myself into trouble on occasions with my own government that made me unpopular in Conservative circles. However, to be fair to many of my Conservative minister colleagues, I did get a good share of government support for local business and its development.

I realized at an early date that some of our terrain is less well-suited for modern factories so I became involved in encouraging development of what was initially a vacant industrial site at Birstall to house Thomas's Pet Food and Spring Ram, the kitchen sink maker, to provide new jobs. Eventually, the site became a retail park that has probably provided even more employment. By ensuring that the area had development status we were able to attract business into various sites in Batley supporting the bedding industry. One of my greater successes was to organize a Business Association that brought local businessmen to Westminster, both socially and to speak directly to ministers.

In this direction I was able to get involved in considerable depth with the wool industry: fighting our corner on International Multifibre issues, discussing and controlling import and export levies on wool and wool products including monitoring imports of unfairly competing textiles. This all led me to the chairmanship of the House of Commons All Party Wool Textile Group, a role I fulfilled for eight years. During this period I was invited to become a Liveryman of the Worshipful Company of Woolmen; an honour as they had, and still have, a limited number of lady Liverymen.

My big industrial challenge at Westminster was always textiles and especially wool. Almost every day when I was the Chairman of the Wool Textile Committee I had some contact with the industry or with a minister on their behalf. Normally we had very good relations with support from government but sometimes involvement with ministers could be difficult and tetchy, as I was reminded when looking through my scrapbook. From the following report in the *Yorkshire Evening Post* in May 1993 I appeared to be giving the government plenty of trouble:

MP mauls Minister about sheep
TORY MP Elizabeth Peacock gave a going-over to one Government Minister – and then to another in a Commons row.
She hit out in protest about the plight of sheep farmers and the wool textile industry.

First in the firing line from Mrs Peacock – who chairs an all-party wool textile group of MPs – was fellow Yorkshire MP David Curry (Skipton and Ripon), followed by Government Minister Sir Hector Monroe.

In clashes about Government action to stop guaranteed prices for wool, Batley and Spen MP Mrs Peacock:

Accused Mr Curry of 'not listening terribly well' during previous Commons exchanges.

Blamed him for an 'insult' to sheep farmers, when he declared that for many the wool fleece was only a side-product!

Told him off for not giving her credit for expert knowledge of the textile and carpet industries.

Clobbered Sir Hector for claiming there had been no protests from the textile industry about the effects of Government action.

Protesters who want the guarantee to be phased out more slowly claim a blow to prices could hit supplies and quality of wool. Some also claim the welfare of sheep could suffer because some farmers might not bother to shear them.

Government Ministers insist farmers have had time to prepare for the ending of the guarantee and that the effects will not be dramatic.

On this occasion we were having a debate about the raw material, wool. More often we had discussions around marketing and export matters. As our wool industry has contracted, so exports have become more important, often depending on import tariffs around the world.

In Batley itself, as the traditional wool and textile industry declined leaving mills empty, a new industry of bed-making developed in these very suitable buildings. I soon discovered their importance as I spoke at their national conference. On several occasions I took their leaders to meet ministers on trade matters. As the selling of beds is closely related to the furniture trade I became interested in their activities and spoke at several of their trade dinners. Not surprisingly this brought me into contact with the timber trade and I looked at some of their activities, particularly those supplying timber for furniture and beds.

By speaking at trade dinners and conferences I could promote the idea of relocating businesses to Batley and Spen, describing how we could explore the benefits of relocating and in particular the availability of a good work force.

As the bed men and the furniture people were joining the timber trade for their annual dinner at Grosvenor House in London I saw an opportunity to promote Batley and Spen as an area for industrial growth when they asked me to speak. Little did I realize the task I had taken on.

The following extract from a trade magazine sums up the event:

Lonely at the top table
She felt a bit lonely at the Timber Trade Federation dinner in March, too. With only 28 women among the 900-strong sea of dinner jackets, and no other females on the top table, Elizabeth Peacock had the dubious privilege of being the first female keynote speaker in the Federation's 100 years.

Considering she had expected an audience of no more than a couple of hundred, the verdict from this most demanding of audiences was that she did a pretty impressive job. In fact, she's the first politician I've heard speak at the Grosvenor who has personal experience of what a rainforest looks like: she had visited Brazil with her husband last year.

Family values
Elizabeth Peacock came late to the Commons: most women MPs do. She remembers a survey in *The Times* just after the 1983 General Election which revealed that the average age of male MPs was about 31, while the average age of female MPs was 45 or 46. The 'motherhood factor' remains significant.

Some might say Elizabeth Peacock has made as much of an impact in her 10 years in Parliament as many a 30-year 'veteran' male backbencher.

But if the odds are against you – female, middle-aged and an outspoken northerner to boot – you probably have to go against the grain to get noticed.

With her own party in its present state of flux, who knows what the future might have in store for the brusquer elements of the Conservative Party. As they say in the Smirnoff adverts – 'anything can happen.'

Despite my many disagreements with Michael Heseltine, I managed to persuade him that urban regeneration was essential for Batley to encourage new business. He responded by finding many millions of pounds for the Batley City Challenge Regeneration Scheme. The scheme certainly helped the town, particularly with the cleaning of lovely stone buildings and the refurbishment of housing. On the new business and new jobs front it was a little disappointing.

From day one at Westminster as I took on the challenge of job and business encouragement, I acknowledged the need for a good and economic supply of energy and services to local businesses. Energy supply has to be available at realistic stable costs and to be locally, nationally and internationally politically ensured with realistic pricing.

British governments never seem to get a long-term policy in place to meet this need. The Conservative governments of the 1980s and 1990s and Tony Blair and Gordon Brown in the 1990s with New Labour did not make much progress. There has been a constant switch between support for gas, oil, coal, nuclear and sustainable energy sources with no real resolution.

Over the years, I have got involved in these constant debates that led me to my serious disagreement with the Conservative government when they attempted to re-structure the British coal industry in a month without a strategic energy policy in place.

My experiences in this sector got me more deeply involved in coal than I might have been because of my extensive knowledge of the industry and more particularly my knowledge of government thinking on the privatization of energy and coal. It was this knowledge that led me to be invited to become a non-executive director of the Coal Investments company.

It was knowledge of government thinking on privatization and industrial matters that I could use to help local businesses and the Yorkshire-wide woollen trade. This was particularly so for energy and utilities such as water when I had direct dealings with Yorkshire Water on water supply and effective effluent treatment and disposal.

With Cheryl Gillan in Taipei looking at local industries.

Meeting local businessman Shabir Daji at his bed-making factory in Batley.

It was not just the larger businesses such as Fox's Biscuits and BBA that took my interest. I saw Angoloco fire-fighting equipment in Hong Kong and more recently in the West Indies. Small businesses are always important as they sometimes grow big, such as Al Murad, the tile business that had one shop in Heckmondwike originally and is now a whole chain. Similarly the Shabi Daji original bed operation has multiplied in size.

One of the things I did as soon as I was elected was to form Batley and Spen Business Association which any local business could join in the knowledge that it was strictly non-political. Its objective was to arrange meetings with ministers locally when they visited but also to meet ministers in London on specific issues. It worked extremely well, so much so that we usually held an annual dinner in London; it really was important for local business contact.

My view
In summary, I am proud of the work I did together with my team in the business area and the benefits we gained for Batley and Spen and for the wider wool textile industry.

However, business never stands still: it has to change and innovate to suit markets as local businesses successfully do with or without politicians.

We did not succeed with everything but I never thought we would.

Parliamentary experiences
The televising of Parliament has tended to show Westminster as a very serious place on the one hand or an out-of-control rabble on the other. Somewhere in between is the norm. In truth parliamentary life throws up experiences almost every day; some funny, some embarrassing, others serious and where you might get a reprimand.

Funny (with reprimand)
One of my first social events after I was elected was to be the guest of honour and speaker at the Business and Professional Women's Annual Lunch at a hotel in Harrogate. I arrived just in time to find the red carpet laid up the steps to the front door but the doorman was just starting to roll it up, so I stepped on it quickly as I was heading towards the door. I heard a voice from behind me say: 'Please don't walk on our red carpet. We don't want it dirtying; the guest speaker has already arrived.' I replied: 'Yes, you are right. Keep rolling, I have just made it.'

Mistaken identity

Often when I went with my husband to a function he was mistakenly recognized as the MP because people were not used to a woman. Once when we went to a military event I was driving. As we arrived at the entry barrier I stopped and wound down the window. A young soldier started to speak to my husband, saying: 'Sir, you can take your car to the front and your chauffeur lady can then park'!

This sort of thing often happened and Brian always thought it funny!

Diplomatic reprimand

As explained elsewhere, I did not travel much on official parliamentary business but I did undertake private visits to various countries that did – eventually – contain some parliamentary or official business.

One year we went for a short break to Cyprus staying in Paphos, just a regular holiday. On about day two the telephone rang in our room and I had the British High Commissioner on the line saying: 'Mrs Peacock, can you confirm that you are the member for Batley and Spen?' 'Yes,' I replied. He was cross!

> Do you not know that I am responsible for your safety while you are on my patch? How can I do that when you have not let me know you are here? Furthermore, the Greek Cypriot government knows you are here and wants to meet you. You should find a way of getting to Nicosia tomorrow for lunch with me and the Greek Cypriots and go to the Green Line with them to understand the situation with the Turkish Cypriots.

I protested that it was a private visit and I was not briefed by the Foreign Office but he persisted. I eventually agreed, my husband 'blew his top' and said a by-election would be needed. In the end we went to Nicosia where we had a good lunch with the High Commissioner who was a Yorkshire man from Ripon. We met the Greek Cypriots and went to the Green Line dividing the city but were not allowed to meet the Turks.

To this day I have never known what the problem was; everyone except my husband was happy. He said he would send a bill to the Foreign Office for wasted time.

Diplomatic embarrassment (1)

We had a similar experience on a private visit to Brazil some years later.

We were back in the Cococabana Palace Hotel in Rio de Janeiro, having been 'up country' from Sao Paulo where Brian had been inspecting orange groves and orange juice-producing factories to ensure juice of first quality and price that was to be supplied to a British supermarket group. Having done the business, we were heading for Manaus and up the Amazon via Brasilia.

We were waiting for a taxi, chatting to the hotel doorman with a group of businessmen stood behind having just completed their meeting. Suddenly one of the men detached himself from the group and I realized we had met before. It was Peter Heap who I had met some years before in Hong Kong where he was the British Trade Commissioner. He had obviously recognized me; he claimed it was my Yorkshire accent. He wanted to know what we were doing in Brazil, so I explained and said rather casually: 'What are you doing here?' The answer came back: 'I am Her Majesty's Ambassador to Brazil based in Brasilia.' He then made a similar speech: I should have arranged to visit him in Brasilia as he was responsible for my welfare, which was difficult if he did not know I was in Brazil. As we were changing planes in Brasilia the next day, he tried to insist that we should visit him. Having explained that we were on a tight schedule, he said: 'Right, I will meet you at Brasilia airport. That will give us two hours to discuss Brazilian issues and I will escort you to your plane to Manaus.'

On the day as our plane came to a halt on the runway we were invited to come to the front to go out first. As we descended the steps, the ambassador's limo shot across the runway with a mini Union flag flying. Out jumped the ambassador and his driver, both grabbing our hand luggage, and off we went to the VIP dining room for lunch and discussion!

Diplomatic embarrassment (2)

There was a similar occurrence in Hong Kong when we flew to Guilin in China on a private visit using China Airlines. Someone must have been reading my passport details because on the return journey as the plane came to a halt at Hong Kong airport I was asked with Brian to come to the front of the plane to exit first, which we did. A diplomatic limo was waiting at the bottom of the steps to take us straight through customs to our hotel on Hong Kong Island.

I never did discover who made the arrangements or even who knew we had gone to China!

Expensive whipping

Private visits abroad can be disrupted by British politics.

I remember being recalled for an emergency debate during the summer recess at the beginning of the Gulf War. We were on holiday in the south of France when we got a call from the whips: 'You must return for the debate as there could be a vote.' On the day the cheapest fare was the equivalent of £500, the cost of which at that time was down to me! At the time there was a flight delay and I did not get to Westminster until the debate was under way. As I arrived in Palace Yard with an expensive taxi heading for the Chamber I spotted my whip waiting for a taxi! I rushed across and asked: 'What is going on?' His answer was: 'The debate has started and they have agreed there will be no vote. You need not have bothered coming!'

I was speechless and penniless!

Pakistan, Kashmir and the North-West Frontier

One of the most interesting visits I made was to Kashmir to make a programme for Pakistan TV in 1994 at the height of the Kashmiri dispute with India. The idea was to visit the camps on the Pakistan/Kashmir border inhabited by refugees from the Indian-held part of Kashmir. The delegation of myself, Michael Colvin MP for Romsey and Waterside, and Lord Waverley would visit the camps, look at conditions and then discuss their findings with Kashmiri and Pakistani politicians; a slightly risky project because of Pakistani/Indian daily shelling and the potential risk diplomatically. I decided with Brian that I should do it if we could both get permission to travel privately in the North-West Frontier region to Peshawar, the Khyber Pass, through the Swat Valley and along the Karakoram Highway to Gilgit in Northern Kashmir and back to Islamabad (Taliban country).

I was keen to do the programme and travel around in Pakistan as I had met Benazir Bhutto on several occasions in London; she was at the time exiled from Pakistan.

We were joined by two charming ladies, Michael's wife Nichola and Lady Waverley, with Raja Najabat Hussain as guide and fixer. So off we went separately, to join up in Islamabad with our TV crew. The first objective was to visit the Refugee Camps along the border with Kashmir, travelling via the very pleasant hill station Murree with its cooler climate. The camps visited were primitive but surprisingly clean, where interviews were given and footage was 'put into the can'. This included non-political contributions from Brian, Nichola and Lady Waverley. The next stop was Muzaffarabad, the capital of Azad Kashmir, for a meeting and dinner with the State Government including the Prime Minister of Azad Kashmir. The plan had been to go on further into Kashmir to the Line of Demarcation but the Pakistani and Indian armies were busy shelling each other and it was considered too dangerous so we had to return to Islamabad. On arrival we discovered a meeting had been arranged with the President of Pakistan who wanted to be briefed on the TV programme; a visit that took most of the day.

As we now had two days to spare, it was the weekend and there was to be a general election within the month, it was decided that I should go electioneering with one of the candidates in the dusty villages around Mirpur. We got a friendly reception at each of the villages, with flowers from the women or flower petals on the paths as we walked; however, the meetings were just for the men. The local candidate spoke and I was encouraged to take part which I did through an interpreter. I never knew whether or not I was accurately translated but it seemed to be acceptable. It was quite an experience, electioneering in Pakistan. I suddenly understood Benazir Bhutto's fascination with the nation's politics.

We had time to visit Mirpur and see the great dam and lake that had flooded the valley and from which many of the families of residents of Batley and Spen came to West Yorkshire in the 1950s. Really successful families have now returned to build houses along the lake shore!

Our TV programme party split up and Brian and I set off on a private trip to Peshawar where we stayed at the Pearl Hotel that has a notice by the front door: 'Will visitors please leave their guns outside.' As Brian discovered when visiting the pharmacy across the road, the pharmacist serves his customers with a Sten gun on the counter. Being collectors of Asian objects, we had to visit the market in Peshawar with a guide. As we wandered around looking at antiques there was a great shout in the street and the sound of gunfire and we were ushered into a shop. Someone along the street had been shoplifting and had run off, causing the offended shopkeeper to open fire; an example of direct law and order!

We did get permission to go up the Khyber Pass to Landi Kotal and the border with Afghanistan as long as we took a Frontier Rifles Guard and went in an official car: a large shining Mercedes with driver that seemed rather odd as we were by choice travelling in a very ordinary people carrier. When we collected our Frontier Rifles Guard from the barracks we noted that his rifle was almost as big as he was. Our driver seemed to be having a bad morning and halfway up the Pass he suddenly stopped the car and said it was too dangerous and would go no further, so Brian in his usual positive style got out of the car and said he would drive. After some discussion the driver realized that as the car would go without him he had better drive but was never happy until we got back to Peshawar. In Landi Kotal the better shops are ship's containers as they can be securely locked. One is a Kit Kat container that had got lost from York!

I will not go into full details of the trip here but we did travel up the beautiful, now troubled, Swat Valley, through the Malakand Pass where Winston Churchill served with the North-West Frontier Force in the early 1900s to Mingora and from here over the Shangla Pass and onto the Karakoram Highway. The word 'highway' is a misnomer as it comprises hundreds of miles of mainly pebbled mountain track cut through the rocks along the hillsides; a truly frightening road linking Islamabad with the Chinese border and really frightening when you meet another vehicle with a drop of hundreds of feet to the valley bottom on one side. Our objective was to visit Gilgit, the home of polo with an historic ground on which the modern game could not be played due to the rough ground and its stone walls. The flight back to Islamabad was awesome over the Karakoram mountain range including Rakaposhi and Nanga Parbat that both rival Everest.

All very stimulating but I never did see the TV programme we made as the Indians did not like it and I could not get a visa to go to India or Indian Kashmir for two years.

My View

I have many other stories of the opportunities that arise as a Member of Parliament, either in your own constituency, at Westminster or travelling around the world. Like it or not, if the British Empire did nothing else, it did bring democracy with a parliamentary system to many parts of the world; a benefit that lives on and something that Britain should be proud of achieving.

Postscript: Michael and Nichola Colvin

There is a very sad ending to the friendship we had developed with Michael and Nichola Colvin, not just on this project but on an earlier visit with them to South Africa to look at the apartheid system then in place under President Botha prior to the release from prison of Nelson Mandela.

In February 2000 there was a serious fire at Michael and Nichola's home in Hampshire that totally destroyed the house and its contents. Michael and Nichola were in the house that night and have never been found.

Brian and I were shattered by this tragedy. The Colvins were wonderful people to know and excellent travelling companions. We miss them.

Chapter 27

General Election
1997

By 1995 I was convinced that we were going to have problems at the next election: people were beginning to say that they wanted a change of government. Also with the new constituency boundaries confirmed with the loss of Heckmondwike I knew it was going to be difficult to win again but I remained confident that something would come along to help.

We all knew there had to be a general election by the summer of 1997 and John Major also knew he was in a fair degree of trouble; the media told him so every day! With Tony Blair 'New Labour' were well ahead in the opinion polls with an aggressive team demanding an opportunity to lead the country. Tory splits on Europe, the number of Conservative misdemeanours and a media stance about overall Conservative competence following the ERM problems of the early 1990s completely drowned out the fact that John had completed his legislative programme and had delivered a very healthy economic climate for Britain with unemployment falling. By December 1996 we had lost our majority in the House of Commons but John soldiered on until March 1997 before calling an election on 1 May in the hope that the continuing improving economy might save us from defeat.

My team, while still very strong, had changed considerably in the years since 1992. I had lost my really experienced stalwarts in Mary Bentley, our constituency secretary and guru of electioneering in the area; also my highly intelligent and workaholic London secretary Lorna Humphreys. They had been replaced by Kath Wrightson carrying out my constituency secretarial work in Cleckheaton and by Martin Casey as my London research assistant and secretary. This was a strong day-to-day team but we lacked election experience.

With the Prime Minister, Spring 1992.

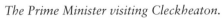

The Prime Minister visiting Cleckheaton.

Michael Howard, Home Secretary speaking at a constituency dinner with President Doug Brewer.

General election, 1997 with Jonathan Peacock, Conservative Candidate for Wakefield.

Rural advertising, 1997.

Mother and son, 1997.

The election team in action, 1997.

Election, 1997.

Locally we had anticipated the date and had planned ahead. We had no one except myself who had acted as an election agent during a general election, so we 'borrowed' Paul Bolton from the Conservative Central Office. As in my earlier general election campaigns our appeal for election funds was widely supported. Our formidable president Doug Brewer got the electioneering troops organized with the usual enthusiasm and vigour we had enjoyed in the 1983/1987/1992 campaigns. I took the stance to assist this process with our slogan 'We can win' but I had at the back of my mind that we would have to be lucky to survive. The media told us every day that 'Britain needed change'.

At the Peacock family level we had an additional campaign to fight from our home in Notton as Jonathan our eldest son had been selected as the Conservative candidate for Wakefield and as soon as the election was called based himself in Notton running a campaign from our house and an office at Zebediah Hinchcliffe's mill in Denby Dale.

Jonathan, who had been my campaign assistant and manager in all my campaigns from 1983 onwards was a well-organized electioneer who knew the political scene well. By 1997 he had become a prospering tax barrister who still wanted the chance of going to Westminster, so threw his hat into the ring to fight David Hinchcliffe for the Wakefield seat, knowing that it would be a long shot but good for experience and so it proved.

It was helpful, though tiring, managing two campaigns from one point but we both luckily had good teams.

When Jonathan was selected to fight Wakefield in the autumn of 1996 there was plenty of press interest, so Brian wrote the following note on the 'Peacock Factor':

PEACOCK POLITICS – TWO PEACOCKS IN YORKSHIRE YORKSHIRE FAMILY DEVELOPS DISTINCTIVE POLITICAL PHILOSOPHY OVER THREE GENERATIONS.
The attached notes have been prepared as the basis for a possible article on the Peacock family and as the precursor for what may become a political pamphlet if the various members of the family can ever sit down long enough to make a personal contribution!

At the next General Election there will be two Peacocks standing for seats in Yorkshire, Elizabeth Peacock in Batley and Spen and Jonathan Peacock in Wakefield: mother and son.

Although this is not a unique situation in the country as a whole (Sally, now Baroness Oppenheim and her son Phillip stood for Parliament at the same election in 1983 and both served as MPs), a mother and son listing is probably unique in Yorkshire.

What is most distinctive, however, is the brand of politics: an unusual brand of fiercely independent Yorkshire Conservatism that has guided three generations of political Peacocks and is referred to by some as 'The Peacock Factor'.

What is this special Conservative philosophy? It is a requirement for a very tough approach to law and order issues, a demand for firm but minimal government, a belief in sound money and free enterprise, and yet a very liberal approach to helping those in genuine need. It is not right or left-wing nor is it middle ground Conservatism – it really is a unique mix.

How did this all come about? The best person to ask seems to be Brian Peacock, husband of Elizabeth and father of Jonathan:

'I suppose the story begins with my father, David Peacock of West and East Marton, who was an Independent Councillor on the former Skipton and District for many years, with Elizabeth's mother who had no real interest in politics but had a fierce determination to ensure that her four daughters had a good start in life from some very trying circumstances.

'My father was so strongly independent that the Liberals thought he was one of them and the Conservatives were sure he was their man; not a bit of it, he was his own man, if somewhat difficult with it! He took a view that party politics had no part to play in local government. Councillors were there to sort out the problems of their patch and its inhabitants; they were positively not there to indulge in party politics. Anyone who had the temerity to argue would end up with a very vigorous response. While he concealed his true allegiance I know he always paid his subscription to the Conservative Party, but like a good Yorkshireman at the second or third time of asking! His political philosophy was born out of problems of the Depression of the 1930s when he was developing a business and trying to bring up a young family. He was always cautious with money and understood all too well the damage inflation could cause to people's lives. Equally, like any businessman, now and then he wanted Government to provide order and a sound legal framework in which to work. He was, as can be imagined, no fan of interference from Government bodies and I think he would have despaired of doing business with some of the "red tape" we suffered in this country in more recent times. The need for help for those in trouble – which he always respected – certainly came from the Depression but he would have no time for those who had the chance to help themselves and failed to do so.

'If I was pushed to classify the philosophy I would say it is more Macmillan of the 1950s than that great Skiptonian, Iain Macleod, but with a firm mix of early-day Thatcher.

'The Elizabeth Peacock version of this philosophy is well known in Batley and Spen and I suspect on a wider basis. Her independent track record in the years since 1983 speaks for itself.

'However, Elizabeth's tendency to plough an independent

political furrow came soon after she was elected in 1981 to the North Yorkshire County Council who were proposing a re-organisation of secondary education in York where we then lived. Being involved in the community of York she had some knowledge of the strength of feeling on the issue, particularly as our two sons attended one of the schools, Nunthorpe Grammar School, that was due for closure under the scheme. She was appalled that a Conservative-controlled council could even consider such a step. As a consequence, a campaign was mounted, votes against the Conservative group's proposals followed, as did several trips to London to lobby the then Secretary of State for Education, Keith Joseph.

'The cause was lost but what it did do was enhance a growing interest in a Parliamentary career, allied with the view that if you thought, having listened to the arguments, that a proposal being made by the Administration was wrong you said so early in the debate and unless very substantial amendments or concessions were made, an opposing vote or at the very least an abstention was the only way to express dissatisfaction.

'Undoubtedly my father's views had some influence on Elizabeth's political positioning; there was general agreement between them on broad policy but often bouts of verbal sparring on the issues of the day.

'Of greater influence, though not political, was Elizabeth's mother's view on life. Dorothy Gates was an extremely hard-working woman from a traditional Durham coal-mining family, who struggled to give four daughters a good basic Convent education while supporting a husband who was crippled by a motorbike accident in his youth. This restricted his ability to do most jobs when his shoe repair business became unprofitable and had to be closed. The Dorothy Gates approach required well-turned-out girls, fed to the limit of her purse, often on home-made baking, all to be accomplished after a full-time job. By this regime a Convent education with its necessary "extras" was achieved, even though it was necessary for Elizabeth and her elder sister to leave before O-levels to bring some additional cash into the household. In this way the younger girls could follow on. For many years Elizabeth used to say that she was disappointed that she did not get any O-levels: "I am sure I could have got some good ones, I might even have got some As." Consequently in 1992 when she was elected a Fellow of the Royal Society for Arts and Commerce, she said: "I was elected on what I have achieved rather than what I missed in my early life."

'I believe that the Elizabeth Peacock "positive approach" to politics really developed when we were asked to help in a By-Election in 1971 in Macclesfield, where we then lived, which brought Nicholas Winterton MP into the House of Commons. Nicholas had, and still has, a dashing and robust approach to his politics and is prepared to say what he thinks and vote how he likes. Elizabeth was impressed during the campaign, so much so she agreed to join the local Conservative Association Executive Committee where the Winterton brand of Conservatism obviously rubbed off! It was certainly Nicholas's encouragement and his style that pushed Elizabeth finally to decide on a career in politics, first at County level and then hopefully at National level. But that was not the first expression of interest in becoming a Member of Parliament. That came many years earlier in the early 1960s, before we were married. We went to a social function organised by the Colne and Nelson Conservative Association and who should show up and ruin the valuable drinking time by speech-making but the local MP David Waddington together with Willie Whitelaw MP. I was not amused but Elizabeth obviously was impressed as I remember her saying: "I think I could do that, I fancy being an MP and I will be one day." At the time I thought it was the wine talking but it progressively became a major objective. This was, for many years when the children were small, a secret project due to the impractical nature of the task and a desire that "mother should be at home when the children are small".

'By 1983 Elizabeth had made it, becoming only the 115th woman to serve in the House of Commons.

'Jonathan Peacock is now at the beginning of a political career that he obviously hopes will develop over the years. He already has a huge advantage in that he has wide experience of the political system, helping in County Council elections from an early age. Throughout his university days and his early time at the Bar a mix of research assistance and speech-drafting were well within his orbit. A lawyer's ability to cut straight to the centre of the issue has a merit in the political arena; the great pity is that we now seem to get too many of them! Jonathan undoubtedly shares the down-to-earth version of Conservatism of his grandfather and mother, even though they disagree – over the breakfast table – on many issues.

'He is tough on law and order and certainly, as a tax barrister, in favour of sound money. His experience as a Governor of an inner city primary school and as a Business Advisor for the Prince's Youth Business Trust has clearly honed a view that everything possible must be done for those in real need. He knows, as we all do, that it is often very difficult to be generous to those in real need and not give unjustified support to those who make a practice of living on the welfare system. This will be of increasing concern into the next century for all politicians, of whatever party, since fewer people of working age will have to fund the present level of support.

'I could not end these notes without mentioning the second member of the third generation team, Nicholas, another barrister with a razor-sharp brain and typical Yorkshire bloody-mindedness. The region's voters may be happy to know that he has no interest in politics or politicians; this is probably a pity as he could possibly be the best orator in the family.

'If I had to sum up the family as a whole?

'We are independent Yorkshire folk.

'As Elizabeth always says: "I am not a rebel. I am an independent Yorkshire woman."

'Yes, we are different; we are not right-wing, we are not left-wing, or middle ground, we are just "different". Maybe this is the 'Peacock Factor'.'

Brian Peacock
November 1996

The national campaign got off to a bad start for the Conservative Party when the *Sun* newspaper changed sides, suddenly announcing that it would support Tony Blair and New Labour.

As in all general election campaigns, there was plenty of argument and noise with the Labour Party homing in on the Conservative split on Europe. In this direction a well-known Yorkshire businessman, Paul Sykes, offered to financially support the campaign of those Tory candidates who opposed the single currency.

Equally enthusiastically, New Labour emphasized Tory sleaze, particularly when BBC broadcaster Martin Bell agreed to stand in Tatton as an independent candidate to oppose Neil Hamilton who was alleged to be involved. When the Labour and Liberal Democrat candidates withdrew to give Bell a clear field, Tatton and the sleaze issue was a media topic right up to polling day and the Conservative Party had little defence.

The Labour Party fought an incredibly well-balanced campaign with good advertising and sound control provided by Peter Mandelson. They were desperate for power and they recognized that the British public wanted change.

Locally we had a good campaign with a good reception wherever we went. We knew from the national scene that we had a problem but we had worked with so many people in Batley and Spen that they regarded us as friends. Clearly friendship and voting on the day are not directly linked!

The candidates fighting me for the seat were very suited to the task as they were also well-known locally. Mike Wood was a local councillor and had gained a reputation as a down-to-earth traditional socialist with a positive approach. He has subsequently demonstrated an independent tendency. Kath Pinnock was equally well-known with a good Liberal following in Cleckheaton.

Clive Lord was once again bravely standing for the Greens; always an optimist. The BNP and Referendum candidates made little impact but I assume they enjoyed the experience.

By polling day we had come to the view that with good luck and a possible late swing nationally we might just hold the seat with the usual wafer-thin margin. How wrong we were. We lost by 6,141 with Mike Wood, a solid old Labour candidate, taking the seat.

Of course I was disappointed because we had worked so hard for fourteen years to keep the seat for the Conservatives and represent all

WINSTON S. CHURCHILL
4 BELGRAVE SQUARE, LONDON SW1X 8PH
TEL: 0171-245 9534   FAX: 0171-245 6798   5/5/97

Dear Elizabeth,

I was most sorry to see that you did not survive the holocaust! I do hope you will have another go and, any way, wish you all good fortune in the years ahead. It was a pleasure doing battle at your side for the miners!

Yours ever,

Winston

Note from Winston Churchill following my Election Defeat in 1997.

constituents, whatever their problems. However, I had recognized the demand for change and acknowledged I had been at Westminster for fourteen years which I might never have achieved without Batley and Spen. More importantly, my team of supporters and activists were totally shocked and shattered by the defeat and the scale of the defeat as they also had noted the friendly reception and promise of votes we received throughout the constituency.

I knew from an early moment at the count that we were in trouble when I saw the boxes being emptied to start counting. Early declarations elsewhere confirmed the party was in difficulty when I heard that my good friends Sir Donald Thompson (Calder Valley) and Sir Marcus Fox (Shipley) had lost their seats. Clearly we did not need the count to confirm we were out and that John Major was out of Downing Street.

The Peacock family did not do any better in Wakefield either. Jonathan, who always recognized he was not going to win and had also noted the national mood for change, said his target was to hold David Hinchcliffe's majority to its existing level of 5,000/6,000. To his disappointment, this was also not to be. He lost by 14,604 but he had campaigned well and gained valuable political experience. With this experience he could if he wished make a political comeback, although I doubt that he will as he has now become one of London's leading tax lawyers.

The scale of John Major's defeat was almost unbelievable, having in 1992 gained the highest Conservative vote in history of 12 million, to the worst electoral defeat of a ruling party in 1997. A complete summary of Labour votes drowned the Conservative Party and swept Tony Blair into Downing Street with a majority for a full term.

While John Major had retained his seat at Huntingdon, his Cabinet colleagues Norman Lamont, Sir Malcolm Rifkind and Michael Portillo had lost theirs and the Conservative Party had no MPs in Scotland or Wales. Tony Blair had a majority of 179 in the new parliament with Labour holding 418 seats, Conservatives 165 and Liberal Democrats 46.

By the afternoon of 2 May 1997 John Major had resigned and gone to watch cricket at the Oval, Tony Blair was Prime Minister and sadly I was no longer the Member of Parliament for Batley and Spen.

I had gone to the count with the usual A and B speeches in my head with a note in my pocket. My greatest regret is that I did not get the opportunity to make a speech of thanks to Batley and Spen or my helpers.

Our declaration of the results was late; many national results had already been announced with well-known figures losing their seats. Consequently the Labour Party was jumping for joy, so when our result was declared there was so much noise that speakers could not be heard. I did not get the chance to say 'thank you', though I did try in the local newspaper.

General election results 1 May 1997

Batley and Spen

Mike Wood	Labour	23,213
Elizabeth Peacock	Conservative	17,072
Kath Pinnock	Liberal Democrat	4,133
E. Wood	Referendum Party	1,691
B. Smith	BNP	472
C. Lord	Green Party	384
Labour majority		6,141

Wakefield

D. Hinchcliffe	Labour	28,977
J.D. Peacock	Conservative	14,373
D. Dale	Liberal Democrat	5,656
S. Shires	Referendum Party	1,480
Labour majority		14,604

National Result	Seats
Labour	418
Conservative	165
Liberal Democrat	46
Others	30
Labour majority	177
Speaker not included	

Life After Westminster

* * *

Chapter 28

Out in the Cold

Yes, we had lost in a big way; a thorough electoral drubbing. The British people wanted change and they voted forcefully for what they wanted. As the count commenced I thought that the government would lose with what would be a 30 to 50 Labour majority. I never considered that Labour would have a 176 majority. In Batley and Spen I had hoped that we had done enough to just hold the seat by hundreds, never thinking we might lose by 6,500. In Wakefield Jonathan thought he would lose by 10,000 but lost by 14,000! However, I had always realized that politics is a dangerous occupation with swings and roundabouts and that most political careers end in tears. At 3.00am when the result was announced there were plenty of Conservative tears.

Everybody was tired, my team was deflated because I had lost and so many big Conservative names had also disappeared. In contrast the Labour supporters were, as they say, 'over the moon' and proceeded to goad my team and make unsavoury comments about me and things began to get out of hand. I know I had spent fourteen years opposing the local Labour Party and naturally they were entitled to get some glee at the scale of our defeat but it all became too unpleasant so we all moved out of the Town Hall to prevent trouble.

I was disappointed with this but I did later get opportunities to thank my supporters and the people of Batley and Spen; however, it was never as spontaneous as it would have been on the night.

That night I did announce, publicly, that this was the last election I would fight, for myself or for anyone else. Little did I realize that I would change my mind in four years' time. It does, however, come as a nasty shock when you lose. It seems to be a massive kick in the teeth from your constituents with whom you have worked for fourteen years.

If you have been electioneering in some form or another for weeks, win or lose you are tired out. If you have won, the adrenaline will keep you going for days; when you lose, the adrenaline supply is turned off. This is what happened to me: I was completely drained for thirty-six to forty-eight hours and could not take part in the media post-mortem of why we lost. Since those two difficult days I have clearly seen why we lost, regardless of party splits and Tory sleaze. The British people had sensibly decided that the Conservative Party had been in power long enough, maybe too long; they had decided they were having a change and they got their way.

Tony Blair had done a good job placing New Labour in the middle ground, thus collecting the 'want a change' vote by the boxful; he saw the opportunity and went for it. The British 'first past the post' electoral system allows the British people to get government change when they decide it is necessary. It is the power held in the hands of the people by our system that has provided periodic changes of government party giving us democratic stability. I might have gone into the House on Margaret Thatcher's coat tails but I was kicked out by Tony Blair's shiny New Labour boot!

However, when you have lost your seat you are given little time to be sorry for yourself. Elections are usually held on Thursdays with a count and result by Friday, a weekend to deal with the drama and back to Westminster on Monday to clear your office. The new members begin arriving by Wednesday and they want your office. This describes my sort of timetable in 1997 and began a trying few weeks that I did not enjoy.

When an MP loses a seat, there is what looks to be a generous so-called resettlement allowance to help reorganize the member's life. It may look generous but in the end it was not. It has to cover the cost of tidying-up a Westminster and a constituency office, including redundancy of staff. This was the part I hated: I had to make both Martin Casey and Kath Wrightson redundant, sorting out details of their payments and negotiating with them to work until we had emptied all the files. This all sounds relatively easy until you consider that I had fourteen years' worth of files, some of which contained confidential information on cases we had handled. The Westminster office had to be emptied first so that the new members could have offices; the files being transferred to the Cleckheaton office and our garage at home for final sorting and destroying. In truth the job has never been finished as I still have a cabinet full of historical interesting letters, papers and newspapers that I am now using for my writing.

The winding-up of a Member's time at Westminster is a major financial task; all the final bills were to be paid and claimed through the Fees Office. Kath Wrightson and Martin Casey had instantly to start looking round for new jobs, as the Fees Office allowed only a limited number of weeks to help me wind up. Margaret Bates soon found that her tasks were completed and she was looking for a new challenge.

The Fees Office was understandably very careful about the details of the wind-up expenses. We certainly would not have been allowed to get into the sort of trouble experienced by members in 2008–09.

From then on, I did not enjoy watching the televised House of Commons with somebody else sitting in 'my seat'!

I am often asked 'Do you miss the House of Commons?' The answer for the first few months was 'yes' but over the years this feeling has disappeared. I have been lucky to have reason to carry on visiting the Palace of Westminster fairly regularly over the years since I lost and I am surprisingly still known by the staff and a few of the policemen who often kindly say: 'Glad to see you, Mrs Peacock. We miss you but you would not like it here now. It's a different House of Commons to the one in Mrs Thatcher's day.'

Nobody seems to be able to say why, but Mrs Thatcher and her government worked the House and its members hard, both night and day. The Tories were welded into a team by committee work and some of us became friendly with opposition members, with whom we were in almost daily contact. Some of these friendships have survived over the years. The House of Commons is a unique place, with the sound and flurry of political battle to the forefront but nevertheless, many long-standing friendships develop.

As the winding-up tasks were completed, I began to think: 'What am I going to do now?' My husband made a short-term suggestion, saying: 'You've spent fourteen years with a daily dose of politics; you are completely tired out. We are going on holiday to New Zealand for several weeks.' We had a wonderful trip that helped the tiredness but it did not answer the question of how I would now fill my time.

I was determined that I would not get involved in politics at any level; I wanted a complete change. I did, however, think that I would like to continue my connection with industry. I had been deeply involved with the wool textile industry and I had been a non-executive director of a stock exchange company, albeit with a disappointing outcome. Initially I did take a few advisory meetings in industry but my involvement never really took off. Industry does not want failed Members of Parliament and in any case, there were too many Conservative MPs who had lost their seats trying to do this sort of work, more than the industry needed.

The Peacock family decided that they would find me something to do. We have a family investment company and I was told: 'Mother, you can look after the company and its projects', which I agreed to do. However, it takes little time and amounts to administration for the most part which was never my interest.

I also thought that as I had experience of government at various levels, I could be useful on a quango or two. I was invited to apply for several interesting government jobs but was never successful. I suspect that I was considered too Tory and a likely rebellious troublemaker who would ask difficult questions if I did not agree with the way things were being done. So I did not rush into anything, other than to get as far away from politics as I could.

After two years of looking, I came to the conclusion that neither industry nor government really want former MPs so began to look elsewhere.

However, I was determined that I must do something useful. Happily, the Lord Lieutenant for West Yorkshire John Lyles, who I had known through his connection with his family carpet wool business, asked me whether I would be willing to serve as a Deputy Lieutenant for West Yorkshire. Naturally, I responded: 'Yes, I would be honoured to do this.' Some months later I was duly appointed. I had already become a Freeman of the City of London and a member of the Worshipful Company of Woolmen. They then honoured me further by appointing me to the Court of the Company, thus getting me on the road to becoming Master in later years.

In 1998/9 these activities were not very time-consuming so I offered to become an assessor for the Duke of York's Community Initiative, reviewing organizations and projects for the Duke's award. This was very interesting as it kept me in touch with the voluntary sector across Yorkshire and proved in some cases to be a challenge.

I was equally determined that I would keep some interest in activities in Batley and Spen, without getting in the way of their new Labour member Mike Wood and certainly not getting involved in local politics.

During my fourteen years as an MP I had taken a real interest in the Scout and Guide movement, probably because I never had the opportunity to become involved as a girl. At an earlier date in 1987 Batley District Scouts had asked me to become their President and I accepted. When I lost my seat they asked me to stay on and I was pleased and honoured to do so. I now serve as President of the Heavy Woollen District Scouts that have the camp site at Woolley near my home. I am now a Scout myself, as the movement thanked me by awarding me the honour of the Silver Acorn after twenty years' services. I am very proud of the award and I have recently received my twenty-five years' Service Certificate.

I had in the main kept away from Conservative politics and involvement, though I had been pressured on occasions to make a contribution to the media via radio, television and newspapers. This I did, attempting to take a non-party political position. I had for a short time been president of Hemsworth Conservative Association and helped reorganize its structure. However, being President of an Association did not suit my style. I did continue to keep in touch with friends who had returned to the House in 1997 and visited Westminster regularly.

As both Angela Rumbold and I had lost our seats, we wondered what to do with the now well-established Westminster Dining Club. The problem was suddenly solved when Cheryl Gillan MP for Amersham said: 'If you do the organizing, I will keep the club going based at the House of Commons as your President.' So the 'old girls' club' lives on to this day with Cheryl as President. I remain joint chairman with Margaret Miller, the chairman of Knightsbridge Furniture, as our other joint chairman since Angela's death.

Chapter 29

General Election
2001

On one visit to Westminster in 2000 I ran into William Hague in the Central Lobby of the House of Commons. William had become leader of the Conservative Party when John Major resigned. His opening greeting was: 'Elizabeth, I have been meaning to speak to you for some time, what are you going to do for the party when the next election is called? Will you stand again for Westminster?' My instant response was: 'After the count in 1997 I said publically I would not stand for election again and I have not changed my mind.'

His equally instant reply was: 'We (the party) would like you to change your mind. We would like you to fight Batley and Spen again, as we think with your experience and the connections you have, you have more chance of regaining the seat than anyone.'

I countered by saying: 'Since the loss of Heckmondwike with the boundary changes and the state of the polls, the chances of us turning over a 6,500 majority are remote.' 'Elizabeth, the party wants you to fight Batley and Spen again. Hopefully your local association will be happy. Think about it and I will get in touch in a few weeks' time,' and off he went.

I reported the discussion to my husband, commenting that I was not changing my mind. His response was: 'You have been such a damned nuisance to the party, you might consider changing your mind. The chance of you winning is slim.' Shortly afterwards, and by chance, I met William again, this time in Yorkshire and he said: 'We want you to fight Batley and Spen and we want a positive answer.' I said: 'If Batley and Spen are happy with the idea, I will give it a go. Our chances of winning are poor but I will as always fight to win.'

Canvassing – General Election, 2001.

Election leaflet, 2001.

I reported these conversations to Doug Brewer and several members of the Executive Committee who in the main were in favour of the idea. I suspect a few thought it was time for someone new. As the party requires, there was a selection process in December 1999 and I was selected to fight again. My old team were happy and straight back into gear looking for an election date. I did discover that not all the members of the Conservative Association were totally convinced that I should be the candidate trying to regain the seat. Some people thought I should have supported Margaret Thatcher 'through thick and thin' in 1990, even though the switch to John Major had given them a Conservative Government for a further five years!

Having been selected as the Conservative candidate, I soon found that I had plenty of time to get back into the old routine of making contact with businesses and other organizations in the constituency. My newspaper cuttings indicate that I was everywhere, reconnecting with people. Obviously we spent time attacking our opponents, particularly our Member of Parliament, Mike Wood. Mike had only spoken twice in the House of Commons since 1997 so we named him 'the quiet one'. We then attacked some of the people that New Labour was attempting to promote in Kirklees and nationally this gave us plenty of scope.

Labour had taken control of Kirklees Council with a 25 per cent increase in council tax, giving us a good area to attack. The Labour government had decided to end the School Assisted Places scheme that had been very successful in our local grammar schools. I therefore pressurized the Conservative Party for a new approach to this problem created by New Labour that was clearly an attack on social mobility. Throughout 2000 and 2001 we harassed the Labour Party on issues that might dent their substantial local majority. We had a go at the control of asylum-seekers and tax issues that are always good for an argument. We developed a positive strategy with a will to win and by the time the election was held in May 2001, we had covered the ground and felt confident we could reduce the majority and win if the election went badly for Labour.

As we commenced the campaign our President got the appeal for funds going and again we got good financial support, especially from local businesses.

I needed an election agent and this time we had in the experienced campaigning team someone suitable: Graham Rhodes was the man and he agreed to be my Agent. He had not been an agent before but was well-

With Kath, my Cleckheaton secretary, in the office.

Meeting Cllr Margaret Bates and residents regarding traffic problems.

organized, good at directing the troops and could keep his paperwork on expenses etc in good shape. I enjoyed working with him on this somewhat difficult task.

The candidates were obviously the sitting member Mike Wood for Labour; Kath Pinnock who with her husband had as a Liberal Democrat worked hard for the people of Kirklees; the long-standing fighter for the Greens, Clive Lord; and Andrew Burton for UKIP.

Locally we seemed to be in constant electioneering mode for most of 2000 and 2001 to the date of the election. The party did want to win the seat back so we had support from shadow ministers in several important areas such as Ann Widdecombe, Theresa May and others.

The local issue topics were the schools, post offices, roads and open-cast coal extraction. In truth, the election never really took off.

On the national scene the Conservative Party had the competent and witty William Hague as leader facing the charismatic Tony Blair, leaving the Lib-Dem Charles Kennedy on the sidelines. From the beginning it was Tony Blair's election to lose and he didn't!

The Conservatives got off on the wrong foot by giving mixed messages on tax if we won the election. These would cost £8 billion but needed substantial spending cuts to be viable. Labour homed in on this and the Tory team lost the argument.

Having lost the initiative, William Hague played 'Europe' and claimed that the country had two weeks to 'save the Pound' from a Labour Party that was heading to join the single currency. I agreed with his views that the Euro was wrong for Britain and hoped this new initiative would sway the electors. Britain heard the message but did not really listen as they had faith in Tony Blair and wanted him back again, regardless of detailed argument. In truth it was rather a dull election, the main national interest being John Prescott's punch-up with a heckler in North Wales.

Locally I rather enjoyed the election as I had nothing to lose and possibly everything to gain, so as a team we had fun. By election day and the count I realized that while we had fought a good local campaign with plenty of support, not enough had been gained nationally for me to win in Batley and Spen. We did not win nationally but the New Labour majority was reduced from 179 to 167. We did not win locally either and Mike Wood was returned to Westminster with his majority reduced from 6,141 to 5,064. Overall this was a disappointing result for two years of effort.

General election June 2001

Batley and Spen

Mike Wood	Labour	19,224
Elizabeth Peacock	Conservative	14,160
Kath Pinnock	Liberal Democrat	3,989
Clive Lord	Green	595
A. Burton	UKIP	574
Labour majority		5,064

National Result	Seats
Labour	412
Conservative	166
Liberal Democrat	52
Others	29
Total	659
Labour majority	167

My View

The Conservative Party was never going to win this election. The British electorate still wanted to punish the Conservatives and more importantly wanted the smooth Tony Blair to continue as Prime Minister. A closer result might have been achieved if the Conservatives had not got themselves into a tangle on tax during the campaign but in the end it did not influence the result.

Could we have done better in Batley and Spen? Our team could not have worked harder and we did regain some of my original support but not as much as we planned. A new candidate might have indicated 'change' but I doubt it; the electors just wanted Blair back regardless.

Chapter 30

New Goals

Jewellery

Over many years I had developed an amateur interest in Victorian and other antique jewellery and decided that I would study the subject in greater depth. To do this, I enrolled at the Gemmological Institute in Hatton Garden to look at precious stones, with particular reference to their use in Victorian and Edwardian jewellery. This extensive course awakened my interest in the use of precious stones but more importantly the use of much more affordable semi-precious stones and freshwater cultured pearls.

This stimulated me to start making my own bead jewellery. I became thoroughly involved with design and manufacture; so much so that what started as a life-changing hobby became a small business.

If you are regularly designing and producing jewellery of this type, even as a hobby, you have to do something with it to finance the new raw material. Luckily several people saw my designs and asked me to make specific one-off pieces for them. As a consequence I commenced selling my designer jewellery, mainly in Yorkshire, under the 'Antonella' name or as special commissions. This keeps me busy sourcing semi-precious stones, cultured pearls and other materials from around the world to create new designs. In truth the enterprise is not very profitable but it gives me the challenge of sourcing and design.

My new interest came to the notice of friends in the media and I did a television programme on antiques for Yorkshire TV with the late Richard Whiteley, who I had known for many years in the political field. We had great fun making the programme that made me study a wider range of antiques generally.

Association of Former Members of Parliament

I had just begun in 2002 to get this enterprise off the ground when I was

Welcoming Sheriff Alderman David Wootton to the Woolmen's Livery Company dinner in 2009 [later Lord Mayor of the City of London].

Master of the Worshipful Company of Woolmen 2009/10 presenting Her Silver Woolsack Trophy to the company.

278

approached by some former colleagues from the House with the idea of helping to start an Association of Former Members of Parliament. The objective of this proposed association was to keep former members in touch with their colleagues, to ensure that the expertise of former members remained available for the benefit of the government of the day and that terms and conditions of former members, particularly their widows/widowers, were properly administered and updated.

Many of the Commonwealth Parliaments already have this sort of body for former members with broadly similar objectives. There was a widespread feeling that Britain, the home of democracy, should have such an organization. Eventually I got involved but on the understanding that I would not be constrained by party politics and pointing out that I would be taking an independent cross-bench approach to the challenge. I joined the initial Steering Group with Joe Ashton (Bassetlaw) and Ted Graham (Lord) former member for Edmonton, Sir Peter Emery (Honiton) and Mr Speaker Michael Martin. This small but dynamic team was prepared to drive the matter forward, despite the difficulties the Speaker was having in the Commons. Administration and organization were placed in the capable hands of Lady Sally Grocott. By some means I found myself in the role of Joint Vice-Chairman, the position I continue to hold.

The Association is now working well, justifying its foundation, and having a membership of about 400 former members, some former backbenchers, former ministers and at least three former Prime Ministers. My role allows me to keep in touch with Westminster and my political friends without the pressure of party constraints and allowing the freedom for my independent views.

This position is particularly helpful as it forces me to follow the activities at Westminster and keep abreast of the current political scene. This is useful as I am from time to time called upon to take part in radio programmes. These cover a wide spectrum of topics and require comment on issues of the day. More importantly, and possibly to my surprise, I remain on a list at BBC Radio 4 as someone who might be worth interviewing on topical issues from news items to *Woman's Hour* programmes. I suspect it is because I am usually prepared to take a robust line on issues and the interviewer stands a chance of getting a different or 'Yorkshire' view.

Royal Society of Arts and Manufactures

In the 1980s I was invited to become a Fellow of the Royal Society of Arts,

Manufactures and Commerce, the RSA, which I accepted on the basis that this historic organization supported not only the arts but also manufactures and commerce that encapsulated my interest in industry. I discovered that the RSA had an enthusiastic branch in Yorkshire chaired by Sir Brian Askew that I joined as it was not always possible for me to be in London.

When I lost my seat I began to get more involved and found the activities of the society of interest and importance as they gave me a wider insight into Yorkshire arts and industry. I must have shown too much interest and involvement because in 2005 I suddenly became Vice-Chairman and was then propelled into becoming the next chairman. The role of Chairman is to plan and lead a programme of events balancing the interests of the Society and this I was happy to do. I was determined to ensure that for the next two or three years while I was Chairman we would have a good look at Yorkshire industry. This we did with some enthusiasm, paying visits to a York Hand-Made Brick company, Smith & Nephew in Hull and a selection of the furniture, Yorkshire textile and bedding industry. I am proud to say we looked thoroughly at Yorkshire industry in those three years without neglecting the arts; a fine balance that I enjoyed leading.

During this time I was elected to represent the Yorkshire RSA region on the Council in London. Again I found this stimulating as it gave me a wider view of the work of the Society, especially during the period when Sir Paul Judge was chairman as he obviously brought commercial bite to the organization.

As I ended my stint as Yorkshire chairman there was something of a revolution in the RSA with a new chairman and CEO, the latter having arrived from the Blair regime in Downing Street. This revolution in my view caused the RSA to divert from its traditional objectives and become a 'think-tank' with defined political ambitions; something the RSA does not need and should not have, even in this changing age.

I realized that I would have little influence in opposing this change so I decided to resign and move on. As I have often found, as one door is closed another one opens and so it happened again. I was invited to take over the chairmanship of the BBC Yorkshire Audience Council with a seat on the English Audience Council that usually met in London.

The BBC
The Audience Council is the body within the BBC Trust structure that

advises the Trust on audience comments and suggestions, the Trust being the Statutory Body that monitors the BBC itself.

The Yorkshire Audience Council is tasked with keeping the Trust informed of radio-listeners' and television-watchers' views on programmes, their content, presentation and acceptability. The Yorkshire challenge looked worthwhile so I said 'yes', particularly as it appeared to be closely related to the work of the National BBC Advisory Committee to which I had been appointed as a Conservative MP. I had enjoyed the work of the committee advising the then BBC Board of Governors with originally 'Duke' (Marmaduke) Hussey and then Tessa Blackstone as Chairman.

The work of the Audience Council was to keep the Trust informed of audience views in their many forms and from the diverse political and ethical points of view. To achieve this balance, we had to maintain a diverse representation from the people of Yorkshire. The work of the council, comprising endless watching, reviewing and providing Yorkshire views on BBC radio and television, was a huge task.

I had on my patch three radio stations (including television): Radio Leeds, Sheffield and York; for some historical reason, not Hull! Of the three, Leeds and Sheffield were well-equipped; however, York was not. To my disgust it was housed in a Portakabin on a temporary site. I considered this to be a disgrace, particularly in one of Britain's major cities and large rural areas. Consequently I spent my time trying to get the BBC to make a decision to invest in the site to provide suitable conditions for broadcasting. It was really difficult to get a positive decision. However, at the end of my term I got a promise that monies would eventually be spent in York. This appeared typical of the BBC national scene, which at the time was all about the move from London to Manchester.

The Audience Council worked well in Yorkshire but seemed ineffective at national level, albeit well-chaired by a Trust member. The work was done but I suspect the chairman had difficulty in getting the audience message across to the Trust. Eventually, I came to the conclusion that the Trust and its chairman at the time were not really interested in the Audience Council.

My View
The BBC needs a radical restructure: currently it is too big and too complex for efficient management and should be reduced to a more manageable size. Parts of the non-broadcasting side of the organization

and some broadcast channels would be better in the commercial sector. The broadcasting output needs a re-think to establish a core business of national news and wide-interest radio and television with a firm input into quality local radio and television. New commercial and minority programmes need to be re-evaluated. Where possible they should be removed from licence-fee support and placed in the private sector, albeit with subscription or government short-term support if necessary. I fully recognize that minority programming is a problem but it has to be viable and not a long-term drain on the licence-fee-payer.

The slimmed-down BBC should deal with its own routine governance within a national regulated media with a truly independent chairman with no political history and a strong team of non-political non-executive directors capable of handling management and operational challenges. It will take a brave government of whatever colour to deal with this task that will become urgent when the licence fee has to be renewed.

The Worshipful Company of Woolmen

Throughout the years since disappearing from Batley and Spen and Westminster I have retained my contact with an interest in the activities of the wool industry. In the early 1990s I had been accepted as a Liveryman of the Worshipful Company of Woolmen and subsequently invited to join the Court with the prospect of becoming only the second female Master in the 800-year history of the Company. I can now claim to be the first 'commoner' to achieve this position as I was Master in 2009/10 and the first female Master of the Woolmen was the Princess Royal in 1994/95.

The duties of the Master are remarkably time-consuming as Presiding over Court Meetings and Dinners of the Woolmen's Livery Company is only part of the task. A full schedule of City of London events requires the Master to be present, particularly on the election of the Sheriffs of the City of London and the election of the Lord Mayor.

The Master's year includes a tour of the major agricultural shows, Bath and the Royal Highland in Edinburgh, the Belfast, the Great Yorkshire and Royal Welsh, to support the sheep industry with the presentation of prizes for sheep-shearing, the shearing of wool from the sheep being an essential part of the 'wool chain' from sheep to clothing. As a further step to encourage the success of the wool industry, the Livery Company supports students who are studying a course that includes using wool. We do hope, of course, that these students will eventually join the industry.

To fulfil the demands of the Master's role I spent a full year either in

London, in Yorkshire liaising with the wool industry or touring the agricultural shows; a very interesting, enjoyable and unique challenge successfully completed.

National Coal Mining Museum of England
I have a determination to keep in touch with Britain's energy policy, regardless of party political influence. The position of coal in this policy continues to interest me; consequently I am happy to be a Patron of the National Coal Mining Museum in Wakefield to support their work and long-term development.

Chapter 31

Epilogue

The story has, I believe, been told but I need to summarize my thoughts on the objectives that stimulated me to write in the first place. To remind the reader and myself, these were to place on record my activities in the political field from the 1970s and to confirm my view of the successes and failures of the Thatcher and Major years.

I believe that I have placed on record my activities in the political field from the 1970s in some detail and there is therefore no need to repeat myself here.

The big question that I ask myself is: 'Elizabeth, if you could turn back the clock, would you play the issues in the same way?' Many others ask the same question. The answer is a straightforward, positive 'yes'. I would still follow my independent line and speak and vote accordingly.

However, looking back at the battles I fought, some look in today's light rather minor matters that I could have ignored. In contrast, others should have been fought harder. The wisdom of time has taught me to be more selective with the ground on which to fight but then make a stronger attack. In other words, I would be more tactical with my opposition.

I believe I need say no more on this aspect, other than to say 'thank you' to all those who endured my behaviour over the years, particularly the President of Batley and Spen Conservative Association, the late Doug Brewer, who was unfailing in his support of me and my activities.

I would couple these thanks with those to my husband Brian and our sons Jonathan and Nicholas who encouraged me to go into politics and then supported me in taking an independent and positive line, regardless of the 'hot water' it got me into!

The question still remains, was I a rebel? I certainly did not conform. I did not set out to rebel but if I did not agree with the matter I was happy to say so in a loud voice. I have always been independently-minded and remain so today. I claimed at the time that I was using common sense and I am convinced that I did.

The second and possibly more important objective was to distil my views on the successes and failures of the Thatcher and Major governments from the great Thatcher landslide of 1983 to the even greater Blair landslide of 1997. The more I reflect on these years, the more I am convinced that the Thatcher and Major years have to be considered together. If they are considered separately, both have serious shortcomings that many would find surprising, particularly in the case of the Thatcher years. Equally, the fact that John Major was considered by some to be a 'grey man' hides many of his real successes. If Major had not followed Thatcher, many of her initiatives could have come to nothing and would have left her period in history subject to query. Taken together, the Thatcher and Major governments changed the face of British politics for the better. This was a turning-point in British history, re-shaping the economy and re-emphasizing Britain's role on the international scene.

Analyzing the period shows a wide spread of successes and failures. From 1975 when Mrs Thatcher became leader of the Conservative Party, she took a positive progressive line within a party that was divided with support remaining for Ted Heath who never seemed to accept her as his successor. Even after she had gained the 1979 election victory and become prime minister, the party remained divided with many continuing to believe she was just temporary and would soon disappear.

Her biggest successes were the Falklands War, the re-structuring of British industry and the taming of trade union power. Her negative areas were the over-generosity of welfare support, the chaos of the poll tax and, I suggest, her relationship with the Cabinet and her advisors.

Prior to the Falklands conflict, Margaret Thatcher and her government were in trouble with poor public support and may not have been re-elected. The Falklands War changed all that. Her brave decision that the Falklands could be regained and the instant moves to achieve this set her apart as a leader of world stature. It was a gamble that paid off, turning her into a renowned international figure and putting the 'Great' back into Great Britain.

The success of the Falklands was recognized by the British electorate in 1983, allowing Margaret to storm to victory with a large majority. This strong parliamentary position then gave her the remit to develop her own policies with a re-shaped Cabinet. These policies, better-known later as Thatcherism, were based on the strength of market forces: 'you cannot buck the market.' An example of this was the privatization of the substantial businesses of British Telecom, British Airways and the gas and electricity utilities being brought into the commercial sector. This substantial inflow of cash into government together with the cash flowing from North Sea oil was used to enhance the welfare sector. This enhancement has been a problem for all subsequent governments and remains so today in a period of austerity. Contrary to popular belief Margaret Thatcher, the so-called 'milk snatcher', was just too soft in the welfare sector. She had cash flowing in and allowed it to be utilized in an array of allowances and payments at levels that have subsequently been found to be unsustainable. Some of the welfare payments were so generous that certain people found it did not pay to work. Governments have since struggled with control of excessive welfare costs stemming from the cash-rich Thatcher era. This is something that is not generally recognized, even in the Conservative Party. The left wing of British politics cannot attribute the description 'too generous' to their hated Thatcher. In defence of the government, it seemed right at the time.

As we have noted, there was anarchy on the British industrial scene in the 1970s so the measures taken by the Thatcher government that brought the miners under control was a significant achievement, albeit necessitating the big fight with Arthur Scargill and his coal miners to establish the new restraining legislation.

An impression we gained on the back benches was that despite Margaret Thatcher's phenomenal international recognition and her personal hard work, there always seemed to be tension at Cabinet level. This is something that Cabinet members of the period never seemed to discuss. Understandably she dropped the 1979 'wets' such as Francis Pym and Edward Heath's followers but later lost major contributors Leon Brittan, Michael Heseltine, Geoffrey Howe and Nigel Lawson. I have always concluded that her positive approach, often high-handed, made her a difficult leader. Certainly in her early government she needed to be positive to get her policies through Cabinet. This positive approach in her last government led to her big mistake: the poll tax.

Certainly a new local tax system was overdue by the late 1980s as the existing rates system was unsatisfactory. The poll tax concept of widening the tax base had merit but it needed the long period of 'tapering-in' that it did not get. The whole project was mismanaged. The opposition and Tory back benches were ignored by the government and the results caused rioting in the streets. The biggest problem was that Mrs Thatcher was surrounded by 'yes men' who did not brief her properly; she refused to listen to others and just pushed on.

The whole thing descended into chaos, with back-benchers assuming that they would lose their seats at the next election and the Cabinet losing faith in Mrs Thatcher, forcing her resignation in a flood of tears.

As already stated, I did support Michael Heseltine in the subsequent leadership election. However, the winner John Major was the right man, as we were to discover as he offered continuity for the Thatcher legacy.

The Major governments of 1990 and 1992 have been decried and written off as failures by many commentators and John was dubbed the 'grey man' of British politics. In my view this is unfair and does not measure the facts. In the early years of his time in Downing Street he with the help of Michael Heseltine corrected the mistakes of the Thatcher period and consolidated the successes. Indeed, if John Major had lost in 1992 and not been able to carry on correcting the problems of the Thatcher era, Margaret's period in Downing Street would have looked significantly less successful. On the contrary, John's stunning election victory in 1992 polling 12 million votes, more than the Conservative Party had ever done before, was historic.

Despite all the trials and tribulations faced by his government, John Major completed all his policy and manifesto commitments and with Ken Clarke re-shaped the economy in such a way that it helped the early days of the Blair government. This was achieved by getting on with the day-to-day business in a sensible free market manner, regardless of external pressures.

On the other hand his government did not get everything right. John and others had eventually persuaded Margaret Thatcher to join the ERM. This proved to be a mistake, as John and Norman Lamont were to find out when Britain was forced out, doing great damage to the Conservative cause.

Where John did get it wrong was in European matters with a highly sceptical party. He started well by keeping us out of the mainstream of Europe with his negotiations on the Maastricht Treaty but failed to build on this independent line. In my opinion a more independent line would have been acceptable to the British people and the Tory Party would not have been so badly split.

By the end of the 1992–97 parliament, the various incidents of Conservative misbehaviour better known as 'Tory sleaze' had put a real tarnish on the party and on John's government. He got the blame but if

The Peacock family.
Back row l-r: Susan Peacock, Nicholas Peacock QC, Jonathan Peacock QC and
Charlotte Peacock.
Front row l-r: Laura and Helena, the author, Brian Peacock, Francesca and Edward.

you analyze these incidents, they were almost all 'private misdemeanours' over which neither the party nor the Prime Minister had any control.

Come the election, we lost very heavily and certainly could never have won. The British people wanted Tony Blair and New Labour regardless. Despite that heavy defeat, the Major years were the saviour of the Thatcher era. Prime Minister John Major deserves a better position in history than many commentators have tried to give him. In my view, he should be congratulated on his achievements because with his help Margaret Thatcher's career ended not with tears but with a smile and we can salute a great lady forever.

The story is now told!

I acknowledge that some readers will not agree with my view of the Thatcher–Major era but I was there at the time and the views expressed here are mine alone.

Brian and I have enjoyed setting it all down on paper, even if in the end no one ever reads it!

In memoriam:
Margaret Thatcher

Great Britain's only female Prime Minister, Margaret Thatcher, died on Monday 8 April 2013 at the age of eighty-seven.

She led the country for eleven years, from 1979 to 1990, serving in office longer than any other twentieth-century British politician.

Baroness Thatcher was given a ceremonial funeral on Wednesday 17 April and, breaking with tradition, this was attended by HM Queen Elizabeth and Prince Philip.

Prime Minister of the United Kingdom
4 May 1979 – 28 November 1990

Leader of the Opposition
11 February 1975 – 4 May 1979

Leader of the Conservative Party
11 February 1975 – 28 November 1990

Secretary of State for Education and Science
20 June 1970 – 4 March 1974

Member of Parliament for Finchley
8 October 1959 – 9 April 1992

Some weeks after the manuscript for this book was delivered to the publisher, the death of Margaret Thatcher was announced. She had been in poor health for some time but her passing was still a shock to the nation.

To my great surprise and honour I was invited to be present in St Paul's for the funeral service. As I have acknowledged elsewhere in the book, I was swept into Westminster in 1983 as part of the Thatcher success.

By attending the funeral I was able to say a last personal 'Thank you' to Margaret for her support despite becoming, in later years, a somewhat controversial and independent member of her party.

I will not repeat what we have said in the book but I pay a final tribute to the finest peace-time political prime minister of the twentieth century and one of the greatest women leaders of all time.

Thank you, Margaret.

Elizabeth Peacock
17 April 2013

Index